NINJA FOODI

Table of Contents

Pork, beef and lamb

Fish

Vegetarian

Meatless

Dessert

30 Days Meal Plan 207

Bonus Recipes

Introduction

It is a single machine that can work for four machines. It alone can do the same job as it is four machines in one. It can do everything that is done by an Instant Pot. It can even do much more than that. Coming towards the cost, Ninja Foodi costs you less than the amount you have to pay for buying all other machines individually. Individual costs when combined exceed the amount you have to pay for Ninja Foodi. Sometimes the ease you feel at things is due to how friendly they behave towards you. It means that the more comfortable it is to use, the more you enjoy using it. Ninja Foodi is very easy to use, and you don't need to put in a lot of brainy capabilities to understand how it would work. It's easy to learn its usage and does not bother you much. There is a digital display given in Ninja Foodi whereas there is no such kind of technologically developed approach in Instant Pot. As the pressure keeps rising within Ninja Foodi, it continuously becomes visible on the digital display. You do not need to worry about it as guessing about pressure in an Instant Pot was only about your approach of making the right clue. Ninja Foodi is reliable because everything is visible on the digital display while in the case of Instant Pot it is not like that. It's all about how accurately you can guess. Apart from other aspects comes the cleaning of Ninja Foodi. It's easy to clean Ninja Foodi and clear it from the food particles and oily content of your food. One who uses it can quickly get a trick of its efficient cleaning.

As our lives get busier, we take on more and more responsibilities. There are never-ending distractions and buzzing entertainment all around us. We've become desperate for anything that would let us cut out a slice of time from a hectic daily schedule and use it in some better way. That's why the Ninja Foodi's multifunctionality is not the only advantage it has to offer.

It's a great cooking device that saves you hours every week. Imagine someone gives you an extra three hours in the sauna at the end of every week. Who wouldn't want that? Ninja Foodi also gives you the freedom to cook your meals and do whatever you need or want to do in the meantime. Don't fancy using multiple pots and risking a house burn down? No problem! Thanks to this smart kitchen robot, you can go clean your home, go to the gym or even go to work for an entire day while your food (and your house!) remain in one piece - all of that without compromising on taste and quality.

One of many other benefits Ninja Foodi offers is that it keeps your meals warm for up to ten hours. So that's another few minutes saved right there if reheating meals is not what particularly enjoy doing.

This cookbook is the only guide you'll ever need to start your adventure with the Ninja Foodi. Hundreds of recipes included inside will keep you entertained for a long time if you want to try them all.

15 Mins

55 Mins

4

INGREDIENTS

- 4 potatoes
- 4 teaspoons butter
- 2 cups cheddar cheese, shredded
- 1 1/4 cups sour cream
- 8 slices bacon, cooked crispy and chopped

Breakfast Potatoes

Method

1. Take out the grill gate and crisper basket.
2. Set Ninja Foodi Grill to bake.
3. Set it to 390 °F.
4. Preheat by selecting "start".
5. Add the potatoes inside.
6. Seal and cook for 45 minutes.
7. Let cool.
8. Make slices on top of the potatoes.
9. Create a small hole.
10. Top with butter and cheese.
11. Put the potatoes back to the pot.
12. Bake at 375 °F for 10 minutes.
13. Top with sour cream and bacon before serving.

Serving Suggestions: Garnish with chopped scallions.
Preparation / Cooking Tips: Preheat the Ninja Foodi Grill before putting the potatoes back to the pot after cheese and butter have been added.

2

Breakfast Casserole

15 Mins

15 Mins

8

Method

1. Add white onion, bell pepper and ground sausage to your Ninja Foodi Grill pot.

2. Spread cheese and then the eggs on top.

3. Season with garlic salt.

4. Whisk eggs, heavy cream, and spices together in a separate bowl.

5. Close Air Crisp lid on the Foodi and set to Air Crisp at 350 °F for 30 minutes.

6. Check after 25 minutes to see if eggs are cooked through. Eggs *may* need as much as 10 extra minutes to finalize cooking.

7. Place remaining 1 cup of cheese on top of casserole and close lid.

8. Heat will melt the cheese

Serving Suggestions: Garnish with chopped parsley.
Preparation / Cooking Tips: You can also place the casserole in a small dish and put it inside the air fryer basket.

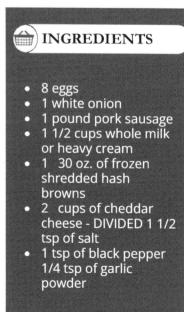

INGREDIENTS

- 8 eggs
- 1 white onion
- 1 pound pork sausage
- 1 1/2 cups whole milk or heavy cream
- 1   30 oz. of frozen shredded hash browns
- 2   cups of cheddar cheese - DIVIDED 1 1/2 tsp of salt
- 1 tsp of black pepper 1/4 tsp of garlic powder

Spicy Sausage & Mushroom Casserole

 15 Mins

 15 Mins

 6

INGREDIENTS

- 1 tablespoon olive oil
- 3/4 cup white onion, diced
- 5 mushrooms, sliced
- 1/2 lb. spicy ground sausage
- 8 eggs, beaten scrambled
- Garlic salt to taste
- 1/4 cup cream of mushroom soup
- 3/4 cup cheddar cheese, shredded

Method

1. In a pan over medium heat, pour the olive oil and cook onion, mushrooms and spicy ground sausage for 5 minutes.
2. Remove from heat and drain oil.
3. Pour eggs and sausage mixture into the Ninja Foodi Grill pot.
4. Season with garlic salt.
5. Spread mushroom soup on top.
6. Sprinkle with cheese.
7. Seal the pot.
8. Set to air fry and cook at 390 °F for 5 minutes.
9. Stir and cook for another 5 minutes.

Serving Suggestions: Sprinkle with chopped chives before serving.
Preparation / Cooking Tips: You can use Alfredo pasta sauce if you don't have the cream of mushroom soup.

15 Mins

10 Mins

6

INGREDIENTS

- 6 eggs
- 1 white onion, diced
- 1 red bell pepper, diced
- 6 mushrooms, chopped
- 2 slices ham, chopped and cooked
- 1 cup cheddar cheese, shredded
- Salt and pepper to taste

Breakfast Omelette

Method

1. Beat-eggs in a bowl.
2. Stir in the rest of the ingredients.
3. Set your Ninja Foodi Grill to air fry.
4. Pour the egg mixture into the pot.
5. Cook at 390 °F for 10 minutes, stirring halfway through. Serving Suggestions: Serve with toasted garlic bread.

Preparation / Cooking Tips: You can also use turkey bacon to replace ham in this recipe.

Breakfast Burrito

15 Mins

30 Mins

12

Method

1. Pour olive oil into a pan over medium heat.
2. Cook potatoes and sausage for 7 to 10 minutes, stirring frequently.
3. Spread this mixture on the bottom of the Ninja Foodi Grill pot.
4. Season with salt and pepper.
5. Pour the eggs and cheese on top.
6. Select the bake setting.
7. Cook at 325 °F for 20 minutes.
8. Top the tortilla with the cooked mixture and roll.
9. Sprinkle cheese on the top side.
10. Add the air fryer basket to the Ninja Foodi Grill.
11. Air fry the burrito at 375 degrees F for 10 minutes.

Serving Suggestions: You can also serve this as a snack.
Preparation / Cooking Tips: The burrito can be made ahead and frozen. Take it out of the freezer 30 minutes before cooking it.

INGREDIENTS

- 1 teaspoon olive oil
- 1 lb. breakfast sausage
- 2 cups potatoes, diced
- Salt and pepper to taste
- 10 eggs, beaten
- 3 cups cheddar cheese, shredded
- 12 tortillas

15 Mins

25 Mins

4

INGREDIENTS

- 3 large potatoes, diced
- 1 tablespoon olive oil
- 1 tablespoon butter
- Garlic salt and pepper to taste
- 3 sprigs thyme
- 2 sprigs rosemary

Roasted Breakfast Potatoes

Method

1. Add potatoes to the Ninja Foodi Grill pot.
2. Toss in olive oil and butter.
3. Season with garlic salt and pepper.
4. Top with the herb sprigs.
5. Seal the pot.
6. Set it to air fry.
7. Cook at 375 °F for 25 minutes.

Serving Suggestions: Garnish with chopped parsley.
Preparation / Cooking Tips: Stir the potatoes halfway through to ensure even cooking.

Bacon

5 Mins   10 Mins   3

Method

1. Pour water to the bottom of the Ninja Foodi Grill pot.
2. Place the grill rack inside.
3. Put the bacon slices on the grill rack.
4. Select air fry function.
5. Cook at 350 °F for 5 minutes per side or until golden and crispy.

Serving Suggestions: Serve with bread and vegetables for a complete breakfast meal.

Preparation / Cooking Tips: Use turkey bacon if you want a breakfast dish that's lower in fat and cholesterol.

INGREDIENTS

- 6 slices bacon
- 2 tablespoons water

8

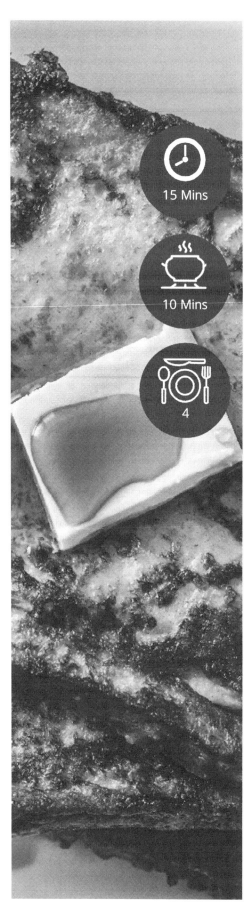

French Toast

15 Mins

10 Mins

4

Method

1. Beat the eggs in a bowl.
2. Stir in milk, cream and honey.
3. Dip the bread slices into the mixture.
4. Add to the grill basket inside the Ninja Foodi Grill.
5. Spread some butter and sprinkle sugar on top of the bread slices.
6. Seal the pot and air fry at 350 °F for 5 to 10 minutes.

Serving Suggestions: Serve with maple syrup.
Preparation / Cooking Tips: It's a good idea to use day-old bread for this recipe.

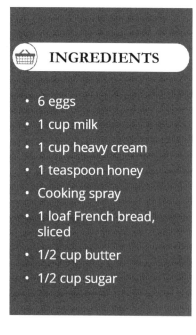

INGREDIENTS

- 6 eggs
- 1 cup milk
- 1 cup heavy cream
- 1 teaspoon honey
- Cooking spray
- 1 loaf French bread, sliced
- 1/2 cup butter
- 1/2 cup sugar

10 Mins

20 Mins

8

INGREDIENTS

- 1 1/2 lb. potatoes, diced
- 1 tablespoon avocado oil
- 1 teaspoon garlic powder
- Salt and pepper to taste

Crispy Garlic Potatoes

Method

1. Toss the potatoes in oil.
2. Season with garlic powder, salt, and pepper.
3. Add the air fryer basket to the Ninja Foodi Grill.
4. Select the air fry setting.
5. Cook at 400 °F for 20 minutes, tossing halfway through.

Serving Suggestions: Sprinkle with chopped turkey bacon crisps.
Preparation / Cooking Tips: You can also season the potatoes with paprika.

French Toast Sticks

INGREDIENTS

- 5 eggs
- 1 cup almond milk
- 1/4 cup sugar
- 1 teaspoon vanilla extract
- 4 tablespoons melted butter
- 4 bread slices, sliced into 12 sticks

10 Mins   10 Mins   12

Method

1. Beat the eggs in a bowl.
2. Stir in milk, sugar, vanilla, and butter.
3. Dip the bread sticks into the mixture.
4. Add these to the air fryer basket and place them inside the Ninja Foodi Grill.
5. Air fry at 350 °F for 8 to 10 minutes.

Serving Suggestions: Sprinkle with cinnamon powder before serving.
Preparation / Cooking Tips: Prepare in advance and freeze for later use.

15 Mins

20 Mins

4

🧺 **INGREDIENTS**

- 6 potatoes, grated
- 1 onion, chopped
- 1 bell pepper, chopped
- 2 teaspoons olive oil
- Salt and pepper to taste

Hash Browns

 **Method**

1. Toss the grated potatoes, onion and bell pepper separately in oil.
2. Season with salt and pepper.
3. Add potatoes to the air fryer.
4. Air fry at 400 °F for 10 minutes.
5. Shake and stir in onion and pepper.
6. Cook for another 10 minutes.

Serving Suggestions: Serve with a side salad.

Preparation / Cooking Tips: Soak the potatoes in water for 30 minutes after grating. Dry completely with paper towels before cooking. Doing this technique results in a crispier hash brown.

Eggs & Avocado

10 Mins

15 Mins

2

Method

1. Scoop out about a tablespoon of avocado flesh to make a hole.
2. Crack an egg on top of the avocado.
3. Season with salt and pepper.
4. Sprinkle with cheese.
5. Air fry at 390 degrees °F for 12 to 15 minutes.

Serving Suggestions: Serve with salsa or hot sauce.
Preparation / Cooking Tips: Scoop out more avocado flesh to create a bigger hole for the egg.

INGREDIENTS

- 1 avocado, sliced in half and pitted
- 2 eggs
- Salt and pepper to taste
- Cheddar cheese, shredded

Sausage Casserole

15 Mins | **20 Mins** | **4**

INGREDIENTS

- 1 lb. hash browns
- 1 lb. ground breakfast sausage, cooked
- 1 white onion, chopped
- 2 red bell peppers, chopped
- 4 eggs, beaten
- Salt and pepper to taste

Method

1. Line the air fryer basket with foil.
2. Add hash browns at the bottom part.
3. Spread sausage, onion, and bell peppers on top.
4. Air fry at 355 °F for 10 minutes.
5. Pour eggs on top and cook for another 10 minutes.
6. Season with salt and pepper.

Serving Suggestions: Garnish with chopped herbs.

Preparation / Cooking Tips: You can also use turkey sausage for this recipe.

10 Mins

15 Mins

2

🛒 **INGREDIENTS**

- 1 large bell pepper, sliced in half
- 1 teaspoon olive oil
- 4 eggs, beaten
- Salt and pepper to taste

Breakfast Bell Peppers

 **Method**

1. Brush the bell pepper halves with oil.
2. Pour eggs into the bell pepper.
3. Sprinkle with salt and pepper.
4. Place these in the air fryer basket.
5. Set the Ninja Foodi Grill to air fry.
6. Cook at 390 °F for 15 minutes.

Serving Suggestions: Sprinkle with chopped parsley before serving.
Preparation / Cooking Tips: You can also crack the eggs into the bell peppers.

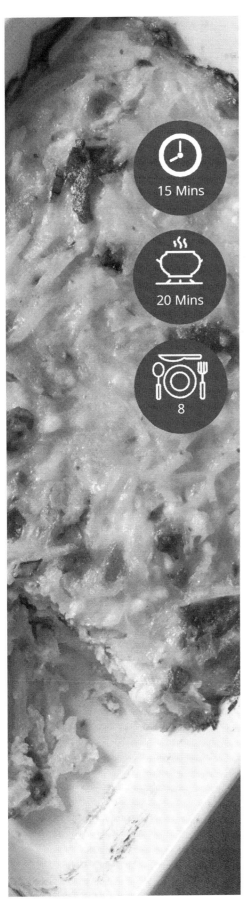

Ham & Cheese Casserole

15 Mins

20 Mins

8

Method

1. Line the air fryer basket with foil.
2. Spread ham on the bottom of the basket.
3. Top with cheese, onion, bell peppers and eggs.
4. Sprinkle with salt and pepper.
5. Choose the air fry function.
6. Cook at 390 degrees F for 15 to 20 minutes.

Serving Suggestions: Sprinkle with grated Parmesan cheese before serving.
Preparation / Cooking Tips: You can also use cheddar cheese in place of Colby Jack cheese

INGREDIENTS

- 1 lb. ham, chopped and cooked
- 2 cups Colby Jack cheese, shredded
- 1 white onion, chopped
- 1 red bell pepper, chopped
- 1 yellow bell pepper, chopped
- 8 eggs, beaten
- Salt and pepper to taste

INGREDIENTS

- 12 organic eggs
- ½ cup unsweetened almond milk
- Salt and ground black pepper, as required
- 1 head cauliflower, shredded
- 1 small onion, chopped
- 1-pound sugar-free ham, chopped
- 8 ounces Cheddar cheese, shredded

15 Mins | 7 Hours | 8

Ham & Cauliflower Casserole

 directions :

1. In a bowl, add the eggs, almond milk, salt and black pepper and beat well.
2. In the bottom of the greased pot of Ninja Foodie, place one-third of the cauliflower.
3. Top with one-third of onion.
4. Sprinkle with salt and black pepper.
5. Top with one-third of ham pieces and a third of the cheese.
6. Repeat the layers twice.
7. Top with the egg mixture evenly.
8. Close the Ninja Foodi with a crisping lid and select "Slow Cooker".
9. Set on "Low" for 6-7 hours.
10. Press "Start/Stop" to begin cooking.
11. Cut into equal-sized wedges and serve hot.

Nutrition :
- Calories: 315
- Fats: 21.1g
- Net Carbs: 4g
- Carbs: 5.8g
- Fiber: 1.8g
- Sugar: 1.8g
- Proteins: 25.6g
- Sodium: 1000mg

Ham & Zucchini Casserole

 15 Mins

 8h 7Mins

 10

directions:

1. Select the "Sauté/Sear" setting of Ninja Foodi and place the butter into the pot.
2. Press "Start/Stop" to begin cooking and heat for about 2-3 minutes.
3. Add the onion and cook for around 4-5 minutes.
4. Add the zucchini and cook for about 1-2 minutes.
5. Meanwhile, in a bowl, add the eggs and cream and beat well.
6. Press "Start/Stop" to stop cooking and stir in the ham, egg mixture, and cheese.
7. Close the Ninja Foodi with a crisping lid and select "Slow Cooker".
8. Set on "Low" for 8 hours.
9. Press "Start/Stop" to begin cooking.
10. Cut into equal-sized wedges and serve hot.

Nutrition :
- Calories: 520
- Fats: 39.7g
- Net Carbs: 5.4g
- Carbs: 7.1g
- Fiber: 1.7g
- Sugar: 2.5g
- Proteins: 34.2g
- Sodium: 1200mg

INGREDIENTS

- 2 tablespoons butter
- 1 onion, chopped
- 1-pound zucchini, chopped
- 1-pound sugar-free ham, cubed
- 12 large organic eggs, beaten
- 1 cup heavy whipping cream
- 16 ounces Cheddar cheese, shredded

10 Mins

4 Hours

4

Spinach Quiche

INGREDIENTS

- 10 ounces frozen chopped spinach, thawed and squeezed
- 4 ounces' feta cheese, shredded
- 2 cups unsweetened almond milk
- 4 organic eggs
- ¼ teaspoon red pepper flakes, crushed
- Salt and ground black pepper, as required

 directions:

1. In the pot of Ninja Foodie, add all the ingredients and mix until well combined.
2. Close the Ninja Foodi with a crisping lid and select "Slow Cooker".
3. Set on "Low" for 4 hours.
4. Press "Start/Stop" to begin cooking.
5. Cut into equal-sized wedges and serve hot.

Nutrition :
- Calories : 174
- Fats : 12.5g
- Net Carbs: 3g
- Carbs: 5.1g
- Fiber: 2.1g
- Sugar: 1.8g
- Proteins: 12.1g
- Sodium: 563mg

10 Mins

1½ hours

12

Nuts Granola

directions:

1. In the greased pot of Ninja Foodie, add all the ingredients and mix until well combined.
2. Close the Ninja Foodi with a crisping lid and select "Slow Cooker".
3. Set on "Low" for 1½-2 hours.
4. Press "Start/Stop" to begin cooking.
5. Move the granola onto an enormous heating sheet and set aside to cool completely before serving.

Nutrition :
- Calories: 184
- Fats: 17.6g
- Net Carbs: 6g
- Carbs: 9g
- Fiber: 3g
- Sugar: 5.8g
- Proteins: 5.3g
- Sodium: 0mg

INGREDIENTS

- 1 cup raw pecans
- 1 cup raw almonds
- 1 cup raw walnuts
- 1½ teaspoons ground cinnamon
- ¼ cup Erythritol

Nuts & Seeds Granola

 INGREDIENTS

- 1/3 cup unsalted butter
- 1 teaspoon liquid stevia
- 1 teaspoon organic vanilla extract
- 1½ cups pumpkin seeds
- 1½ cups sunflower seeds
- ½ cup raw pecans, chopped roughly

- ½ cup raw hazelnuts, chopped roughly
- ½ cup raw walnuts, chopped roughly
- ½ cup raw almonds, chopped roughly
- 1 teaspoon ground cinnamon

directions:

1. Select "Sauté/Sear" setting of Ninja Foodi and place the butter into the pot.
2. Press "Start/Stop" to begin cooking and heat for about 2-3 minutes.
3. Add the fluid stevia and vanilla concentrate and mix to combine.
4. Immediately, press "Start/Stop" to stop cooking
5. Now, add the remaining ingredients and stir to combine.
6. Close the Ninja Foodi with a crisping lid and select "Slow Cooker".
7. Set on "Low" for 2 hours, stirring after every 30 minutes.
8. Press "Start/Stop" to begin cooking.
9. Move the granola onto an enormous heating sheet and set aside to cool completely before serving.

15 Mins

2 hours

12

Nutrition :
- Calories: 315
- Fats: 29.3g
- Net Carbs: 4.2g
- Carbs: 7.6g
- Fiber: 3.4g
- Sugar: 1.1g
- Proteins: 8.7g
- Sodium: 40mg

Chocolaty Granola

INGREDIENTS

5 cups unsweetened coconut, shredded

1 cup almonds, chopped

1/3 cups sunflower seeds

1/3 cups pumpkin seeds

¼ cup cacao nibs

2½ ounces coconut oil, melted

3 tablespoons Erythritol

4 tablespoons cocoa powder unsweetened

1 tablespoon lemon zest, grated finely

directions:

1. In the pot of Ninja Foodi, add all ingredients and mix well.
2. Close the Ninja Foodi with a crisping lid and select "Slow Cooker".
3. Set on "High" for 2 hours.
4. Press "Start/Stop" to begin cooking.
5. Stir the mixture after every 15 minutes.
6. Move the granola onto an enormous heating sheet and set it aside to cool completely before serving

Nutrition :

- Calories: 268
- Fats: 27.1g
- Net Carbs: 2.5g
- Carbs: 6.6g
- Fiber: 3.5g
- Sugar: 2.3g
- Proteins: 3.1g
- Sodium: 15mg

15 Mins

2 hours

20

Zucchini & Coconut Bread

 INGREDIENTS

- 2½ cups zucchini, shredded
- ½ teaspoon salt
- 1 1/3 cups almond flour
- 2/3 cup coconut, shredded
- ½ cup Erythritol
- ¼ cup unflavored whey protein powder
- 2 teaspoons organic baking powder
- 2 teaspoons ground cinnamon
- ½ teaspoon ground ginger
- ¼ teaspoon ground nutmeg
- 3 large organic eggs
- ¼ cup butter, melted
- ¼ cup water
- ½ teaspoon organic vanilla extract
- ½ cup walnuts, chopped

directions:

1. Arrange a large sieve in a sink.
2. Place the zucchini in a sieve and sprinkle with salt. Set aside to drain for about 1 hour.
3. With your hands, squeeze out the moisture from zucchini.
4. In a large bowl, add the almond flour, coconut, Erythritol, protein powder, baking powder and spices and mix well.
5. Add the zucchini, eggs, coconut oil, water, and vanilla extract and mix until well combined.
6. Fold in the walnuts.
7. In the bottom of a greased Ninja Foodie, place the mixture.
8. Close the Ninja Foodi with a crisping lid and select "Slow Cooker".
9. Set on "Low" for 2½-3 hours.
10. Press "Start/Stop" to begin cooking.
11. Keep the bread inside for about 5-10 minutes.
12. Carefully, remove the bread from the pot and place it onto a wire rack to cool completely before slicing.
13. Cut the bread into desired-sized slices and serve.

Nutrition :
- Calories: 224
- Fats: 19.1g
- Net Carbs: 3.7g
- Carbs: 6.8g
- Fiber: 3.1g
- Sugar: 1.6g
- Proteins: 10g
- Sodium: 180mg

15 Mins

3 hours

10

Carrot Bread

INGREDIENTS

- 1 cup almond flour
- 1/3 cup coconut flour
- 1½ teaspoons organic baking powder
- ½ teaspoon baking soda
- ½ teaspoon xanthan gum
- 1 teaspoon ground cinnamon
- ¼ teaspoon ground cloves
- ¼ teaspoon ground nutmeg
- ¼ teaspoon salt
- 1 cup Erythritol
- 1/3 cup coconut oil, softened
- 3 organic eggs
- 1 teaspoon organic vanilla extract
- ½ teaspoon organic almond extract
- 2 cups plus 2 tablespoons carrots, peeled and shredded

directions:

1. In a bowl, add the flours, baking powder, baking soda, spices and salt and mix well.
2. In another large bowl, add the Erythritol, coconut oil, eggs and both extracts and beat until well combined.
3. Add the flour mixture and mix until just combined.
4. Fold in the carrots.
5. Place the mixture into a greased 8x4-inch silicone bread pan.
6. Arrange a "Reversible Rack" in the pot of Ninja Foodi.
7. Place the pan over the "Reversible Rack".
8. Close the Ninja Foodi with a crisping lid and select "Slow Cooker".
9. Set on "Low" for 3 hours.
10. Press "Start/Stop" to begin cooking.
11. Place the bread pan onto a wire rack for about 5-10 minutes.
12. Carefully, remove the bread from the pan and place it onto the wire rack to cool completely before slicing.
13. Cut the bread into desired-sized slices and serve.

15 Mins

3 hours

12

Nutrition :
- Calories: 133
- Fats: 11.9g
- Net Carbs: 3g
- Carbs: 4.8g
- Fiber: 1.8g
- Sugar: 1.4g
- Proteins: 3.6g
- Sodium: 178mg

Savory Cauliflower Bread

INGREDIENTS

- 12 ounces cauliflower florets
- 2 large organic eggs
- 2 cups mozzarella cheese, shredded and divided
- 3 tablespoons coconut flour
- Salt and ground black pepper, as required
- 2 garlic cloves, minced

directions:

1. In the food processor, add cauliflower and blend until a ricelike consistency is achieved.
2. Transfer the cauliflower rice into a large bowl.
3. Add 1 cup of the cheese, eggs, coconut flour, salt and black pepper and mix until well combined.
4. In a greased pot of Ninja Foodie, place the cauliflower mixture and press firmly.
5. Sprinkle with garlic and the remaining cheese evenly.
6. Close the Ninja Foodi with a crisping lid and select "Slow Cooker".
7. Set on "High" for 2-4 hours.
8. Press "Start/Stop" to begin cooking.
9. Keep the bread inside for about 5-10 minutes.
10. Carefully, remove the bread from the pot and place it onto a platter.
11. Cut the bread into desired-sized slices and serve warm.

15 Mins

4 hours

8

Nutrition:
- Calories: 72
- Fats: 3.3g
- Net Carbs: 2.9g
- Carbs: 5.9g
- Fiber: 3g
- Sugar: 1.5g
- Proteins: 5.2g
- Sodium: 104mg

Pecan & Coconut Porridge

INGREDIENTS

- 1 cup pecan halves
- ½ cup unsweetened dried coconut shreds
- ¼ cup pumpkin seeds, shelled
- 1 cup water
- 2 teaspoons butter, melted
- 4-6 drops liquid stevia

directions:

1. In the food processor, add the walnuts, coconut and pumpkin seeds and pulse for about 30 seconds.
2. In the pot of Ninja Foodie, place the pecan mixture and the remaining ingredients and stir to combine.
3. Close the Ninja Foodi with a crisping lid and select "Slow Cooker".
4. Set on "High" for 1 hour.
5. Press "Start/Stop" to begin cooking.
6. Serve warm.

Nutrition:
- Calories: 317
- Fats: 31.5g
- Net Carbs: 2.9g
- Carbs: 7.5g
- Fiber: 4.6g
- Sugar: 1.8g
- Proteins: 5.8g
- Sodium: 19mg

15 Mins

1 hours

4

Pumpkin Porridge

INGREDIENTS

- 1 cup unsweetened almond milk, divided
- 2 pounds pumpkin, peeled and cubed into ½-inch size
- 6-8 drops liquid stevia
- ½ teaspoon ground allspice
- 1 tablespoon ground cinnamon
- 1 teaspoon ground nutmeg
- ¼ teaspoon ground cloves

directions:

1. In the pot of Ninja Foodie, place ½ cup of almond milk and remaining ingredients and stir to combine.
2. Close the Ninja Foodi with a crisping lid and select "Slow Cooker".
3. Set on "Low" for 4-5 hours.
4. Press "Start/Stop" to begin cooking.
5. Stir in the remaining almond milk and with a potato masher, mash the mixture completely.
6. Serve warm.

Nutrition:
- Calories: 48
- Fats: 0.9g
- Net Carbs: 6g
- Carbs: 10g
- Fiber: 4g
- Sugar: 3.8g
- Proteins: 1.4g
- Sodium: 29mg

15 Mins

5 hours

4

Sausage & Veggies Casserole

 INGREDIENTS

- 2½ cups cauliflower florets
- 12 organic eggs
- ¾ cup unsweetened almond milk
- 1 teaspoon dried oregano, crushed
- ¾ teaspoon paprika
- Salt, as required
- 1 red ringer pepper, seeded and cleaved finely
- 1-pound gluten-free cooked sausages cut into slices
- 1½ cups Cheddar cheese, grated

 directions:

1. In an enormous dish of bubbling water, cook cauliflower for about 2-3 minutes.
2. Expel from the warmth and channel the cauliflower completely.
3. Set aside to cool.
4. In a bowl, add the eggs, almond milk, and oregano, paprika and salt and beat until well combined.
5. In the bottom of a greased pot of Ninja Foodie, place the cauliflowers, followed by the bell pepper, sausage slices, and Cheddar cheese.
6. Top with the egg mixture evenly.
7. Close the Ninja Foodi with a crisping lid and select "Slow Cooker".
8. Set on "Low" for 6-7 hours.
9. Press "Start/Stop" to begin cooking.
10. Cut into equal-sized wedges and serve hot.

Nutrition :
- Calories: 389
- Fats: 30.1g
- Net Carbs: 2.8g
- Carbs: 4g
- Fiber: 1.2g
- Sugar: 2.2g
- Proteins: 25.2g
- Sodium: 695mg

15 Mins

7h 3 Mins

8

Appetizers & Snacks

Honey Mustard Chicken Tenders

5 Mins **3 Mins** **4**

 directions:

1. Grab a bowl, using a whisk mix the mustard, olive oil, honey, and pepper into it
2. Add the chicken and toss to coat
3. Grind the walnut in your food processor
4. Supplement the flame broil mesh and close the hood
5. Pre-heat Ninja Foodi by pressing the "GRILL" option and setting it to "HIGH" for 4 minutes
6. Toss the chicken tenders in the ground walnuts to coat them lightly
7. Grill the chicken tender for 3 minutes
8. Serve hot and enjoy!

Nutrition:
- Calories: 444 kcal
- Carbs: 26 g
- Fat: 20 g.
- Protein: 6 g

 INGREDIENTS

- 2 pounds chicken tenders
- 1/2 cup Dijon mustard
- 1/2 cup walnuts
- 2 tablespoons honey
- 2 tablespoons olive oil
- 1 teaspoon black pepper, ground

- 2 small eggplants cut into slices
- 1/4 cup olive oil
- 2 tablespoons lime juice
- 3 teaspoons Cajun seasoning

5-10 Mins

10 Mins

8

Cajun Eggplant Appetizer

 directions :

1. Coat the eggplant slices with oil, lemon juices and Cajun seasoning add the chicken wings and combine well to coat
2. Arrange the grill grate and close the lid
3. Pre-heat Ninja Foodi by pressing the "GRILL" option and setting it to "MED" and timer to 10 minutes
4. Let it pre-heat until you hear a beep
5. Arrange the eggplant slices over the grill grate, lock lid and cook for 5 minutes
6. Flip the chicken and close the lid, cook for 5 minutes more
7. Serve warm and enjoy!

Nutrition:
- Calories: 362 kcal
- Carbs: 16 g
- Fat: 11 g.
- Protein: 8 g

Fajita Skewers

10 Mins   14 Mins   8

directions:

- Thread the steak, tortillas, scallions, and pepper on the skewers
- Drizzle olive oil, salt, black pepper over the skewers
- Pre-heat Ninja Foodi by pressing the "GRILL" option and setting it to "MED"
- Once preheated, open the lid and place 4 skewers on the grill
- Cover the lid and grill for 7 minutes
- Keep rotating skewers for every 2 minutes
- Serve warm and enjoy!

Nutrition:
- Calories: 353 kcal
- Carbs: 11 g
- Fat: 7.5 g.
- Protein: 13.1 g

INGREDIENTS

- 1-pound sirloin steak, cubed
- Olive oil, for drizzling
- 1 bunch scallions cut into large pieces
- 4 large bell pepper, cubed
- 1 pack tortillas, torn
- Salt to taste
- Black pepper, grounded

Honey Asparagus

 10 Mins
 15 Mins
 4

directions:

1. Take a bowl and add asparagus, oil, salt, honey, pepper, tarragon, and toss well
2. Pre heat Ninja Foodi by pressing the "GRILL" option and setting it to "MED" and timer to 8 minutes
3. Let it pre heat until you hear a beep
4. Arrange asparagus over grill grate, lock lid and cook for 4 minutes, flip asparagus and cook for 4 minutes more
5. Serve and enjoy!

Nutrition:
- Calories: 240 kcal
- Carbs: 31 g
- Fat: 15 g.
- Protein: 7 g

INGREDIENTS

- 2 pounds asparagus, trimmed
- 1/2 teaspoon pepper
- 1 teaspoon salt
- 1/4 cup honey
- 2 tablespoons olive oil
- 4 tablespoons tarragon, minced

 INGREDIENTS

- 1-pound potato, peeled
- 1 tablespoon olive oil
- 1 teaspoon dried dill
- 1 teaspoon dried oregano
- 1/4 teaspoon chili flakes

 10 Mins

 20 Mins

 4

Crispy Potato Cubes

 directions :

1. Pre-heat Ninja Foodi by squeezing the "AIR CRISP" alternative and setting it to "400 °F" and timer to 20 minutes
2. Let it pre-heat until you hear a beep
3. Cut potatoes into cubes
4. Sprinkle potato cubes with dill, oregano and chili flakes
5. Transfer to Foodi Grill and cook for 15 minutes
6. Stir while cooking, once they are crunchy
7. Serve and enjoy!

Nutrition:
- Calories: 119 kcal
- Carbs: 20 g
- Fat: 4 g.
- Protein: 12 g

- 1/4 teaspoon salt
- 1 egg
- 3/4 cup milk
- 1 tablespoon baking powder
- 3/4 cup breadcrumbs
- 1 large onion
- 1 cup flour
- 1 teaspoon paprika

10 Mins

10 Mins

4

Healthy Onion Rings

 directions :

1. Pre-heat Ninja Foodi by squeezing the "AIR CRISP" alternative and setting it to "340 °F" and timer to 10 minutes
2. Let it pre-heat until you hear a beep
3. Take a bowl and whisk the egg, milk, salt, flour, and paprika together
4. Slice the onion and separate it into rings
5. Grease your Ninja Foodi Grill with cooking spray
6. Then dip the onion rings into batter and coat with breadcrumbs
7. Arrange them in Ninja Foodi Grill Cooking Basket
8. Cook for 10 minutes
9. Serve and enjoy!

Nutrition:
- Calories: 450 kcal
- Carbs: 56 g
- Fat: 13 g.
- Protein: 30 g

Lemon-Garlic Shrimp Caesar Salad

10 Mins   5 Mins   4

 directions:

1. Add the flame broils mesh and closes the hood. Pre-heat Ninja Foodi by pressing the "GRILL" option and setting it to "MAX" and timer to 5 minutes
2. Take a large bowl; toss the shrimp with the lemon juice, garlic, salt, and pepper
3. Let it marinate while the grill is preheating
4. Once it pre-heat until you hear a beep
5. Arrange the shrimp over the grill grate lock lid and cook for 5 minutes
6. Toss the romaine lettuce with the Caesar dressing
7. Once cooked completely, remove the shrimp from the grill
8. Sprinkle with parmesan cheese
9. Serve and enjoy!

Nutrition:
- Calories: 279 kcal
- Carbs: 17 g
- Fat: 11 g.
- Protein: 30 g

 INGREDIENTS

- 1-pound fresh jumbo shrimp
- 2 heads romaine lettuce, chopped
- 3/4 cup Caesar dressing
- 1/2 cup parmesan cheese, grated
- 1/2 lemon juice
- 3 garlic cloves, minced
- Sea salt
- Black pepper, grounded

 INGREDIENTS

- 6 slices bacon, chopped
- 1-pound Brussels sprouts, halved
- 1/2 teaspoon black pepper
- 1 tablespoon of sea salt
- 2 tablespoons olive oil, extra-virgin

 5-10 Mins

 12 Mins

 4

Bacon Brussels Delight

 directions :

1. Take a mixing bowl and toss the Brussels sprouts, olive oil, bacon, salt, and black pepper
2. Arrange the crisping basket inside the pot
3. Pre-heat Ninja Foodi by squeezing the "AIR CRISP" setting at 390 °F and timer to 12 minutes
4. Let it pre-heat until you hear a beep
5. Arrange the Brussels sprout mixture directly inside the basket
6. Close the top lid and cook for 6 minutes, then shake the basket
7. Close the top lid and cook for 6 minutes more
8. Serve warm and enjoy!

Nutrition:
- Calories: 279 kcal
- Carbs: 12.5 g
- Fat: 18.5 g.
- Protein: 14.5 g

Seared Tuna Salad

 10 Mins
 6 Mins
 4

directions:

1. Supplement the flame broil mesh and close the hood
2. Pre-heat Ninja Foodi by pressing the "GRILL" option at and setting it to "MAX" and timer to 6 minutes
3. Take a small bowl, whisk together the rice vinegar, salt, and pepper
4. Slowly pour in the oil while whisking until vinaigrette is fully combined
5. Season the fish with salt and pepper, sprinkle with the sesame oil
6. Once it pre-heat until you hear a beep
7. Arrange the shrimp over the grill grate lock lid and cook for 6 minutes
8. Do not flip during cooking
9. Once cooked completely, top salad with tuna strip
10. Drizzle the vinaigrette over the top
11. Serve immediately and enjoy!

Nutrition:
- Calories: 427 kcal
- Carbs: 5 g
- Fat: 30 g.
- Protein: 36 g

INGREDIENTS

1/2-pounds ahi tuna, cut into four strips

- 2 tablespoons sesame oil
- 1(10 ounces) bag baby greens
- 2 tablespoons of rice wine vinegar
- 6 tablespoons extra-virgin olive oil
- 1/2 English cucumber, sliced
- 1/4 teaspoon of sea salt
- 1/2 teaspoon ground black pepper

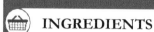
- 8 small Portobello mushrooms, trimmed with gills removed
- 1 tomato, sliced
- 2 tablespoons canola oil
- 1/2 cup pesto
- 1/2 cup micro greens
- 2 tablespoons balsamic vinegar
- 8 slider buns

10 Mins

8 Mins

4

Portobello and Pesto Sliders

 directions :

1. Addition the flame broils mesh and closes the hood
2. Pre-heat Ninja Foodi by pressing the "GRILL" option at and setting it to "HIGH" and timer to 8 minutes
3. Brush the mushrooms with oil and balsamic vinegar
4. Once it pre-heat until you hear a beep
5. Arrange the mushrooms over the grill grate lock lid and cook for 8 minutes
6. Once cooked, removed the mushrooms from the grill and layer on the buns with tomato, pesto, and micro greens
7. Serve immediately and enjoy!

Nutrition:
- Calories: 373 kcal
- Carbs: 33 g
- Fat: 22 g.
- Protein: 12 g

Crispy Rosemary Potatoes

10 Mins

20 Mins

4

directions:

1. Take a large bowl and add all the listed ingredients, toss well and coat them well
2. Pre-heat Ninja Foodi by squeezing the "AIR CRISP" alternative and setting it to "390 °F" and clock to 20 minutes
3. Let it pre-heat until you hear a beep
4. Once preheated, add potatoes to the cooking basket
5. Lock and cook for 10 minutes, making sure to shake the basket and cook for 10 minutes more
6. Once done, check the crispiness, if it's alright, serve away.
7. If not, cook for 5 minutes more
8. Enjoy!

Nutrition:
- Calories: 232 kcal
- Carbs: 39 g
- Fat: 7 g.
- Protein: 4 g

INGREDIENTS

- 2 pounds baby red potatoes, quartered
- 2 tablespoons extra virgin olive oil
- 1/4 cup dried onion flakes
- 1/2 teaspoon onion powder
- 1/2 teaspoon garlic powder
- 1/4 teaspoon celery powder
- 1/4 teaspoon freshly ground black pepper
- 1/2 teaspoon dried parsley
- 1/2 teaspoon salt

Simple Crispy Brussels

 **INGREDIENTS**

- 1-pound Brussels sprouts, halved
- 2 tablespoons olive oil, extra virgin
- 1/2 teaspoon ground black pepper
- 1 teaspoon salt
- 6 slices bacon, chopped

directions:

1. Take a mixing bowl and add Brussels, olive oil, salt, pepper, and bacon
2. Pre-heat Ninja Foodi by squeezing the "AIR CRISP" alternative and setting it to "390 °F and clock to 12 minutes
3. Let it pre-heat until you hear a beep
4. Arrange the Brussels over basket and lock lid, cook for 6 minutes, shake and cook for 6 minutes more
5. Serve and enjoy.

Nutrition:
- Calories: 279 kcal
- Carbs: 12 g
- Fat: 18 g.
- Protein: 14 g

10 Mins

12 Mins

4

Sweet Potato Wedges

 INGREDIENTS

- 2 sweet potatoes, sliced into wedges
- 1 tablespoon vegetable oil
- 1 teaspoon smoked paprika
- 1 tablespoon honey
- Salt and pepper to taste

Method

1. Add an air fryer basket to your Ninja Foodi Grill.
2. Choose air fry setting.
3. Preheat at 390 °F for 25 minutes.
4. Add sweet potato wedges to the basket.
5. Cook for 10 minutes.
6. Stir and cook for another 10 minutes.
7. Toss in paprika and honey.

Preparation / Cooking Tips: Soak sweet potato wedges in cold water for 30 minutes, and then drain and pat dry before seasoning.

10 Mins

20 Mins

4

Crispy Pickles

 INGREDIENTS

- 1 cup all-purpose flour
- 3 eggs
- 1 cup breadcrumbs
- Garlic salt to taste
- 12 dill pickle spears
- Cooking spray

 Method

1. Dip pickles in flour, eggs, and then in a mixture of breadcrumbs and garlic salt.
2. Arrange on a plate.
3. Place inside the freezer for 30 minutes.
4. Add a crisper basket to the Ninja Foodi Grill.
5. Choose air fry function.
6. Add pickles to the basket.
7. Spray with oil.
8. Cook at 375 °F for 18 to 20 minutes.
9. Flip and cook for another 10 minutes.

Serving Suggestions: Mix mayo, mustard and ketchup. Serve with fried pickles.

Preparation / Cooking Tips: Pat the pickles dry with a paper towel before breading.

15 Mins

30 Mins

4

Grilled Tomato Salsa

INGREDIENTS

- 1 onion, sliced
- 1 jalapeño pepper, sliced in half
- 5 tomatoes, sliced
- 2 tablespoons oil
- Salt and pepper to taste
- 1 cup cilantro, trimmed and sliced
- 1 tablespoon lime juice
- 1 teaspoon lime zest
- 2 tablespoons ground cumin
- 3 cloves garlic, peeled and sliced

Method

1. Coat onion, jalapeño pepper, and tomatoes with oil.
2. Season with salt and pepper.
3. Add the grill grate to your Ninja Foodi Grill.
4. Press the grill setting.
5. Choose the max temperature and set it to 10 minutes.
6. Press start to preheat.
7. Add vegetables to the grill.
8. Cook for 5 minutes per side.
9. Transfer to a plate and let it cool.
10. Add vegetable mixture to a food processor.
11. Stir in the remaining ingredients.
12. Blend until smooth.

15 Mins

10 Mins

4 to 8

Serving Suggestions: Serve with nacho chips.

Preparation / Cooking Tips: You can also add chili powder to the food processor if you want your salsa spicy.

Parmesan French Fries

 INGREDIENTS

- 1 lb. French fries
- 1/2 cup mayonnaise
- 2 cloves garlic, minced
- 1 tablespoon oil
- Salt and pepper to taste
- 1 teaspoon garlic powder
- 1/2 cup Parmesan cheese, grated
- 1 teaspoon lemon juice

Method

1. Add a crisper basket to your Ninja Foodi Grill.
2. Select the air fry function.
3. Set it to 375 °F for 22 minutes.
4. Press start to preheat.
5. Add fries to the basket.
6. Cook for 10 minutes.
7. Shake and cook for another 5 minutes.
8. Toss in oil and sprinkle with Parmesan cheese.
9. Mix the remaining ingredients in a bowl.
10. Serve fries with this sauce.

Serving Suggestions: Sprinkle chopped parsley and serve.
Preparation / Cooking Tips: Buy frozen fries for convenience.

15 Mins

15 Mins

6

Fish Sticks

 INGREDIENTS

- 16 oz. tilapia fillets, sliced into strips
- 1 cup all-purpose flour
- 2 eggs
- 1 1/2 cups breadcrumbs
- Salt to taste

 Method

1. Dip fish strips in flour and then in eggs.
2. Mix breadcrumbs and salt.
3. Coat fish strips with breadcrumbs.
4. Add fish strips to a crisper plate.
5. Place the crisper plate inside the basket.
6. Choose the air fry setting.
7. Cook fish strips at 390 °F for 12 to 15 minutes, flipping once halfway done.

Serving Suggestions: Serve with tartar sauce and ketchup.
Preparation / Cooking Tips: You can use other types of white fish for this recipe.

15 Mins

15 Mins

8

Homemade Fries

15 Mins

45 Mins

6

 **Method**

1. Toss potato strips in oil.
2. Add the crisper plate to the air fryer basket inside the Ninja Foodi Grill.
3. Choose the air fry function. Set it to 390 °F for 3 minutes.
4. Press start to preheat.
5. Add potato strips to the crisper plate.
6. Cook for 25 minutes.
7. Stir and cook for another 20 minutes.

Serving Suggestions: Serve with ketchup and mayo.
Preparation / Cooking Tips: Soak potato strips in cold water for 30 minutes before cooking.

INGREDIENTS

- 1 lb. large potatoes, sliced into strips
- 2 tablespoons vegetable oil
- Salt to taste

20 Mins

15 Mins

6

Fried Garlic Pickles

 Method

1. In a bowl, combine flour, baking powder, water and salt.
2. Add more water if the batter is too thick.
3. Put the cornstarch in a second bowl, and mix breadcrumbs and garlic powder in a third bowl.
4. Dip pickles in cornstarch, then in the batter and finally dredge with breadcrumb mixture.
5. Add crisper plate to the air fryer basket inside the Ninja Foodi Grill.
6. Press the air fry setting.
7. Set it to 360 °F for 3 minutes.
8. Press start to preheat.
9. Add pickles to the crisper plate.
10. Brush with oil.
11. Air fry for 10 minutes.
12. Flip, brush with oil, and cook for another 5 minutes.

Serving Suggestions: Serve with ketchup or sweet chili sauce.

Preparation / Cooking Tips: Dry pickles before coating with breading.

INGREDIENTS

- 1/4 cup all-purpose flour
- Pinch baking powder
- 2 tablespoons water
- Salt to taste
- 20 dill pickle slices
- 2 tablespoons cornstarch
- 1 1/2 cups panko bread crumbs
- 2 teaspoons garlic powder
- 2 tablespoons canola oil

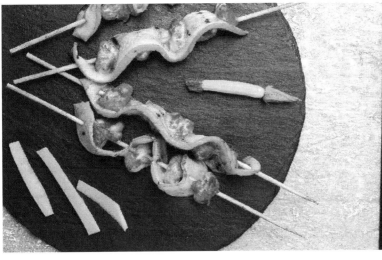

1h 10 Mins

30 Mins

8

Zucchini Strips with Marinara Dip

INGREDIENTS

- 2 zucchinis, sliced into strips
- Salt to taste
- 1 1/2 cups all-purpose flour
- 2 eggs, beaten
- 2 cups bread crumbs
- 2 teaspoons onion powder
- 1 tablespoon garlic powder
- 1/4 cup Parmesan cheese, grated
- 1/2 cup marinara sauce

Method

1. Season zucchini with salt.
2. Let sit for 15 minutes.
3. Pat dry with paper towels.
4. Add flour to a bowl.
5. Add eggs to another bowl.
6. Mix the remaining ingredients except for marinara sauce in a third bowl.
7. Dip zucchini strips in the first, second, and third bowls.
8. Cover with foil and freeze for 45 minutes.
9. Add crisper plate to the air fryer basket inside the Ninja Foodi Grill.
10. Select the air fry function.
11. Preheat to 360 °F for 3 minutes.
12. Add zucchini strips to the crisper plate.
13. Air fry for 20 minutes.
14. Flip and cook for another 10 minutes.
15. Serve with marinara dip.

Serving Suggestions: Serve with a side salad.

Preparation / Cooking Tips: Use reduced-sodium marinara sauce as a dip.

Ranch Chicken Fingers

15 Mins   20 Mins   4

 Method

1. Coat chicken strips with olive oil.
2. Sprinkle all sides with ranch seasoning.
3. Cover with foil and refrigerate for 1 to 2 hours.
4. In a bowl, mix breadcrumbs and salt.
5. Dredge the chicken strips with seasoned breadcrumbs.
6. Add crisper plate to the air fryer basket inside the Ninja Foodi Grill.
7. Choose the air fry setting.
8. Set it to 390 °F.
9. Preheat for 3 minutes.
10. Add chicken strips to the crisper plate.
11. Cook for 15 to 20 minutes, flipping halfway through.

Serving Suggestions: Serve with ketchup and mayo.
Preparation / Cooking Tips: Arrange chicken strips on the crisper plate on a single layer.

 INGREDIENTS

- 2 lb. chicken breast fillet, sliced into strips
- 1 tablespoon olive oil
- 1 oz. ranch dressing seasoning mix
- 4 cups breadcrumbs
- Salt to taste

15 Mins

10 Mins

4

Peanut Butter & Banana Snacks

Method

1. Spread peanut butter on 4 bread slices.
2. Spread jam on the remaining bread slices.
3. Add bananas and make 4 sandwiches.
4. In a bowl, mix cinnamon and sugar.
5. Select the air fry function in your Ninja Foodi Grill.
6. Set it to 390 °F for 3 minutes.
7. Add crisper plate to the air fryer basket.
8. Spray sandwiches with oil and sprinkle with the cinnamon mixture.
9. Air fry sandwiches for 6 minutes.
10. Flip and cook for 3 more minutes.

Serving Suggestions: Serve with chocolate hazelnut spread.
Preparation / Cooking Tips: Use creamy peanut butter for this recipe.

INGREDIENTS

- 1 cup peanut butter
- 8 slices whole wheat bread
- 1 cup jam
- 2 bananas, sliced
- 2 teaspoons ground cinnamon
- 1/4 cup white sugar
- Cooking spray

20 Mins

30 Mins

4

Greek Potatoes

INGREDIENTS

- 1 lb. potatoes, sliced into wedges
- 2 tablespoons olive oil
- 1 teaspoon paprika
- 2 teaspoons dried oregano
- Salt and pepper to taste
- 1/4 cup onion, diced
- 2 tablespoons lemon juice
- 1 tomato, diced
- 1/4 cup black olives, sliced
- 1/2 cup feta cheese, crumbled

Method

1. Add crisper plate to the air fryer basket inside the Ninja Foodi Grill.
2. Choose the air fry setting.
3. Set it to 390 °F.
4. Preheat for 3 minutes.
5. While preheating, toss potatoes in oil.
6. Sprinkle with paprika, oregano, salt and pepper.
7. Add potatoes to the crisper plate.
8. Air fry for 18 minutes.
9. Toss and cook for another 5 minutes.
10. Add onion and cook for 5 minutes.
11. Transfer to a bowl.
12. Stir in the rest of the ingredients.

Serving Suggestions: Garnish with fresh dill.
Preparation / Cooking Tips: Use freshly squeezed lemon juice.

Garlic Parmesan Fries

INGREDIENTS

- 3 potatoes, sliced into sticks
- 2 tablespoons vegetable oil, divided
- 1/4 cup Parmesan cheese, grated
- 2 cloves garlic, minced
- 1 teaspoon garlic powder
- Salt to taste

Method

1. Coat potato strips with half of the oil.
2. Add crisper plate to the air fryer basket inside the Ninja Foodi Grill.
3. Select the air fry function.
4. Preheat at 360 degrees F for 3 minutes.
5. Add fries to the crisper plate
6. Cook for 12 minutes.
7. Flip and cook for another 5 minutes.
8. Combine the remaining ingredients in a bowl.
9. Toss fries in the mixture and serve.

Serving Suggestions: Sprinkle with chopped parsley before serving.
Preparation / Cooking Tips: Use russet potatoes for this recipe.

15 Mins

20 Mins

4

Bacon & Sausages

 **INGREDIENTS**

- 4 sausages
- 8 bacon slices

Method

1. Add crisper plate to the air fryer basket inside the Ninja Foodi Grill.
2. Press the air fry setting.
3. Preheat at 360 °F for 3 minutes.
4. Wrap 2 bacon slices around each sausage.
5. Add these to the crisper plate.
6. Cook for 10 minutes per side.

Serving Suggestions: Serve with ketchup and mustard.
Preparation / Cooking Tips: Use Italian sausage for this recipe.

 10 Mins
 20 Mins
 4

10 Mins

10 Mins

4

Crunchy Parmesan Asparagus

Method

1. Mix flour and salt in a bowl.
2. Add eggs to a second bowl.
3. Combine Parmesan cheese and breadcrumbs in a third bowl.
4. Dip asparagus spears in the first, second and third bowls.
5. Spray with oil.
6. Add crisper plate to the air fryer basket inside the Ninja Foodi Grill.
7. Set it to air fry.
8. Preheat at 390 °F for 3 minutes.
9. Add asparagus to the plate.
10. Air fry for 5 minutes per side.

Serving Suggestions: Serve with ranch dressing as a dip.
Preparation / Cooking Tips: Dry asparagus thoroughly before breading.

INGREDIENTS

- 1/4 cup all-purpose flour
- Salt to taste
- 2 eggs, beaten
- 1/4 cup Parmesan cheese, grated
- 1/2 cup breadcrumbs
- 1 cup asparagus, trimmed
- Cooking spray

10 Mins

5 Mins

16

INGREDIENTS

- 1 pack bacon slices
- 12 bell peppers, sliced in half
- 8 oz. cream cheese

Bacon Bell Peppers

 **Method**

1. Stuff bell pepper halves with cream cheese.
2. Wrap with bacon slices.
3. Preheat Ninja Foodi Grill to 500 °F.
4. Add bell peppers to the grill.
5. Grill for 3 to 5 minutes.

Serving Suggestions: Sprinkle with chopped parsley before serving.
Preparation / Cooking Tips: You can use toothpicks to secure bacon and simply remove these before serving.

Chapter

9

Desserts

Fudge Brownies

 INGREDIENTS

- 1/2 cup all-purpose flour
- Pinch salt
- 1/4 cup cocoa powder
- 2 eggs

- 1/2 cup brown sugar
- 1/2 cup white sugar
- 1 tablespoon vanilla extract

- 1 tablespoon water
- 3/4 cup butter, melted
- 6 oz. chocolate chips, melted

 Method

1. Combine flour, salt, and cocoa powder in a bowl.
2. Beat eggs in another bowl.
3. Stir in sugars, vanilla, and water.
4. Add butter and chocolate chips to the mixture.
5. Slowly add dry ingredients to this mixture.
6. Mix well.
7. Spray a small baking pan with oil.
8. Pour batter into the pan.
9. Add crisper plate to the air fry basket in the Ninja Foodi Grill.
10. Choose the air fry setting.
11. Preheat at 300 °F for 3 minutes.
12. Add a small baking pan to the crisper plate.
13. Cook for 1 hour.

 20 Mins

 1 Hour

 6

Serving Suggestions: Serve with milk.

Preparation / Cooking Tips: Use unsweetened cocoa powder.

Baked Apples

INGREDIENTS

- 2 apples, sliced in half
- 1 tablespoon lemon juice
- 4 teaspoons brown sugar
- 1/4 cup butter, sliced into small cubes

Method

1. Add crisper plate to the air fryer basket inside the Ninja Foodi Grill.
2. Choose the air fry function.
3. Preheat it to 325 °F for 3 minutes.
4. Add apples to the crisper plate.
5. Drizzle with lemon juice and sprinkle with brown sugar.
6. Place butter cubes on top.
7. Air fry for 45 minutes.

Serving Suggestions: Top with caramel syrup or crushed graham crackers.
Preparation / Cooking Tips: Poke apples with a fork before cooking.

15 Mins

45 Mins

4

Strawberry & Cake Kebabs

 INGREDIENTS

- 1 pack white cake mix
- 2 cups strawberries, sliced in half
- 2 tablespoons honey
- 1/4 cup sugar

- Cooking spray

Method

1. Cook cake mix according to the directions in the box.
2. Insert the grill grate in the Ninja Foodi Grill.
3. Choose the grill setting.
4. Preheat at 325 °F for 15 minutes.
5. While waiting, slice the cake into cubes.
6. Toss strawberries in honey and sugar.
7. Thread cake cubes and strawberries alternately onto skewers.
8. Grill for 3 minutes per side.

Serving Suggestions: Serve with vanilla ice cream.

Preparation / Cooking Tips: When preparing a cake mix, you can replace water with pudding to make the cake thicker.

15 Mins

6 Mins

5

Grilled Donuts

INGREDIENTS

- 1/4 cup milk
- 1 teaspoon vanilla extract
- 2 cups powdered sugar
- 16 oz. prepared biscuit dough
- Cooking spray

Method

1. In a bowl, mix milk, vanilla, and sugar.
2. Cut rings from the prepared dough.
3. Refrigerate for 5 minutes.
4. Add grill grate to the Ninja Foodi Grill.
5. Choose the grill setting.
6. Set it to medium
7. Preheat for 6 minutes.
8. Spray round dough with oil.
9. Add to the grill and cook for 4 minutes.
10. Dip in the milk mixture and grill for another 4 minutes.

Serving Suggestions: Sprinkle with cinnamon sugar or chocolate sprinkles before serving.

 15 Mins

 10 Mins

 8

Grilled Apple Pie

 30 Mins

 30 Mins

 8

 INGREDIENTS

- 8 cups cold water
- 1 tablespoon lemon juice
- 8 apples, diced
- 1/2 cup brown sugar
- 1/2 teaspoon ground cinnamon
- 1/2 teaspoon ground ginger
- 3 tablespoons all-purpose flour
- 1/2 cup applesauce
- 1 frozen pie crust

 Method

1. In a bowl, mix water, lemon juice and apples.
2. Let sit for 10 minutes.
3. Drain and pat dry.
4. Add grill grate to Ninja Foodi Grill.
5. Press the grill setting.
6. Set it to the max and preheat for 8 minutes.
7. Coat apples with sugar.
8. Grill for 8 minutes without flipping.
9. In a bowl, combine the remaining ingredients.
10. Stir in grilled apples.
11. Pour the mixture into a small baking pan.
12. Top with the pie crust.
13. Select the bake setting.
14. Cook pie at 350 °F for 20 minutes.

Serving Suggestions: Serve with vanilla ice cream.

Preparation / Cooking Tips: Defrost pie crust before using.

Peanut Butter Cups

INGREDIENTS

- 4 graham crackers
- 4 peanut butter cups
- 4 marshmallows

Method

1. Add a crisper plate to the air fryer basket of your Ninja Foodi Grill.
2. Choose the air fry function.
3. Preheat at 360 °F for 3 minutes.
4. Break the crackers in half.
5. Add crackers to the crisper plate.
6. Top with the peanut butter cups.
7. Cook for 2 minutes.
8. Sprinkle mushrooms on top and cook for another 1 minute.

Preparation / Cooking Tips: You can also use chocolate spread in place of peanut butter cups if you like.

5 Mins

5 Mins

4

Cookies

- 4 oz. cookie dough

Method

1. Choose the air fry setting in your Ninja Foodi Grill.
2. Set it to 350 °F.
3. Preheat it for 1 minute.
4. Line air fryer basket with parchment paper.
5. Create 6 cookies from the dough.
6. Add these to the air fryer basket.
7. Place the air fryer basket inside the unit.
8. Cook for 8 to 10 minutes.

Serving Suggestions: Serve with warm milk.

Preparation / Cooking Tips: Make sure there is enough space between the cookies.

10 Mins

10 Mins

65

Fried Oreos

INGREDIENTS

- 8 oz. crescent rolls (refrigerated)
- 16 Oreos
- 3 tablespoons peanut butter

Method

1. Spread dough onto a working surface.
2. Slice into 8 rectangles.
3. Slice each rectangle into 2.
4. Add cookie on top of the dough.
5. Spread with peanut butter.
6. Wrap the dough around the Oreos.
7. Place these in the air fryer basket inside the Ninja Foodi Grill.
8. Choose the air fry setting.
9. Air fry at 320 °F for 5 minutes.

Serving Suggestions: Dust with powdered sugar before serving.
Preparation / Cooking Tips: You can also use this recipe for other sandwich cookies.

10 Mins

5 Mins

8

Cinnamon Apple Chips

 INGREDIENTS

- 1 apple, sliced thinly
- 2 teaspoons vegetable oil
- 1 teaspoon ground cinnamon
- Cooking spray

Method

1. Coat the apple slices in oil and sprinkle with cinnamon.
2. Spray the air fryer basket with oil.
3. Choose the air fry setting in the Ninja Foodi Grill.
4. Air fry the apples at 375 °F for 12 minutes, flipping once or twice.

Serving Suggestions: Serve with almond yogurt dip.

Preparation / Cooking Tips: Use a mandolin to slice the apples very thinly.

10 Mins

12 Mins

4

Strawberry Pop Tarts

INGREDIENTS

- 8 oz. strawberries
- 1/4 cup granulated sugar
- 1 refrigerated pie crust
- Cooking spray

Method

1. Combine strawberries and sugar in a pan over medium heat.
2. Cook while stirring for 10 minutes.
3. Let it cool.
4. Spread pie crust on your kitchen table.
5. Slice into rectangles.
6. Add strawberries on top of the rectangles.
7. Brush edges with water.
8. Wrap and seal.
9. Spray tarts with oil.
10. Add tarts to the air fryer basket.
11. Choose the air fry setting in your Ninja Foodi Grill.
12. Air fry at 350 °F for 10 minutes.
13. Let it cool before serving.

Serving Suggestions: Sprinkle with colorful candy sprinkles before serving.
Preparation / Cooking Tips: You can also use other berries for this recipe.

20 Mins

20 Mins

6

Chicken

&

Turkey

Chicken & Zucchini

 INGREDIENTS

- 1/4 cup olive oil
- 1 tablespoon lemon juice
- 2 tablespoons red wine vinegar
- 1 teaspoon oregano
- 1 tablespoon garlic, chopped
- 2 chicken breast fillet, sliced into cubes

- 1 zucchini, sliced
- 1 red onion, sliced
- 1 cup cherry tomatoes, sliced
- Salt and pepper to taste

directions:

1. In a bowl, mix the olive oil, lemon juice, vinegar, oregano and garlic.
2. Pour half of the mixture into another bowl.
3. Toss chicken in half of the mixture.
4. Cover and marinate for 15 minutes.
5. Toss the veggies in the remaining mixture.
6. Season both chicken and veggies with salt and pepper.
7. Add chicken to the air fryer basket.
8. Spread veggies on top.
9. Select the air fry function.
10. Seal and cook at 380 °F for 15 to 20 minutes.

Serving Suggestions: Garnish with lemon wedges.

Preparation / Cooking Tips: If you want to marinate longer, cover and refrigerate for 1 hour.

30 Mins

20 Mins

6

Chicken Quesadilla

INGREDIENTS

- 4 tortillas
- Cooking spray
- 1/2 cup sour cream
- 1/2 cup salsa
- Hot sauce
- 12 oz. chicken breast fillet, chopped and grilled
- 3 jalapeño peppers, diced
- 2 cups cheddar cheese, shredded
- Chopped scallions

directions:

1. Add grill grate to the Ninja Foodi Grill.
2. Close the hood.
3. Choose the grill setting.
4. Preheat for 5 minutes.
5. While waiting, spray tortillas with oil.
6. In a bowl, mix sour cream, salsa, and hot sauce. Set aside.
7. Add tortilla to the grate.
8. Grill for 1 minute.
9. Repeat with the other tortillas.
10. Spread the toasted tortilla with the salsa mixture, chicken, jalapeño peppers, cheese and scallions.
11. Place a tortilla on top. Press.
12. Repeat these steps with the remaining 2 tortillas.
13. Take the grill out of the pot.
14. Choose the roast setting.
15. Cook the quesadillas at 350 °F for 25 minutes.

Serving Suggestions: Let cool a little before slicing and serving.
Preparation / Cooking Tips: Poke holes in the tortillas to prevent ballooning.

20 Mins

20 Mins

8

Buffalo Chicken Wings

INGREDIENTS

- 2 lb. chicken wings
- 2 tablespoons oil
- 1/2 cup Buffalo sauce

 directions:

1. Coat the chicken wings with oil.
2. Add these to an air fryer basket.
3. Choose the air fry function.
4. Cook at 390 °F for 15 minutes.
5. Shake and then cook for another 15 minutes.
6. Dip in Buffalo sauce before serving.

Serving Suggestions: Serve with blue cheese dressing.
Preparation / Cooking Tips: Dry your chicken wings with paper towels before cooking

15 Mins

30 Mins

4

Fried Chicken

- 2 tablespoons onion powder
- 2 tablespoons garlic powder
- 1 tablespoon mustard powder
- 2 tablespoons chili powder
- Salt and pepper to taste

- 4 cups buttermilk
- 8 chicken thighs
- 2 cups all-purpose flour
- 3/4 cup vegetable oil
- 2 tablespoons sugar

- 3 tablespoons paprika

directions:

1. Mix the spice powders, salt and pepper in a bowl.
2. Transfer half of the mixture to another bowl.
3. Pour in buttermilk to the second bowl and mix well.
4. Coat the chicken pieces with this mixture.
5. Cover and marinate in the refrigerator for 8 hours.
6. Add flour to the remaining spice blend.
7. Toss the chicken in this mixture.
8. Add to the air fryer basket.
9. Select the air fryer function.
10. Cook at 360 °F for 25 to 30 minutes.
11. Coat chicken with oil.
12. Cook for another 15 minutes.

Serving Suggestions: Serve with mustard or ketchup.

Preparation / Cooking Tips: Extend cooking time if you want your chicken crispier but be careful not to overcook.

8h 20 Mins

45 Mins

6

Mustard Chicken

 INGREDIENTS

- 1/4 cup Dijon mustard
- 1/4 cup cooking oil
- Salt and pepper to taste
- 2 tablespoons honey
- 1 tablespoon dry oregano
- 2 teaspoons dry Italian seasoning
- 1 tablespoon lemon juice
- 6 chicken pieces

 directions:

1. Combine all the ingredients except chicken in a bowl.
2. Mix well.
3. Toss the chicken in the mixture.
4. Add a roasting rack to your Ninja Foodi Grill.
5. Choose roast function.
6. Set it to 350 °F.
7. Cook for 30 minutes.
8. Flip and cook for another 15 to 20 minutes.

Serving Suggestions: Serve with hot sauce.

Preparation / Cooking Tips: Use freshly squeezed lemon juice.

20 Mins

50 Mins

4

Honey & Rosemary Chicken

 INGREDIENTS

- 1 teaspoon paprika
- Salt to taste
- 1/2 teaspoon baking powder
- 2 lb. chicken wings
- 1/4 cup honey

- 1 tablespoon lemon juice
- 1 tablespoon garlic, minced
- 1 tablespoon rosemary, chopped

directions:

1. Choose the air fry setting in your Ninja Foodi Grill.
2. Set it to 390 °F.
3. Set the time to 30 minutes.
4. Press start to preheat.
5. While waiting, mix the paprika, salt and baking powder in a bowl.
6. Add the wings to the crisper basket.
7. Close and cook for 15 minutes.
8. Flip and cook for another 15 minutes.
9. In a bowl, mix the remaining ingredients.
10. Coat the wings with the sauce and cook for another 5 minutes.

Serving Suggestions: Serve with the remaining sauce.

Preparation / Cooking Tips: You can also add crushed red pepper to the spice mixture.

15 Mins

35 Mins

Grilled Chicken with Veggies

 INGREDIENTS

- 2 chicken thighs and legs
- 2 tablespoons oil, divided
- Salt and pepper to taste
- 1 onion, diced
- 1/4 cup mushrooms, sliced
- 1 cup potatoes, diced
- 1 tablespoon lemon juice
- 1 tablespoon honey
- 4 sprigs fresh thyme, chopped
- 2 cloves garlic, crushed and minced

 directions:

1. Add the grill grate to your Ninja Foodi Grill.
2. Put the veggie tray on top of the grill grate.
3. Close the hood.
4. Choose the grill function and set it to high.
5. Press start to preheat.
6. Brush the chicken with half of the oil.
7. Season with salt and pepper.
8. Toss the onion, mushrooms and potatoes in the remaining oil.
9. Sprinkle with salt and pepper.
10. Add chicken to the grill grate.
11. Add the potato mixture to the veggie tray.
12. Close the hood and cook for 10 to 15 minutes.
13. Flip chicken and toss potatoes.
14. Cook for another 10 minutes.

Serving Suggestions: Serve chicken with the veggies on the side. Garnish with herb sprigs.

Preparation / Cooking Tips: Add more cooking time if you want skin crispier.

20 Mins

25 Mins

2

Grilled Garlic Chicken

 INGREDIENTS

- 3 lb. chicken thigh fillets
- Garlic salt to taste

 directions:

1. Add grill plate to the Ninja Foodi Grill.
2. Preheat to medium heat.
3. Sprinkle chicken with garlic salt on both sides.
4. Cook for 8 to 10 minutes.
5. Flip and cook for another 7 minutes.

Serving Suggestions: Serve with hot sauce and mustard. Serve with fries on the side.

Preparation / Cooking Tips: Add cooking time to make the skin crispier.

10 Mins

20 Mins

8

Grilled Balsamic Chicken Breast

 INGREDIENTS

- 1/4 cup olive oil
- 2 tablespoons balsamic vinegar
- 3 teaspoon garlic, minced
- 3 tablespoons soy sauce
- 1 tablespoon Worcestershire sauce
- 1/4 cup brown sugar
- Salt and pepper to taste
- 4 chicken breast fillets

 directions:

1. In a bowl, mix all the ingredients except chicken.
2. Reserve 1/4 cup of the mixture for later.
3. Marinate the chicken breast in the remaining mixture for 30 minutes.
4. Add grill grate to the Ninja Foodi Grill.
5. Set it to grill and for 25 minutes.
6. Add the chicken breast and close the hood.
7. Cook for 10 minutes.
8. Flip and cook for another 5 minutes.
9. Baste with the remaining sauce. Cook for 5 more minutes.
10. Serve with the remaining sauce if any.

Serving Suggestions: Let chicken rest for 5 minutes before serving.
Preparation / Cooking Tips: For thick chicken breast fillets, flatten with a meat mallet.

45 Mins

45 Mins

4

Barbecue Chicken Breast

INGREDIENTS

- 4 chicken breast fillets
- 2 tablespoons vegetable oil
- Salt and pepper to taste
- 1 cup barbecue sauce

directions:

1. Add grill grate to the Ninja Foodi Grill.
2. Close the hood.
3. Choose the grill setting.
4. Preheat to medium for 25 minutes.
5. Press start.
6. Brush chicken breast with oil.
7. Sprinkle both sides with salt and pepper.
8. Add chicken and cook for 10 minutes.
9. Flip and cook for another 10 minutes.
10. Brush chicken with barbecue sauce.
11. Cook for 5 minutes.
12. Brush the other side and cook for another 5 minutes.

Serving Suggestions: Serve with mashed potato and gravy.
Preparation / Cooking Tips: You can also use homemade barbecue sauce simply by mixing ketchup, sugar, minced garlic, lemon juice and soy sauce.

15 Mins

50 Mins

4

Chicken, Potatoes & Cabbage

 INGREDIENTS

- 1 cup apple cider vinegar
- 2 lb. chicken thigh fillets
- 6 oz. barbecue sauce
- 2 lb. cabbage, sliced into wedges and steamed
- 1 lb. potatoes, roasted
- Salt and pepper to taste

 directions:

1. Pour the apple cider vinegar into the inner pot.
2. Add grill grate to the Ninja Foodi Grill.
3. Place the chicken on top of the grill.
4. Sprinkle both sides with salt and pepper.
5. Grill the chicken for 15 to 20 minutes per side at 350 °F.
6. Baste the chicken with the barbecue sauce.
7. Serve the chicken with potatoes and cabbage.

Serving Suggestions: Serve with hot sauce and mustard.
Preparation / Cooking Tips: You can also brush veggies with barbecue sauce if you like.

30 Mins

40 Mins

8

 30 Mins

 1h 10 Mins

 6

INGREDIENTS

- 1 whole chicken
- 1/2 teaspoon onion powder
- 1 teaspoon garlic powder
- 1 teaspoon paprika
- Salt and pepper to taste
- 2 drops liquid smoke
- 1 cup water
- 2 tablespoons butter
- 1/4 cup flour
- 2 cups chicken broth

Basting Butter

- 2 tablespoons butter
- Dash garlic powder

Roasted Chicken

Method

1. Season chicken with a mixture of onion powder, garlic powder, paprika, salt, and pepper.
2. Add the chicken to the air frying basket.
3. Combine liquid smoke and butter.
4. Pour into the pot of your Ninja Foodi grill.
5. Seal the unit and cook at 350 °F for 45 minutes.
6. Drain the pot.
7. Sprinkle chicken with butter and flour.
8. Air fry at 400 °F for 15 minutes.
9. Baste with a mixture of the basting butter ingredients.
10. Cook for another 10 minutes.

Serving Suggestions: Serve with a vegetable side dish.

Preparation / Cooking Tips: Pat the chicken dry before seasoning.

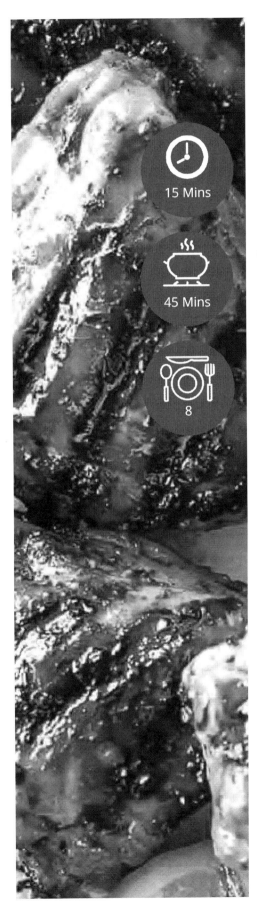

15 Mins

45 Mins

8

Sugar Glazed Chicken

Method

1. Combine all the ingredients except chicken.
2. Reserve 1/4 cup of this mixture for later.
3. Marinate the chicken with the remaining mixture for 30 minutes.
4. Add grill grate to your Ninja Foodi Grill.
5. Select the grill button.
6. Set it to 25 minutes.
7. Add chicken to the grill.
8. Close the hood.
9. Cook for 10 minutes.
10. Flip and cook for 5 minutes.
11. Brush with the remaining mixture.
12. Cook for another 5 minutes.

Serving Suggestions: Let chicken rest for 10 minutes before slicing and serving.

Preparation / Cooking Tips: You can also add a dash of hot sauce.

INGREDIENTS

- 1 tablespoon olive oil
- 1/2 tablespoon apple cider vinegar
- 3 teaspoon garlic, minced
- 1 tablespoon honey
- 1/4 cup light brown sugar
- 1/3 cup soy sauce
- 8 chicken thigh fillets

Lemon Garlic Chicken

 15 Mins

 40 Mins

 4

INGREDIENTS

- 4 chicken breast fillets
- 1 tablespoon lemon juice
- 1 tablespoon melted butter
- 1 teaspoon garlic powder
- Salt and pepper to taste

Method

1. Mix lemon juice and melted butter in a bowl.
2. Brush both sides of the chicken with this mixture.
3. Season with garlic powder, salt and pepper.
4. Insert grill grate to your Ninja Foodi Grill.
5. Place chicken on top of the grill.
6. Close the hood.
7. Grill at 350 °F for 15 to 20 minutes per side.

Serving Suggestions: Garnish with lemon slices.

Preparation / Cooking Tips: You can also use margarine in place of butter.

30 Mins

30 Mins

6

INGREDIENTS

- 6 chicken thigh fillets
- 3 tablespoons ranch dressing
- Garlic salt and pepper

Grilled Ranch Chicken

 Method

1. Spread both sides of chicken with ranch dressing.
2. Sprinkle with garlic salt and pepper.
3. Set your Ninja Foodi Grill to grill.
4. Preheat it to medium.
5. Add chicken to the grill grate.
6. Cook for 15 minutes per side.

Serving Suggestions: Serve with additional ranch dressing.
Preparation / Cooking Tips: Marinate the chicken for 15 to 25.

Basil and Garlic Chicken Legs

10 Mins

35 Mins

4

directions:

1. Pre-heat Ninja Foodi by squeezing the "AIR CRISP" alternative and setting it to "350 °F" and timer to 20 minutes
2. Coat chicken with oil using a brush and drizzle with the rest of the ingredients
3. Transfer to Ninja Foodi Grill
4. Add lemon slices around the chicken legs
5. Close the oven
6. Cook for 20 minutes
7. Serve and enjoy!

Nutrition :
- Calories: 240
- Fat: 18 g
- Saturated Fat: 4 g
- Carbohydrates: 3 g
- Fiber: 2 g
- Sodium: 1253 mg

INGREDIENTS

- 4 chicken legs
- 4 teaspoons basil, dried
- 2 teaspoons garlic, minced
- 2 tablespoons olive oil
- 1 lemon, sliced
- Pinch of pepper and salt

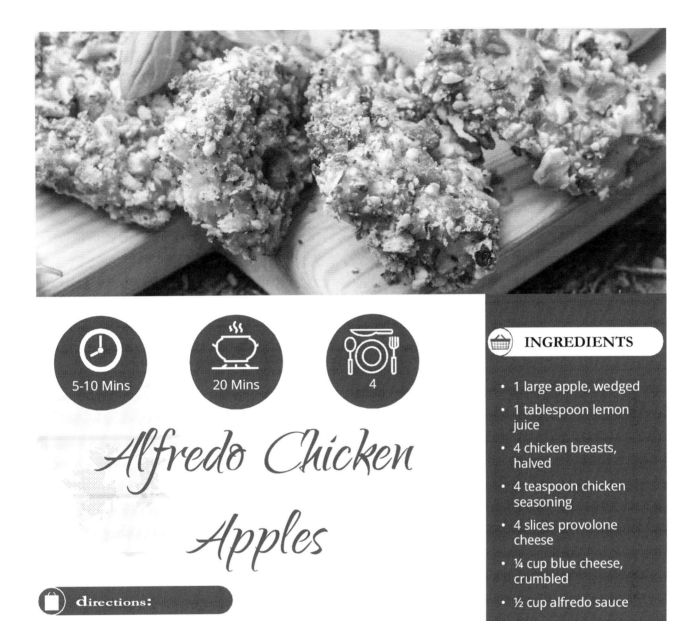

5-10 Mins

20 Mins

4

Alfredo Chicken Apples

INGREDIENTS

- 1 large apple, wedged
- 1 tablespoon lemon juice
- 4 chicken breasts, halved
- 4 teaspoon chicken seasoning
- 4 slices provolone cheese
- ¼ cup blue cheese, crumbled
- ½ cup alfredo sauce

directions:

1. Take a bowl and add chicken, season it well
2. Take another bowl and add in apple, lemon juice
3. Pre-heat Ninja Foodi by pressing the "GRILL" option and setting it to "MED" and timer to 20 minutes
4. Let it pre-heat until you hear a beep
5. Arrange chicken over Grill Grate, lock lid and cook for 8 minutes, flip and cook for 8 minutes more
6. Grill apple in the same manner for 2 minutes per side (making sure to remove chicken beforehand)
7. Serve chicken with pepper, apple, blue cheese, and alfredo sauce
8. Enjoy!

Nutrition:
- Calories: 247
- Fat: 19 g
- Saturated Fat: 6 g
- Carbohydrates: 29 g
- Fiber: 6 g
- Sodium: 853 mg
- Protein: 14 g

Hearty Chicken Zucchini Kabobs

 **INGREDIENTS**

- 1-pound chicken breast, boneless, skinless and cut into cubes of 2 inches
- 2 tablespoons Greek yogurt, plain
- 4 lemons juice
- 1 lemon zest
- ¼ cup extra-virgin olive oil

- 2 tablespoons oregano
- 1 red onion, quartered
- 1 zucchini, sliced
- 4 garlic cloves, minced
- 1 teaspoon of sea salt
- ½ teaspoon ground black pepper

 directions:

1. Take a mixing bowl, add the Greek yogurt, lemon juice, oregano, garlic, zest, salt, and pepper, combine them well
2. Add the chicken and coat well, refrigerate for 1-2 hours to marinate
3. Arrange the grill grate and close the lid
4. Pre-heat Ninja Foodi by pressing the "GRILL" option and setting it to "MED" and timer to 7 minutes
5. Take the skewers, thread the chicken, zucchini, and red onion and thread alternatively
6. Let it pre-heat until you hear a beep
7. Arrange the skewers over the grill grate lock lid and cook until the timer reads zero
8. Baste the kebabs with a marinating mixture in between
9. Take out your when it reaches 165 °F
10. Serve warm and enjoy!

Nutrition:
- Calories: 277
- Fat: 15 g
- Saturated Fat: 4 g
- Carbohydrates: 10 g
- Fiber: 2 g
- Sodium: 146 mg

10 Mins

15 Mins

4

Sweet and Sour Chicken BBQ

INGREDIENTS

- 6 chicken drumsticks
- ¾ cup of sugar
- 1 cup of soy sauce
- 1 cup of water
- ¼ cup garlic, minced
- ¼ cup tomato paste
- ¾ cup onion, minced
- 1 cup white vinegar
- Salt and pepper, to taste

directions:

1. Take a Ziploc bag and add all ingredients to it
2. Marinate for at least 2 hours in your refrigerator
3. Insert the crisper basket, and close the hood
4. Pre-heat Ninja Foodi by squeezing the "AIR CRISP" alternative at 390 °F for 40 minutes
5. Place the grill pan accessory in the air fryer
6. Flip the chicken after every 10 minutes
7. Take a saucepan and pour the marinade into it and heat over medium flame until sauce thickens
8. Brush with the glaze
9. Serve warm and enjoy!

Nutrition:
- Calories: 460
- Fat: 20 g
- Saturated Fat: 5 g
- Carbohydrates: 26 g
- Fiber: 3 g
- Sodium: 126 mg
- Protein: 28 g

10 Mins

40 Mins

4

10 Mins

15 Mins

4

Delicious Maple Glazed Chicken

 INGREDIENTS

- 2 pounds chicken wings, bone-in
- 1 teaspoon black pepper, ground
- ¼ cup teriyaki sauce
- 1 cup maple syrup
- 1/3 cup soy sauce
- 3 garlic cloves, minced
- 2 teaspoons garlic powder
- 2 teaspoons onion powder

 directions:

1. Take a mixing bowl, add garlic, soy sauce, black pepper, maple syrup, garlic powder, onion powder, and teriyaki sauce, combine well
2. Add the chicken wings and combine well to coat
3. Arrange the grill grate and close the lid
4. Pre-heat Ninja Foodi by pressing the "GRILL" option and setting it to "MED" and timer to 10 minutes
5. Let it pre-heat until you hear a beep
6. Arrange the chicken wings over the grill grate lock lid and cook for 5 minutes
7. Flip the chicken and close the lid, cook for 5 minutes more
8. Cook until it reaches 165 °F

9. Serve warm and enjoy!

Nutrition:
- Calories: 543
- Fat: 26 g
- Saturated Fat: 6 g
- Carbohydrates: 46 g
- Fiber: 4 g
- Sodium: 648 mg
- Protein: 42 g

5-10 Mins

18 Mins

4

Hot and Sassy BBQ Chicken

directions:

1. Take a bowl and add BBQ sauce, lime juice, honey, pepper, salt, hot sauce, and mix well
2. Take another mixing bowl and add ½ cup sauce and chicken mix well and add the remaining ingredients
3. Let it sit for 1 hour to marinate
4. Pre-heat Ninja Foodi by pressing the "GRILL" option and setting it to "MED" and timer to 18 minutes
5. Let it pre-heat until you hear a beep
6. Arrange the chicken over grill grate, cook until the timer reaches zero and internal temperature reaches 165 °F
7. Serve and enjoy!

Nutrition:
- Calories: 423
- Fat: 13 g
- Saturated Fat: 6 g
- Carbohydrates: 47 g
- Fiber: 4 g
- Sodium: 698 mg
- Protein: 22 g

INGREDIENTS

- 2 tablespoons honey
- 1-pound chicken drum-stick
- 1 tablespoon hot sauce
- 2 cups BBQ sauce
- Juice of 1 lime
- Pepper and salt as needed

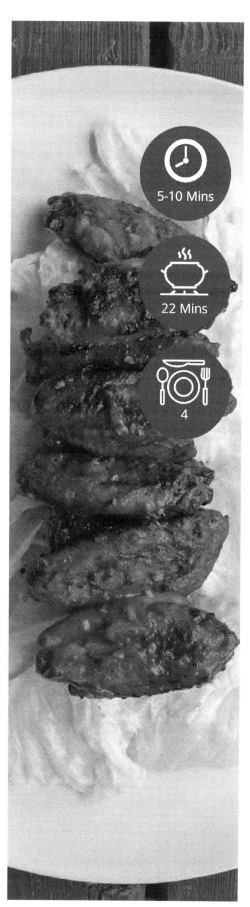

Moroccan Roast Chicken

5-10 Mins

22 Mins

4

 directions:

1. Take your food processor and add garlic, yogurt, salt, and oil and blend well
2. Take a mixing bowl and add chicken, red pepper flakes, paprika, cumin, parsley, garlic, and mix well
3. Let it marinate for 2-4 hours
4. Pre-heat Ninja Foodi by pressing the "ROAST" option and setting it to "400 °F" and the timer to 23 minutes
5. Let it pre-heat until you hear a beep
6. Arrange chicken directly inside your cooking pot and lock lid, cook for 15 minutes, flip and cook for the remaining time
7. Serve and enjoy with yogurt dip!

Nutrition:
- Calories: 321
- Fat: 24 g
- Saturated Fat: 5 g
- Carbohydrates: 6 g
- Fiber: 2 g
- Sodium: 602 mg
- Protein: 21 g

INGREDIENTS

- 3 tablespoons plain yogurt
- 4 skinless, boneless chicken thighs
- 4 garlic cloves, chopped
- ½ teaspoon salt
- 1/3 cup olive oil
- ½ teaspoon fresh flat-leaf parsley, chopped
- 2 teaspoons ground cumin
- 2 teaspoons paprika
- ¼ teaspoon crushed red pepper flakes

Classic Honey Soy Chicken

- 4 boneless, skinless chicken bosoms cut into little pieces
- 4 garlic cloves, smashed
- 1 onion, diced
- ½ cup honey
- 2 tablespoon lime juice
- 2 teaspoon sesame oil
- 3 tablespoon soy sauce
- 1 tablespoon water
- 1 tablespoon cornstarch
- 1 teaspoon rice vinegar
- Black pepper and salt to taste

 directions:

1. In a mixing bowl, add the honey, sesame oil, lime juice, soy sauce, and rice vinegar. Combine well.
2. Take Ninja Foodi multi-cooker, arrange it over a cooking platform, and open the top lid.
3. In the pot, add the onion, chicken, and garlic; add the soy sauce mixture and stir gently.
4. Seal the multi-cooker by locking it with the pressure lid; ensure to keep the pressure release valve locked/sealed.
5. Select "PRESSURE" mode and select the "HI" pressure level. Then, set the timer to 15 minutes and press "STOP/START"; it will start the cooking process by building up inside pressure.
6. At the point when the clock goes off, brisk discharge pressure by adjusting the pressure valve to the VENT. After pressure gets released, open the pressure lid.
7. In a bowl, mix water and cornstarch until well dissolved.
8. Select "SEAR/SAUTÉ" mode and select the "MD" pressure level; add the cornstarch mixture in the pot and combine it, stir-cook for 2 minutes.
9. Serve warm.

5-10 Mins

18 Mins

4

Nutrition:
- Calories: 493
- Fat: 8.5g
- Saturated Fat: 1g
- Trans Fat: 0g
- Carbohydrates: 44.5g
- Fiber: 5g
- Sodium: 712mg
- Protein: 41.5g

INGREDIENTS

1. 1 (14.5 ounces) can black beans, rinsed and drained

2. 14 ounces canned whole tomatoes, chopped

3. 2 cups corn kernels

4. ¼ cup cheddar cheese, shredded

5. 5 chicken thighs, boneless, skinless

6. 5 cups chicken broth

7. 1 tablespoon ground cumin

8. ½ teaspoon dried oregano

9. 2 tablespoon tomato puree

10. 1 tablespoon chili powder

11. 3 cloves garlic, minced

12. 2 stemmed jalapeno peppers, cored and chopped

13. Fresh cilantro, chopped to garnish

 5-10 Mins

 15 Mins

 6

Mexican Chicken Soup

 directions:

1. Take Ninja Foodi multi-cooker, arrange it over a cooking platform, and open the top lid.

2. In the pot, add the chicken, chicken stock, cumin, oregano, garlic, tomato puree, tomatoes, chili powder, and jalapeno peppers; stir the mixture.

3. Seal the multi-cooker by locking it with the pressure lid; ensure to keep the pressure release valve locked/sealed.

4. Select "PRESSURE" mode and select the "HI" pressure level. Then, set the timer to 10 minutes and press "STOP/START"; it will start the cooking process by building up inside pressure.

5. At the point when the clock goes off, brisk discharge pressure by adjusting the pressure valve to the VENT. After pressure gets released, open the pressure lid.

6. Shred the chicken and include it back in the pot.

7. Select "SEAR/SAUTÉ" mode and select "MD: HI" pressure level; add the beans and corn and combine, stir-cook for 4 minutes.

8. Add the cilantro and cheese on top; serve warm.

Nutrition:
- Calories: 408
- Fat: 15g
- Saturated Fat: 3g
- Trans Fat: 0g
- Carbohydrates: 31g
- Fiber: 9g
- Sodium: 548mg
- Protein: 34g

INGREDIENTS

- 2 large eggs
- 2 teaspoons garlic powder
- 1 teaspoon salt
- ½ teaspoon ground black pepper
- ¾ cup coconut aminos
- 1-pound chicken tenders
- Cooking spray as needed

Baked Coconut Chicken

directions:

1. Pre-heat Ninja Foodi by squeezing the "AIR CRISP" alternative and setting it to "400 °F" and timer to 12 minutes
2. Take a large-sized baking sheet and spray it with cooking spray
3. Take a wide dish and add garlic powder, eggs, pepper, and salt
4. Whisk well until everything is combined
5. Add the almond meal and coconut and mix well
6. Take your chicken tenders and dip them in the egg followed by dipping in the coconut mix
7. Shake off any excess
8. Transfer them to your Ninja Foodi Grill and spray the tenders with a bit of oil.
9. Cook for 12-14 minutes until you have nice golden-brown texture
10. Enjoy!

Nutrition:
- Calories: 180
- Fat: 1 g
- Saturated Fat: 0 g
- Carbohydrates: 3 g
- Fiber: 1 g
- Sodium: 214 mg
- Protein: 0 g

10 Mins | 12 Mins | 4

INGREDIENTS

- 1 and ¼ pounds chicken breast, cut into pieces
- 1 can corn
- ¼ teaspoon garlic powder
- 1 can black beans, drained and rinsed
- 1 tablespoon oil
- 2 tablespoons chili powder
- 1 bell pepper, chopped
- ¼ teaspoon garlic powder
- ¼ teaspoon salt

Chicken Chili and Beans

directions:

1. Pre-heat Ninja Foodi by squeezing the "AIR CRISP" alternative and setting it to "360 °F" and timer to 15 minutes
2. Place all the ingredients in your Ninja Foodi Grill cooking basket/alternatively, you may use a dish to mix the ingredients and then put the dish in the cooking basket
3. Stir to mix well
4. Cook for 15 minutes
5. Serve and enjoy!

Nutrition:
- Calories: 220
- Fat: 4 g
- Saturated Fat: 1 g
- Carbohydrates: 24 g
- Fiber: 2 g
- Sodium: 856 mg
- Protein: 20 g

10 Mins

15 Mins

4

INGREDIENTS

- 2 teaspoons ground coriander
- 1/2 teaspoon garlic salt
- 1/4 teaspoon ground black pepper
- 12 chicken wings
- 1 tablespoon canola oil

Sauce:
- 1/4 cup butter, melted
- 3 tablespoons honey
- 1/2 cup orange juice
- 1/3 cup Sriracha chili sauce
- 2 tablespoons lime juice
- 1/4 cup chopped cilantro

5-10 Mins

10 Mins

5-6

Grilled Orange Chicken

directions:

1. Coat chicken with oil and season with the spices; refrigerate for 2 hours to marinate.
2. Combine all the sauce ingredients and set them aside.
   Optionally, you can stir-cook the sauce mixture for 3-4 minutes in a sauce- pan.
3. Take Ninja Foodi Grill, organize it over your kitchen stage, and open the top cover.
4. Organize the barbecue mesh and close the top cover.
5. Click "GRILL" and choose the "MED" grill function. Adjust the timer to 10 minutes and afterward press "START/STOP." Ninja Foodi will begin pre-warming.
6. Ninja Foodi is preheated and prepared to cook when it begins to signal. After you hear a blare, open the top.
7. Organize the chicken over the grill grate.
8. Close the top lid and cook for 5 minutes. Now open the top lid, flip the chicken.
9. Close the top lid and cook for 5 more minutes.

Nutrition:
- Calories: 327
- Fat: 14g
- Saturated Fat: 3.5g
- Trans Fat: 0g
- Carbohydrates: 19g
- Fiber: 1g
- Sodium: 258mg
- Protein: 25g

INGREDIENTS

- 8 ounces cremini mushrooms, sliced
- 1 can (10.5 ounce) cream of celery soup
- 2 tablespoons butter
- 1-pound ground turkey
- 16 ounces peas
- 1 cup sour cream
- ¾ cup grated Parmesan cheese
- 4 cups chicken stock
- 1 (10-ounce) package egg noodles
- Kosher salt
- Freshly ground black pepper

5-10 Mins   35 Mins

4

Turkey Cream Noodles

 directions:

1. Take Ninja Foodi multi-cooker, arrange it over a cooking platform, and open the top lid.
2. In the pot, add the butter; Select "SEAR/SAUTÉ" mode and select "MD: HI" pressure level. Press "STOP/START." After about
   4-5 minutes, the butter will melt.
3. Add the mushrooms, turkey, and stir-cook for about 8-10 minutes to brown evenly.
4. Add the condensed soup and stock; stir and simmer for 15 minutes.
5. Add the egg noodles and peas; stir-cook for 8-10 minutes until the noodles are cooked well.
6. Add the sour cream and Parmesan cheese; stir the mixture, season with salt and pepper.

Nutrition:
- Calories: 752
- Fat: 19.5g
- Saturated Fat: 9g
- Trans Fat: 0g
- Carbohydrates: 38g
- Fiber: 7.5g
- Sodium: 1542mg
- Protein: 52g

Turkey Bean Chili

INGREDIENTS

- 2 garlic cloves, minced
- 1 ½ pounds turkey, ground
- 1 tablespoon extra-virgin olive oil
- 1 onion, chopped
- 1 tablespoon oregano, dried
- 1 tablespoon ground cumin
- 3 cans (15-ounce) of cannellini beans, rinsed and drained
- ⅛ teaspoon sea salt
- ⅛ teaspoon black pepper, freshly ground
- 4 cups chicken broth
- 1 pack biscuits

5-10 Mins

30 Mins

6

directions:

1. Take Ninja Foodi multi-cooker, arrange it over a cooking platform, and open the top lid.
2. In the pot, add the oil; Select "SEAR/SAUTÉ" mode and select "MD: HI" pressure level.
3. Press "STOP/START." After about 4-5 minutes, the oil will start simmering.
4. Add the onions, garlic, and cook (while stirring) for 2-3 minutes until they become softened and translucent.
5. Add the turkey, cumin, oregano, beans, broth, salt, and black pepper; stir the mixture.
6. Seal the multi-cooker by locking it with the pressure lid; ensure to keep the pressure release valve locked/sealed.
7. Select "PRESSURE" mode and select the "HI" pressure level. Then, set the timer to 10 minutes and press "STOP/START"; it will start the cooking process by building up inside pressure.
8. At the point when the clock goes off, speedy discharge pressure by adjusting the pressure valve to the VENT. After pressure gets released, open the pressure lid.
9. Arrange the biscuits in a single layer over the mixture.
10. Seal the multi-cooker by locking it with the crisping lid; ensure to keep the pressure release valve locked/sealed.
11. Select "BROIL" mode and select the "HI" pressure level. Then, set the timer to 15 minutes and press "STOP/START"; it will start the cooking process by building up inside pressure.
12. At the point when the clock goes off, speedy discharge pressure by adjusting the pressure valve to the VENT.
13. After pressure gets released, open the pressure lid.

Nutrition:
- Calories: 543
- Fat: 18g
- Saturated Fat: 6
- Trans Fat: 0g
- Carbohydrates: 51g
- Fiber: 15g
- Sodium: 1357mg
- Protein: 42g

Chicken Bean Bake

INGREDIENTS

- ½ red onion, diced
- ½ red bell pepper, diced
- 1 tablespoon extra-virgin olive oil
- 2 (8-ounce) boneless, skinless chicken breasts cut into 1-inch cubes
- 1 cup white rice
- 1 (15-ounce) can corn, rinsed
- 1 (10-ounce) can roasted tomatoes with chiles
- 1 (15-ounce) can black beans, rinsed and drained
- 1 (1-ounce) packet taco seasoning
- 2 cups shredded Cheddar cheese
- 2 cups chicken broth
- Kosher salt
- Black pepper (ground)

directions:

1. Take Ninja Foodi multi-cooker, arrange it over a cooking platform, and open the top lid. In the pot, add the oil, select "SEAR/SAUTÉ" mode and select "MD: HI" pressure level. Press "STOP/START." After about 4-5 minutes, the oil will start simmering.
2. Put in the chicken and mix for about 2-3 minutes to brown evenly.
3. Add the onion and bell pepper, stir-cook until softened for 2 minutes. Add the rice, tomatoes, beans, corn, taco seasoning, broth, salt, and pepper, combine well.
4. Seal the multi-cooker by locking it with the pressure lid; ensure to keep the pressure release valve locked/sealed.
5. Select "PRESSURE" mode and select the "HI" pressure level. Then, set the timer to 7 minutes and press "STOP/START," it will start the cooking process by building up inside pressure.
6. When the timer goes off, quickly release pressure by adjusting the pressure valve to the VENT, after pressure gets released, open the pressure lid. Add the cheese on top.
7. Seal the multi-cooker by locking it with the Crisping Lid; ensure to keep the pressure release valve locked/sealed.
8. Select "BROIL" mode and select the "HI" pressure level. Then, set the timer to 8 minutes and press "STOP/START," it will start the cooking process by building up inside pressure.
9. When the timer goes off, quickly release pressure by adjusting the pressure valve to the VENT, after pressure gets released, open the Crisping Lid.

5-10 Mins

20 Mins

8

Nutrition:
- Calories: 312
- Fat: 15.5g
- Saturated Fat: 6g
- Trans Fat: 0g
- Carbohydrates: 24.5g
- Fiber: 5g
- Sodium: 652mg
- Protein: 24g

Turkey Yogurt Meal

INGREDIENTS

- 14 ounces yogurt
- 1 tablespoon ginger, grated
- 2 turkey breasts, skinless, boneless and cubed
- 1 yellow onion, chopped
- 1 teaspoon turmeric powder
- 2 teaspoons olive oil
- Black pepper (ground) and salt to taste

directions:

1. Take Ninja Foodi multi-cooker, arrange it over a cooking platform, and open the top lid.
2. In the pot, add the oil, select "SEAR/SAUTÉ" mode and select "MD: HI" pressure level. Press "STOP/START." After about 4-5 minutes, the oil will start simmering.
3. Add the onions and cook (while stirring) until they become softened and translucent for 4 minutes.
4. Add the ginger and turmeric, stir-cook for 1 more minute. Add remaining ingredients, stir gently.
5. Seal the multi-cooker by locking it with the pressure lid; ensure to keep the pressure release valve locked/sealed.
6. Select "PRESSURE" mode and select the "HI" pressure level. Then, set the timer to 20 minutes and press "STOP/START," it will start the cooking process by building up inside pressure.
7. When the timer goes off, naturally release inside pressure for about 8-10 minutes, then, quick-release pressure by adjusting the pressure valve to the VENT
8. Serve warm.

5-10 Mins

20 Mins

4

Nutrition:
- Calories: 176
- Fat: 4.5g
- Saturated Fat: 0g
- Trans Fat: 0g
- Carbohydrates: 7g
- Fiber: 0g
- Sodium: 854mg
- Protein: 21g

Exotic Pilaf Chicken

 INGREDIENTS

- 1 tablespoon unsalted butter
- 4 boneless, skin-on chicken thighs
- 1 (6-ounce) box rice pilaf
- 1 ¾ cups water
- 1 tablespoon extra-virgin olive oil
- 1 teaspoon garlic powder
- 1 teaspoon kosher salt

directions:

1. Take Ninja Foodi multi-cooker, arrange it over a cooking platform, and open the top lid.
2. In the pot, add water, butter, and pilaf, and place a reversible rack inside the pot. Place the chicken thighs over the rack.
3. Seal the multi-cooker by locking it with the pressure lid, ensure to keep the pressure release valve locked/sealed.
4. Select "PRESSURE" mode and select the "HI" pressure level. Then, set the timer to 4 minutes and press "STOP/START," it will start the cooking process by building up inside pressure.
5. When the timer goes off, quickly release pressure by adjusting the pressure valve to the VENT. After pressure gets released, open the pressure lid.
6. In a mixing bowl, combine the olive oil, salt, and garlic powder. Brush thickens with this mixture.
7. Seal the multi-cooker by locking it with the Crisping Lid, ensure to keep the pressure release valve locked/sealed.
8. Select "BROIL" mode and select the "HI" pressure level. Then, set the timer to 10 minutes and press "STOP/START," it will start the cooking process by building up inside pressure.
9. When the timer goes off, quickly release pressure by adjusting the pressure valve to the VENT. After pressure gets released, open the Crisping Lid. Serve warm the chicken with cooked pilaf.

5-10 Mins

15 Mins

4

Nutrition :
- Calories: 425
- Fat: 26g
- Saturated Fat: 8.5g
- Trans Fat: 0g
- Carbohydrates: 12g
- Fiber: 1.5g
- Sodium: 524mg
- Protein: 23g

Chicken Zucchini Kebabs

 INGREDIENTS

- Juice of 4 lemons
- Grated zest of 1 lemon
- 1-pound boneless, skinless chicken breasts, cut into cubes of 2 inches
- 2 tablespoons plain Greek yogurt

- ¼ cup extra-virgin olive oil
- 4 garlic cloves, minced
- 1 teaspoon sea salt
- ½ teaspoon ground black pepper
- 2 tablespoons dried

  oregano
- 1 red onion, quartered
- 1 zucchini, sliced

directions:

1. In a mixing bowl, add the Greek yogurt, oil, lemon juice, zest, garlic, oregano, salt, and pepper. Combine the ingredients to mix well with each other.
2. Add the chicken and coat well. Refrigerate for 1-2 hours to marinate.
3. Take Ninja Foodi Grill, arrange it over your kitchen platform, and open the top lid.
4. Arrange the grill grate and close the top lid.
5. Press "GRILL" and select the "MED" grill function. Adjust the timer to 14 minutes and then press "START/STOP." Ninja Foodi will start pre-heating.
6. Take the skewers, thread the chicken, red onion, and zucchini. Thread alternatively.
7. Ninja Foodi is preheated and ready to cook when it starts to beep. After you hear a beep, open the top lid.
8. Arrange the skewers over the grill grate.
9. Close the top lid and allow it to cook until the timer reads zero. Baste the kebabs with a marinating mixture in between. Cook until the food thermometer reaches 165°F.
10. Serve warm.

5-10 Mins

15 Mins

4

Nutrition:
- Calories: 277
- Fat: 15.5g
- Saturated Fat: 2g
- Trans Fat: 0g
- Carbohydrates: 9.5g
- Fiber: 2g
- Sodium: 523mg
- Protein: 25g

103

Turkey Tomato Burgers

INGREDIENTS

- 2/3 cup sun-dried tomatoes, chopped
- 1/4 teaspoon salt
- 1/4 teaspoon pepper
- 1 large red onion, chopped
- 1 cup crumbled feta cheese
- 2 pounds lean ground turkey
- 6 burger buns of your choice, sliced in half

directions:

1. In a mixing bowl, add all the ingredients. Combine the ingredients to mix well with each other.
2. Prepare six patties from the mixture.
3. Take Ninja Foodi Grill, arrange it over your kitchen platform, and open the top lid.
4. Arrange the grill grate and close the top lid.
5. Press "GRILL" and select the "MED" grill function. Adjust the timer to 14 minutes and then press "START/STOP." Ninja Foodi will start pre-heating.
6. Ninja Foodi is preheated and ready to cook when it starts to beep. After you hear a beep, open the top lid.
7. Arrange the patties over the grill grate.
8. Close the top lid and cook for 7 minutes. Now open the top lid, flip the patties.
9. Close the top lid and cook for 7 more minutes.
10. Serve warm with ciabatta rolls. Add your choice of toppings: lettuce, tomato, cheese, ketchup, cheese, etc.

Nutrition:
- Calories: 298
- Fat: 16g
- Saturated Fat: 2.5g
- Trans Fat: 0g
- Carbohydrates: 32g
- Fiber: 4g
- Sodium: 321mg
- Protein: 27.5g

5-10 Mins

40 Mins

6

Pork, Beef
&
Lamb

INGREDIENTS

- 4 boneless pork chops
- Ocean salt and ground dark pepper to taste
- ¼ cup apple cider vinegar
- ¼ cup soy sauce
- 3 tablespoons Worcestershire sauce
- 2 cups ketchup
- ¾ cup bourbon
- 1 cup packed brown sugar
- ½ tablespoon dry mustard powder

Bourbon Pork Chops

directions:

1. Take Ninja Foodi Grill, orchestrate it over your kitchen stage, and open the top cover. Orchestrate the flame broil mesh and close the top cover.
2. Click "GRILL" and choose the "MED" grill function. Adjust the timer to 15 minutes and click "START/STOP."
3. Ninja Foodi is preheated and prepared to cook when it begins to signal. After you hear a signal, open the top.
4. Arrange the pork chops over the grill grate.
5. Close the top lid and cook for 8 minutes. Now open the top lid, flip the pork chops.
6. Close the top lid and cook for 8 more minutes. Check the pork chops for doneness, cook for 2 more minutes if required.
7. In a saucepan, heat the soy sauce, sugar, ketchup, bourbon, vinegar, Worcestershire sauce, and mustard powder; stir-cook until boils.
8. Reduce the heat and simmer for 20 minutes to thicken the sauce.
9. Coat the pork chops with salt and ground black pepper. Serve warm with the prepared sauce.

Nutrition:
- Calories: 346
- Fat: 13.5g
- Saturated Fat: 4g
- Trans Fat: 0g
- Carbohydrates: 27g
- Fiber: 0.5g
- Sodium: 1324mg
- Protein: 27g

5-10 Mins

20 Mins

4

INGREDIENTS

- 2 pounds pork, cut into ⅛-inch slices
- 5 minced garlic cloves
- 3 tablespoons minced green onion
- 1 yellow onion, sliced
- ½ cup soy sauce
- ½ cup brown sugar
- 3 tablespoons Korean red chili paste or regular chili paste
- 2 tablespoons sesame seeds
- 3 teaspoons black pepper
- Red pepper flakes to taste

Korean Chili Pork

directions:

1. Take a zip-lock bag, add all the ingredients. Shake well and refrigerate for 6-8 hours to marinate.
2. Take Ninja Foodi Grill, orchestrate it over your kitchen stage, and open the top.
3. Mastermind the barbecue mesh and close the top cover.
4. Click "GRILL" and choose the "MED" grill function. flame broil work. Modify the clock to 8 minutes and afterward press " START/STOP." Ninja Foodi will begin to warm up.
5. Ninja Foodi is preheated and prepared to cook when it begins to signal. After you hear a signal, open the top.
6. Fix finely sliced pork on the barbeque mesh.
7. Cover and cook for 4 minutes. Then open the cover, switch the side of the pork.
8. Cover it and cook for another 4 minutes.
9. Serve warm with chopped lettuce, optional.

Nutrition:
- Calories: 621
- Fat: 31g
- Saturated Fat: 12.5g
- Trans Fat: 0g
- Carbohydrates: 29g
- Fiber: 3g
- Sodium: 1428mg
- Protein: 53g

5-10 Mins

8 Mins

4

Lettuce Cheese Steak

- 4 (8-ounce) skirt steaks
- 6 cups romaine lettuce, chopped
- ¾ cup cherry tomatoes halved
- ¼ cup blue cheese, crumbled
- Ocean salt and Ground Black Pepper
- 2 avocados, peeled and sliced
- 1 cup croutons
- 1 cup blue cheese dressing

directions:

1. Coat steaks with black pepper and salt.
2. Take Ninja Foodi Grill, mastermind it over your kitchen stage, and open the top. Organize the barbecue mesh and close the top.
3. Click "GRILL" and choose the "HIGH" function. Change the clock to 8 minutes and afterward press "START/STOP." Ninja Foodi will begin pre-warming.
4. Ninja Foodi is preheated and prepared to cook when it begins to blare. After you hear a blare, open the top cover.
5. Fix finely the 2 steaks on the barbeque mesh.
6. Close the top cover and cook for 4 minutes. Presently open the top cover, flip the steaks.
7. Close the top cover and cook for 4 additional minutes. Cook until the food thermometer comes to 165°F. Cook for 3-4 more minutes if needed. Grill the remaining steaks.
8. In a mixing bowl, add the lettuce, tomatoes, blue cheese, and croutons. Combine the ingredients to mix well with each other.
9. Serve the steaks warm with the salad mixture, blue cheese dressing, and avocado slices on top.

Nutrition:
- Calories: 576
- Fat: 21g
- Saturated Fat: 8.5g
- Trans Fat: 0g
- Carbohydrates: 23g
- Fiber: 6.5g
- Sodium: 957mg
- Protein: 53.5g

5-10 Mins

16 Mins

5-6

INGREDIENTS

- 4 ounces cream cheese
- 4 slices bacon, cooked and crumbled
- 2 seeded jalapeño peppers, stemmed, and minced
- ½ cup shredded Cheddar cheese
- ½ teaspoon chili powder
- ¼ teaspoon paprika
- ¼ teaspoon ground black pepper
- 2 pounds ground beef
- 4 hamburger buns
- 4 slices pepper Jack cheese
- Optional - Lettuce, sliced tomato, and sliced red onion

Grilled Beef Burgers

directions:

1. In a mixing bowl, combine the peppers, Cheddar cheese, cream cheese, and bacon until well combined.
2. Prepare the ground beef into 8 patties. Add the cheese mixture onto four of the patties; arrange a second patty on top of each to prepare four burgers. Press gently.
3. In another bowl, combine the chili powder, paprika, and pepper. Sprinkle the mixture onto the sides of the burgers.
4. Take Ninja Foodi Grill, organize it over your kitchen stage, and open the top cover.
5. Organize the flame broil mesh and close the top cover.
6. Press "Flame broil" and select the "HIGH" barbecue work. Change the clock to 4 minutes and afterward press "START/STOP." Ninja Foodi will begin pre-warming.
7. Ninja Foodi is preheated and prepared to cook when it begins to blare. After you hear a blare, open the top. Arrange the burgers over the grill grate.
8. Close the top lid and allow it to cook until the timer reads zero. Cook for 3-4 more minutes, if needed.
9. Cook until the food thermometer reaches 145°F. Serve warm.
10. Serve warm with buns. Add your choice of toppings: pepper Jack cheese, lettuce, tomato, and red onion.

Nutrition:
- Calories: 783
- Fat: 38g
- Saturated Fat: 16g
- Trans Fat: 0g
- Carbohydrates: 25g
- Fiber: 3g
- Sodium: 1259mg
- Protein: 57.5g

5-10 Mins

10 Mins

4

INGREDIENTS

- ½ diced onion
- 2 cup chicken broth
- 1-pound chopped sausage roll
- 1 tablespoon olive oil
- 2 cup almond milk
- ½ cup parmesan cheese
- 3 cup chopped kale fresh
- 28-ounce tomatoes, crushed
- 1 tablespoon minced garlic
- 1 teaspoon oregano, dried
- ¼ teaspoon salt

Kale Sausage Soup

directions:

1. Take Ninja Foodi multi-cooker, arrange it over a cooking platform, and open the top lid.
2. Select "SEAR/SAUTÉ" mode and select "MD: HI" pressure level. Press "STOP/START." After about 4-5 minutes, the unit is ready to cook.
3. Add the sausage and stir-cook to brown evenly. Add the spices, onions, kale, tomatoes, milk, and chicken broth. Stir the mixture.
4. Seal the multi-cooker by locking it with the pressure lid; ensure to keep the pressure release valve locked/sealed.
5. Select "PRESSURE" mode and select the "HI" pressure level. Then, set the timer to 10 minutes and press "STOP/START"; it will start the cooking process by building up inside pressure.
6. When the timer goes off, naturally release inside pressure for about 8-10 minutes. Then, quick-release pressure by adjusting the pressure valve to the VENT. Serve warm with the cheese on top and enjoy!

Nutrition:
- Calories: 162
- Fat: 10.5g
- Saturated Fat: 4g
- Trans Fat: 0g
- Carbohydrates: 2g
- Fiber: 0.5g
- Sodium: 624mg
- Protein: 19g

5-10 Mins

10 Mins

4

Spinach Beef Meatloaf

directions:

1. Take a baking pan; grease it with some cooking spray, vegetable oil, or butter. Take Ninja Foodi multi-cooker, arrange it over a cooking platform, and open the top lid.

2. In a blending bowl, include the entirety of the listed ingredients except for cheese and spinach.

3. Place the mixture over a wax paper; top with spinach, cheese, and roll it to form a nice meatloaf. Remove wax paper and add the mixture to the baking pan.

4. In the pot, add water and place a reversible rack inside the pot. Place the pan over the rack.

5. Seal the multi-cooker by locking it with the crisping lid; ensure to keep the pressure release valve locked/sealed.

6. Select "BAKE/ROAST" mode and adjust the 380°F temperature level. Then, set the timer to 70 minutes and press "STOP/START";

INGREDIENTS

- ¼ cup tomato puree or crushed tomatoes
- 1-pound lean ground beef
- ½ cup onion, chopped
- 2 garlic cloves, minced
- ½ cup green bell pepper, seeded and chopped
- 2 eggs, beaten
- 1 cup cheddar cheese, grated
- 3 cups spinach, chopped
- 1 teaspoon dried thyme, crushed
- 6 cups mozzarella cheese, grated
- Black pepper to taste

Nutrition:

- Calories: 426
- Fat: 16.5g
- Saturated Fat: 2g
- Trans Fat: 0g
- Carbohydrates: 5.5g
- Fiber: 1g
- Sodium: 743mg
- Protein: 48.5g

5-10 Mins

70 Mins

6

Steak Pineapple Mania

directions:

1. Rub the fillets with the oil evenly, then season with the salt and black pepper.
2. Take Ninja Foodi Grill, arrange it over your kitchen platform, and open the top lid.
3. Arrange the grill grate and close the top lid.
4. Press "GRILL" and select the "HIGH" grill function. Adjust the timer to 8 minutes and then press "START/STOP." Ninja Foodi will start preheating.
5. Ninja Foodi is preheated and ready to cook when it starts to beep. After you hear a beep, open the top lid.
6. Arrange the fillets over the grill grate. Close the top lid and cook for 4 minutes. Now open the top lid, flip the fillets.
7. Close the top lid and cook for 4 more minutes. Cook until the food thermometer reaches 125°F.
8. In a mixing bowl, add the pineapple, onion, and jalapeño. Combine well. Add the lime juice, cilantro, chili powder, and coriander. Combine again.
9. Serve the fillets warm with the pineapple mixture on top.

Nutrition :
- Calories: 536
- Fat: 22.5g
- Saturated Fat: 7g
- Trans Fat: 0g
- Carbohydrates: 21g
- Fiber: 4g
- Sodium: 286mg
- Protein: 58g

5-10 Mins

8 Mins

4-5

INGREDIENTS

- ½ medium pineapple, cored and diced
- 1 jalapeño pepper, seeded, stemmed, and diced
- 1 medium red onion, diced
- 4 (6-8-ounce) filet mignon steaks
- 1 tablespoon canola oil
- Sea salt and ground black pepper to taste
- 1 tablespoon lime juice
- ¼ cup chopped cilantro leaves
- Chili powder and ground coriander to tast

Avocado Salsa Steak

INGREDIENTS

- 1 cup cilantro leaves
- 2 ripe avocados, diced
- 2 cups salsa Verde
- 2 beef flank steak, diced
- 1/2 teaspoon salt
- 1/2 teaspoon pepper
- 2 medium tomatoes, seeded and diced

directions:

1. Rub the beef steak with salt and black pepper to season well.
2. Take Ninja Foodi Grill, orchestrate it over your kitchen stage, and open the top cover.
3. Orchestrate the flame broil mesh and close the top cover.
4. Press "Barbecue" and select the "MED" flame broil work. Alter the clock to 18 minutes and afterward press "START/STOP." Ninja Foodi will begin pre-warming.
5. Ninja Foodi is preheated and prepared to cook when it begins to signal. After you hear a blare, open the top. Arrange the diced steak over the grill grate.
6. Close the top lid and cook for 9 minutes. Now open the top lid, flip the diced steak.
7. Close the top lid and cook for 9 more minutes.
8. In a blender, blend the salsa and cilantro. Serve the grilled steak with the blended salsa, tomato, and avocado.

Nutrition:
- Calories: 523
- Fat: 31.5g
- Saturated Fat: 9g
- Trans Fat: 0g
- Carbohydrates: 38.5g
- Fiber: 2g
- Sodium: 301mg
- Protein: 41.5g

5-10 Mins

18 Mins

4

Fish & Seafood
Grilled Citrus Fish

- 2 tablespoons oil
- 2 tablespoons honey
- 1 tablespoon orange juice
- 1 tablespoon lemon juice
- 1 teaspoon orange zest
- 1 teaspoon lemon zest
- 1 teaspoon garlic, minced
- 1 teaspoon ginger, minced
- 1 tablespoon parsley, minced
- Salt and pepper to taste
- 2 white fish fillets

 **Method**

1. Add grill grate to the Ninja Foodi Grill.
2. Choose the grill function.
3. Set it to high.
4. Set the time to 15 minutes and press start.
5. Mix all the ingredients except fish fillets.
6. Spread half of the mixture on both sides of the fish.
7. Add fish fillets to the grill grate.
8. Close the hood and grill for 15 minutes, brushing with the remaining mixture.

Serving Suggestions: Serve with steamed veggies. Garnish with lemon and orange slices.

Preparation / Cooking Tips: You can use halibut or any white fish fillet for this recipe.

 20 Mins

 15 Mins

 2

10 Mins

10 Mins

4

INGREDIENTS

- 4 salmon fillets
- 1 cup teriyaki sauce

Teriyaki Salmon

 Method

1. Coat fish fillet with teriyaki sauce.
2. Cover and refrigerate for 12 hours.
3. Add grill grate to the Ninja Foodi Grill.
4. Select the grill setting. Set it to high.
5. Set the time to 10 minutes.
6. Press start to preheat.
7. Put the fish fillets on the grill.
8. Cook for 6 minutes.
9. Flip and cook for 2 minutes.

Serving Suggestions: Garnish with white sesame seeds or chopped scallions.

Preparation / Cooking Tips: You can also use barbecue sauce for this recipe.

15 Mins

5 Mins

6

Crispy Fish Fillet

Method

1. Place olive oil, mustard, and salt in a bowl and whisk to combine. Add crushed butter crackers and bread crumbs to another bowl and stir to combine.
2. Working in small batches, coat fish fillets in mustard mixture. Transfer fillets to bread crumb mixture, tossing well to evenly coat. Set aside.
3. Insert crisper plate in basket. Preheat unit by selecting AIR FRY, setting temperature to 390°F, and setting time to 3 minutes. Select START/STOP to begin preheating.
4. Spray breaded fillets liberally with cooking spray. Once unit is preheated, place fillets on the crisper plate.
5. Select AIR FRY, set temperature to 390°F, and set time to 8 minutes. Select START/STOP to begin cooking.
6. After 4 minutes, remove basket and flip fillets. Reinsert basket to resume cooking.
7. When cooking is complete, serve fish immediately.

Serving Suggestions: Serve with stir-fried vegetables and with sweet chili sauce.

Preparation / Cooking Tips: Dry the fish fillets with a paper towel before seasoning and dredging with breadcrumbs.

INGREDIENTS

- 2 tablespoons olive oil
- 1/2 cup Dijon mustard
- 1 teaspoon kosher salt
- 2 cups butter crackers, crushed
- 1 cup plain bread crumbs
- 4 uncooked cod or haddock fillets (6 ounces each)
- Cooking spray

Herbed Salmon

15 Mins   10 Mins   2

INGREDIENTS

- 2 salmon fillets
- 2 tablespoons olive oil
- 1 teaspoon Herbes de Provence
- 1/4 teaspoon smoked paprika
- Salt and pepper to taste
- 1 tablespoon butter
- 1/2 teaspoon lemon juice

 Method

1. Coat the salmon with olive oil.
2. Sprinkle with herbs, paprika, salt and pepper.
3. Insert grill grate to the Ninja Foodi Grill.
4. Set it to high. Set it to 10 minutes.
5. Press start to preheat.
6. Add fish to the grill.
7. Grill for 3 to 5 minutes per side.
8. Top the fish with butter and drizzle with lemon juice before serving.

Serving Suggestions: Garnish with lemon slices and chopped parsley.

Preparation / Cooking Tips: Press the fish onto the grill if you want it to have grill marks.

10 Mins

12 Mins

4

INGREDIENTS

- ¼ cup vegetable oil
- 1 cup breadcrumbs
- 4 flounder fillets
- 1 egg, beaten

Crumbed Flounder Fillet

Method

1. Set Ninja Foodi Grill to air fry.
2. Preheat to 350 °F.
3. Combine oil and breadcrumbs in a bowl.
4. Mix until crumbly.
5. Coat the fish with egg and dredge with the breadcrumb mixture.
6. Add fish fillets to the air fryer basket.
7. Cook for 12 minutes.

Serving Suggestions: Garnish with lemon wedges.

Preparation / Cooking Tips: You can also use olive oil in place of vegetable oil.

45 Mins

15 Mins

4

INGREDIENTS

- 1/2 teaspoon ginger powder
- 1/2 teaspoon garlic powder
- 1 tablespoon honey
- 4 tablespoons coconut aminos
- Salt and pepper to taste
- 3 salmon fillets

Salmon with Coconut Aminos

Method

1. In a bowl, mix ginger powder, garlic powder, honey, coconut aminos, salt and pepper.
2. Coat the salmon fillets with this mixture.
3. Marinate for 30 minutes, covered in the refrigerator.
4. Add fish to the air fryer basket.
5. Set your Ninja Foodi Grill to air fry.
6. Cook at 390 °F for 10 to 15 minutes.

Serving Suggestions: Garnish with lemon slices.

Preparation / Cooking Tips: Do not overcrowd the air fryer basket to ensure even cooking. Cook in batches if necessary.

Beer-Battered Cod

15 Mins

15 Mins

4

Method

1. Mix flour, baking soda, cornstarch, egg, and beer in a bowl.
2. Sprinkle cod fillets with paprika, cayenne, salt, and pepper.
3. Dip in the flour mixture.
4. Drizzle with oil.
5. Add to the air fryer basket.
6. Choose the air fry setting in your Ninja Foodi Grill.
7. Cook at 390 °F for 12 to 15 minutes.

Serving Suggestions: Serve with coleslaw.
Preparation / Cooking Tips: Refrigerate flour mixture for 20 minutes before using.

INGREDIENTS

- 1 cup all-purpose flour
- ½ teaspoon baking soda
- 2 tablespoons cornstarch
- 1 egg, beaten
- 6 oz. beer
- 4 cod fillets
- ½ teaspoon paprika
- Pinch cayenne pepper
- Salt and pepper to taste
- Vegetable oil

20 Mins

10 Mins

8

INGREDIENTS

- 2 lb. shrimp, deveined
- 2 tablespoons olive oil
- 1 tablespoon Old Bay Seasoning
- Garlic salt to taste

Grilled Shrimp

 **Method**

1. Preheat your grill to medium.
2. Brush shrimp with olive oil.
3. Season with Old Bay seasoning and garlic salt.
4. Cook for 3 to 5 minutes per side.

Serving Suggestions: Serve with grilled corn.
Preparation / Cooking Tips: Add cayenne pepper if you want your shrimp spicier.

10 Mins

15 Mins

6

Shrimp Boil

INGREDIENTS

- 12 oz. shrimp, peeled and deveined
- 14 oz. smoked sausage, sliced
- 4 corn on cobs, sliced into 4
- 3 cups potatoes, sliced in half and boiled
- 1/8 cup Old Bay seasoning
- 1/4 cup white onion, diced
- Cooking spray

 **Method**

1. Mix all the ingredients in the inner pot of the Ninja Foodi Grill.
2. Spray mixture with oil.
3. Set the unit to air fry.
4. Air fry at 390 °F for 5 to 7 minutes.
5. Stir and cook for another 6 minutes.

Serving Suggestions: Sprinkle with dried herbs before serving.

Preparation / Cooking Tips: Check the dish halfway through cooking to see if it's cooking evenly.

Honey Garlic Shrimp

15 Mins

30 Mins

6

INGREDIENTS

- 1/2 cup tamari
- 1/2 cup honey
- 1 clove garlic, crushed
- 1 teaspoon fresh ginger
- 2 tablespoons ketchup
- 2 tablespoons corn-starch
- 16 oz. shrimp, peeled and deveined
- 16 oz. frozen vegetables

Method

1. Add tamari, honey, garlic, ginger, and ketchup in a pan over medium heat.
2. Simmer for 10 minutes.
3. Stir in cornstarch and simmer for 5 minutes.
4. Dip shrimp in the sauce.
5. Add shrimp to the air fryer basket.
6. Set your Ninja Foodi Grill to air fry.
7. Air fry at 355 °F for 10 to 12 minutes.

Serving Suggestions: Serve with hot brown rice.

Preparation / Cooking Tips: You can also use pre-peeled shrimp to save time.

10 Mins

10 Mins

2

INGREDIENTS

- 2 salmon fillets
- Pinch paprika
- Salt and pepper to taste

Grilled Paprika Salmon

Method

1. Insert grill grate to the Ninja Foodi Grill.
2. Choose the grill function.
3. Set it to high and preheat for 10 minutes.
4. Season salmon with paprika, salt and pepper.
5. Add salmon to the grill.
6. Cook for 5 minutes per side.

Serving Suggestions: Serve with pasta salad.
Preparation / Cooking Tips: You can also use white fish fillet for this recipe.

15 Mins

12 Mins

2

Crispy Fish Sandwich

INGREDIENTS

Tartar Sauce
- 1/4 cup mayonnaise
- 1 teaspoon pickle juice
- 2 tablespoons dill pickles, chopped

Fish Sandwiches
- 2 white fish fillets
- 2 teaspoons Old Bay Seasoning
- 2 tablespoons flour
- 1 egg, beaten
- 1/2 cup breadcrumbs
- 2 slices low-fat cheese slices
- 2 burger buns

 Method

1. Mix mayo, pickle juice and dill pickles in a bowl.
2. Cover and place inside the refrigerator.
3. Add seasoning and flour to a dish.
4. Beat egg in a bowl.
5. Put breadcrumbs in the third bowl.
6. Coat fish fillets with flour mixture.
7. Dip in egg and then dredge with breadcrumbs.
8. Add fish fillets to the air fryer basket.
9. Set Ninja Foodi Grill to air fry.
10. Cook at 350 °F for 10 to 12 minutes.
11. Add crispy fish to burger buns.
12. Top with tartar sauce and cheese.

Serving Suggestions: Serve with cucumber and tomato salad.
Preparation / Cooking Tips: Use low-fat or fat-free mayonnaise.

Shrimp Fajitas

20 Mins

20 Mins

12

Method

1. Spray air fryer basket with oil.
2. Mix shrimp, onion, and bell peppers in a bowl.
3. Spray with oil and season with taco seasoning.
4. Set your Ninja Foodi Grill to air fry.
5. Add shrimp mixture to the air fryer basket.
6. Air fry at 390 °F for 10 to 12 minutes.
7. Shake and cook for another 10 minutes.
8. Spread on top of tortillas.

Serving Suggestions: Serve with hot sauce.

Preparation / Cooking Tips: If you're going to use frozen shrimp, add 3 to 5 more minutes of cooking time.

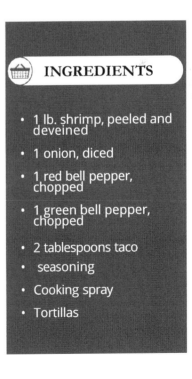

INGREDIENTS

- 1 lb. shrimp, peeled and deveined
- 1 onion, diced
- 1 red bell pepper, chopped
- 1 green bell pepper, chopped
- 2 tablespoons taco
- seasoning
- Cooking spray
- Tortillas

Shrimp Bang Bang

 INGREDIENTS

- 1/2 cup all-purpose flour
- 2 eggs, beaten
- 2 tablespoons olive oil
- 1 cup breadcrumbs
- Salt and pepper to taste

- 1 teaspoon garlic powder
- 1 lb. shrimp, peeled and deveined
- 1/2 cup mayonnaise
- 1/2 cup sweet chili sauce

- 1 tablespoon lime juice
- 1 tablespoon hot pepper sauce
- Salt to taste
- 2 teaspoons honey

 Method

1. Add flour to a bowl.
2. Put the eggs in a second bowl.
3. Mix the breadcrumbs, salt, pepper, and garlic powder in the third bowl.
4. Coat shrimp with flour and then with egg.
5. Dredge with breadcrumb blend.
6. Set Ninja Foodi Grill to air fry.
7. Cook at 400 °F for 15 minutes.
8. Shake and cook for another 15 minutes.
9. Combine the rest of the ingredients in a bowl.
10. Dip the shrimp in this mixture and serve.

15 Mins   30 Mins

4

Serving Suggestions: Serve with more hot sauce if desired.

Preparation / Cooking Tips: Use light mayonnaise for this recipe.

Grilled Lemon Pepper Shrimp

INGREDIENTS

- 1 lb. shrimp, peeled and deveined
- Cooking spray
- Pinch lemon pepper seasoning

Method

1. Spray the shrimp with oil.
2. Sprinkle with lemon pepper seasoning.
3. Set Ninja Foodi Grill to air fry.
4. Cook at 350 °F for 3 to 5 minutes per side.

Serving Suggestions: Serve with mango salsa.
Preparation / Cooking Tips: Marinate shrimp for 15 minutes before cooking.

15 Mins

10 Mins

4

Coconut Baked Trout

 INGREDIENTS

- 2 tablespoons parsley, chopped
- 2 teaspoons olive oil
- 2 teaspoons garlic, minced
- 4 trout fillets, skinless and boneless
- 1/2 cup coconut milk
- Black pepper (ground)
- and salt to taste

directions

1. Take a baking pan, grease it with some cooking spray, vegetable oil, or butter. Add all the ingredients and combine well.
2. Take Ninja Foodi multi-cooker, arrange it over a cooking platform, and open the top lid.
3. In the pot, add water and place a reversible rack inside the pot. Place the pan over the rack.
4. Seal the multi-cooker by locking it with the Crisping Lid, ensure to keep the pressure release valve locked/sealed.
5. Select "BAKE/ROAST" mode and adjust the 380°F temperature level. Then, set the timer to 15 minutes and press "STOP/START," it will start the cooking process by building up inside pressure.
6. When the timer goes off, quickly release pressure by adjusting the pressure valve to the VENT. After pressure gets released, open the Crisping Lid. Serve warm.

5-10 Mins

15 Mins

4

Nutrition:
- Calories: 320
- Fat: 16g
- Saturated Fat: 4g
- Trans Fat: 0g
- Carbohydrates: 17g
- Fiber: 2.5g
- Sodium: 954mg
- Protein: 28.5g

Wholesome Broccoli Shrimp

INGREDIENTS

- 3 garlic cloves, minced
- ¼ cup white wine
- 2 tablespoons unsalted butter
- 1 shallot, minced
- ½ cup chicken stock
- ½ teaspoon Black pepper (ground)
- 1 ½ pounds frozen
- shrimp, thawed
- Juice of ½ lemon
- ½ teaspoon of sea salt

directions

1. Take Ninja Foodi multi-cooker, arrange it over a cooking platform, and open the top lid.

2. In the pot, add the butter, Select "SEAR/SAUTÉ" mode and select "MD: HI" pressure level. Press "STOP/START." After about 4-5 minutes, the butter will melt.

3. Add the shallots and cook (while stirring) until they become softened and translucent for 2-3 minutes.

4. Add the garlic and cook for 1 minute. Add the wine and stir gently. Mix in the chick-en stock, lemon juice, salt, pepper, broccoli, and shrimp.

5. Seal the multi-cooker by locking it with the pressure lid, ensure to keep the pressure release valve locked/sealed.

6. Select "PRESSURE" mode and select the "HI" pressure level. Then, set the timer to 1 minute and press "STOP/START," it will start the cooking process by building up inside pressure.

7. When the timer goes off, quickly release pressure by adjusting the pressure valve to the VENT. After pressure gets released, open the pressure lid. Serve warm.

5-10 Mins

2 Mins

4

Nutrition:
- Calories: 286
- Fat: 7.5g
- Saturated Fat: 3.5g
- Trans Fat: 0g
- Carbohydrates: 10g
- Fiber: 3g
- Sodium: 657mg
- Protein: 38g

Creamed Salmon

 INGREDIENTS

- 2 garlic cloves, minced
- 2 tablespoons butter, melted
- 1 tablespoon chives, chopped
- 1-pound salmon, boneless, skinless and cubed
- 1/4 cup heavy cream
- Black pepper (ground) and salt to taste

 directions:

1. Take Ninja Foodi multi-cooker, arrange it over a cooking platform, and open the top lid.
2. In the pot, add the butter, Select "SEAR/SAUTÉ" mode and select "MD: HI" pressure level. Press "STOP/START." After about 4-5 minutes, the butter will melt.
3. Add the chives, garlic, and cook (while stirring) until they become softened for 2 minutes.
4. Add the remaining ingredients, stir gently.
5. Seal the multi-cooker by locking it with the pressure lid, ensure to keep the pressure release valve locked/sealed.
6. Select "PRESSURE" mode and select the "HI" pressure level. Then, set the timer to 12 minutes and press "STOP/START," it will start the cooking process by building up inside pressure.
7. When the timer goes off, naturally release inside pressure for about 8-10 minutes. Then, quick-release pressure by adjusting the pressure valve to the VENT. Serve warm.

Nutrition:
- Calories: 286
- Fat: 19g
- Saturated Fat: 9g
- Trans Fat: 0g
- Carbohydrates: 2g
- Fiber: 0g
- Sodium: 930mg
- Protein: 24g

 5-10 Mins

 14 Mins

 4

Cream Mussels with Bread

INGREDIENTS

- 3 garlic cloves, minced
- 1 cup cherry tomatoes, halved
- 2 tablespoons vegetable oil
- 2 shallots, sliced
- 2 cups heavy cream

- 1 ½ teaspoons cayenne pepper
- 1 ½ teaspoon Black pepper (ground)
- 2 pounds mussels, scrubbed and debeard-

ed
- 2 cups white wine
- 1 loaf sourdough bread, cut into slices

directions:

1. Take Ninja Foodi multi-cooker, arrange it over a cooking platform, and open the top lid.
2. In the pot, add the oil, Select "SEAR/SAUTÉ" mode and select "MD: HI" pressure level. Press "STOP/START." After about 4-5 minutes, the oil will start simmering.
3. Add the shallots, garlic, and cherry tomatoes and cook (while stirring) until they become softened and translucent for 4-5 minutes.
4. Add the mussels, wine, heavy cream, cayenne, black pepper, stir gently.
5. Seal the multi-cooker by locking it with the pressure lid, ensure to keep the pressure release valve locked/sealed.
6. Select the "STEAM" mode and select the "HI" pressure level. Then, set the timer to 20 minutes and press "STOP/START," it will start the cooking process by building up inside pressure.
7. When the timer goes off, quickly release pressure by adjusting the pressure valve to the VENT. After pressure gets released, open the pressure lid. Serve warm with bread.

Nutrition:
- Calories: 842
- Fat: 26g
- Saturated Fat: 13g
- Trans Fat: 0g
- Carbohydrates: 56g
- Fiber: 3.5g
- Sodium: 1123mg
- Protein: 39g

5-10 Mins

25 Mins

4

Cod Sandwich

directions:

1. In a blending bowl, whisk the eggs and beer. In another bowl, whisk the cornstarch, flour, chili powder, cumin, salt, and pepper.

2. First, coat the cod fillets with the egg mixture and then with the flour mixture.

3. Take Ninja Foodi multi-cooker, arrange it over a cooking platform, and open the top lid.

4. In the pot, place the Crisping Basket, coat it with some cooking oil. In the basket, add the fillets.

5. Seal the multi-cooker by locking it with the crisping lid, ensure to keep the pressure release valve locked/sealed.

6. Select the "AIR CRISP" mode and adjust the 375°F temperature level. Then, set the timer to 15 minutes and press "STOP/ START," it will start the cooking process by building up inside pressure.

7. When the timer goes off, quickly release pressure by adjusting the pressure valve to the VENT. After pressure gets released, open the Crisping Lid.

8. Arrange four bread slices and spread the tartar sauce over, place the fillets, and add the remaining slices on top. Serve fresh.

Nutrition:
- Calories: 511
- Fat: 12.5g
- Saturated Fat: 2g
- Trans Fat: 0g
- Carbohydrates: 56.5g
- Fiber: 3g
- Sodium: 1147mg
- Protein: 36g

5-10 Mins

15 Mins

4

INGREDIENTS

- 1 cup cornstarch
- 1 cup all-purpose flour
- 2 eggs
- 8 ounces ale
- 1 teaspoon sea salt
- 1 teaspoon black pepper (ground)
- ½ tablespoon chili powder
- 1 tablespoon ground cumin
- Tartar sauce
- 8 slices sandwich bread
- 4 (5-6 ounce) cod fillets, cut into 16 half-inch strips

Classic Honey Salmon

 directions:

1. Take Ninja Foodi multi-cooker, arrange it over a cooking platform, and open the top lid.
2. In the pot, add the oil, salmon, and other ingredients. Stir gently.
3. Seal the multi-cooker by locking it with the pressure lid, ensure to keep the pressure release valve locked/sealed.
4. Select "PRESSURE" mode and select the "HI" pressure level. Then, set the timer to 10 minutes and press "STOP/START," it will start the cooking process by building up inside pressure.
5. When the timer goes off, naturally release inside pressure for about 8-10 minutes. Then, quick-release pressure by adjusting the pressure valve to the VENT. Serve warm.

Nutrition:
- Calories: 268
- Fat: 13g
- Saturated Fat: 1g
- Trans Fat: 0g
- Carbohydrates: 9g
- Fiber: 0.5g
- Sodium: 936mg
- Protein: 29g

5-10 Mins

10 Mins

4

 INGREDIENTS

- 1 tablespoon olive oil
- 2 tablespoons honey
- 1-pound salmon fillets, boneless, skinless and cubed
- 1/4 cup lime juice
- Black pepper (ground) and salt to taste

INGREDIENTS

- 1 (14-ounce) package smoked sausage or kielbasa, sliced into 1-inch pieces
- 4 cups water
- 2 pounds red potatoes, diced
- 3 ears corn, cut crosswise into thirds
- 2 ½ tablespoons Creole seasoning
- 1-pound medium (21–30 count) shrimp, peeled and deveined

Sausage Potato Shrimp

directions:

1. Take Ninja Foodi multi-cooker, arrange it over a cooking platform, and open the top lid.
2. In the pot, add the potatoes, corn, sausage, water, and Creole seasoning. Stir gently.
3. Seal the multi-cooker by locking it with the pressure lid, ensure to keep the pressure release valve locked/sealed.
4. Select "PRESSURE" mode and select the "HI" pressure level. Then, set the timer to 5 minutes and press "STOP/START," it will start the cooking process by building up inside pressure.
5. When the timer goes off, quickly release pressure by adjusting the pressure valve to the VENT. After pressure gets released, open the pressure lid.
6. Select "SEAR/SAUTÉ" mode and select the "LO" pressure level, add the shrimps and combine. Stir-cook for 4-5 minutes. Serve warm.

Nutrition:
- Calories: 426
- Fat: 18g
- Saturated Fat: 5.5g
- Trans Fat: 0g
- Carbohydrates: 37.5g
- Fiber: 6g
- Sodium: 987mg
- Protein: 37.5g

5-10 Mins

10 Mins

6

INGREDIENTS

- 1 teaspoon garlic powder
- 1 teaspoon cumin, ground
- 4 mackerel fillets, boneless
- 1 tablespoon canola oil
- Juice of 1 lime
- Black pepper (ground) and salt to taste

Crispy Garlic Mackerel

directions:

1. Take Ninja Foodi multi-cooker, arrange it over a cooking platform, and open the top lid.
2. In the pot, arrange a reversible rack and place the Crisping Basket over the rack. In the basket, add the fish and other ingredients, combine well.
3. Seal the multi-cooker by locking it with the crisping lid, ensure to keep the pressure release valve locked/sealed.
4. Select the "AIR CRISP" mode and adjust the 370°F temperature level. Then, set the timer to 12 minutes and press "STOP/START," it will start the cooking process by building up inside pressure. Flip the fish after 6 minutes.
5. When the timer goes off, quickly release pressure by adjusting the pressure valve to the VENT. After pressure gets released, open the Crisping Lid. Serve warm with chopped salad greens (optional).

Nutrition:
- Calories: 411
- Fat: 31.5g
- Saturated Fat: 8g
- Trans Fat: 0g
- Carbohydrates: 8g
- Fiber: 1g
- Sodium: 1025mg
- Protein: 22g

5-10 Mins

12 Mins

4

Shrimp Pie Meal

INGREDIENTS

- 1 celery stalk, diced
- 1 carrot, peeled and diced
- ¼ cup unsalted butter
- ½ large onion, diced
- 16 ounces shrimp, cleaned, tailed removed, and deveined
- ¾ cup chicken stock
- 8 ounces chorizo, fully cooked, cut into ½-inch rounds
- ¼ cup all-purpose flour
- 1 tablespoon Cajun spice mix
- ½ cup heavy (whipping) cream
- 1 refrigerated store-bought pie crust
- Sea salt
- Black pepper (ground)

directions:

1. Take Ninja Foodi multi-cooker, arrange it over a cooking platform, and open the top lid.
2. In the pot, add the butter, Select "SEAR/SAUTÉ" mode and select "MD: HI" pressure level. Press "STOP/START." After about
   4-5 minutes, the butter will melt.
3. Add the onions, celery, carrot, and sausage and cook (while stirring) until they become softened and translucent for 3 minutes.
4. Mix the flour and cook for 2 minutes. Add the shrimp, stock, Cajun spice mix, cream, salt and pepper, stir cook for 3 minutes.
5. In the pie crust, add the filling mixture and fold the edges. Make cuts on top for steam escape. Add the pie to the pot.
6. Seal the multi-cooker by locking it with the Crisping Lid, ensure to keep the pressure release valve locked/sealed.
7. Select "BROIL" mode and select the "HI" pressure level. Then, set the timer to 10 minutes and press "STOP/START," it will start the cooking process by building up inside pressure.
8. When the timer goes off, quickly release pressure by adjusting the pressure valve to the VENT. After pressure gets released, open the Crisping Lid. Serve warm.

Nutrition :
- Calories: 479
- Fat: 32.5g
- Saturated Fat: 12g
- Trans Fat: 0g
- Carbohydrates: 18g
- Fiber: 1.5g

5-10 Mins

18 Mins

6

Juicy Rosemary Garlic Salmon

INGREDIENTS

- ¼ teaspoon pepper
- 1 garlic clove, minced
- ¼ teaspoon salt
- ¼ teaspoon fresh rosemary, minced
- 1 teaspoon lemon zest, grated
- 2 salmon fillets, 6 ounces each

directions:

1. Take a mixing bowl and add all listed ingredients except salmon, mix well
2. Add salmon and combine, let it sit for 15 minutes
3. Pre-heat Ninja Foodi by pressing the "GRILL" option and setting it to "MED" and timer to 6 minutes
4. Let it pre-heat until you hear a beep
5. Arrange salmon over grill grate, lock lid and cook for 3 minutes
6. Flip and cook for 3 minutes more, serve and enjoy!

Nutrition:
- Calories: 250
- Fat: 8 g
- Saturated Fat: 3g
- Carbohydrates: 22 g
- Fiber: 3 g
- Sodium: 370 mg
- Protein: 36 g

5-10 Mins

12 Mins

3

INGREDIENTS

- 1 large whole egg
- 1 teaspoon Dijon mustard
- ½ cup breadcrumbs
- 1-pound cod filets
- ¼ cup all-purpose flour
- 1 tablespoon dried parsley
- 1 teaspoon paprika
- ½ teaspoon pepper

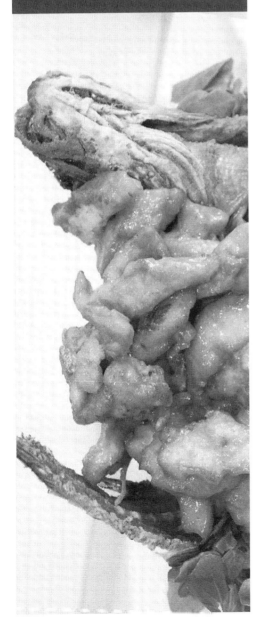

Mustard Crispy Cod

 directions:

1. Take fish filets and cut them into 1-inch wide strips
2. Take a blending bowl and speed in eggs, include mustard and consolidate well
3. Add flour in another bowl
4. Take another bowl and include breadcrumbs, dried parsley, paprika, dark pepper and join well
5. Coat strips with flour, at that point cover with egg blend, and cover with scraps finally
6. Pre-heat Ninja Foodi by squeezing the "AIR CRISP" alternative and setting it to "390 °F" and clock to 10 minutes
7. Let it pre-heat until you hear a beep
8. Arrange strips directly inside basket, lock lid, and cook until the timer runs out
9. Serve and enjoy!

Nutrition:
- Calories: 200
- Fat: 4 g
- Saturated Fat: 1 g
- Carbohydrates: 17 g
- Fiber: 1 g
- Sodium: 214 mg
- Protein: 24 g

 5-10 Mins
 10 Mins
 3

INGREDIENTS

- 2 teaspoons cayenne pepper
- 2 pounds salmon fillets
- 2 teaspoon salt
- 6 tablespoons butter, melted
- 1 and ¼ teaspoon onion salt
- 2 tablespoons lemon pepper
- 1 teaspoon white pepper, ground
- 1 teaspoon black pepper, ground
- 1 teaspoon dry basil
- 1 teaspoon ancho chili powder
- 1 teaspoon dry oregano
- Lemon wedges and dill sprigs

Buttery Spiced Grilled Salmon

directions:

1. Season salmon fillets with butter, take a mixing bowl, and add the listed ingredients
2. Coat salmon fillets with the mixture
3. Pre-heat Ninja Foodi by pressing the "GRILL" option and setting it to "MED" and timer to 10 minutes
4. Let it pre-heat until you hear a beep
5. Arrange prepared fillets over grill grate, let them cook for 5 minutes, flip and cook for 5 minutes more
6. Serve and enjoy!

Nutrition:
- Calories: 300
- Fat: 8 g
- Saturated Fat: 2 g
- Carbohydrates: 17 g
- Fiber: 1 g
- Sodium: 342 mg
- Protein: 26 g

5-10 Mins

10 Mins

4

INGREDIENTS

- 1 shallot, minced
- ¼ cup mayonnaise, low carb
- 12 ounces lump crabmeat
- ¼ cup parsley, minced
- 2 tablespoons Dijon mustard
- 2 tablespoons almond flour
- 1 lemon, zest
- 1 egg, beaten
- Pepper and salt as needed

Crispy Crabby Patties

directions:

1. Take a mixing bowl and add all ingredients, mix well and prepare four meat from the mixture
2. Pre-heat Ninja Foodi by squeezing the "AIR CRISP" choice and setting it to "375 ° F" and timer to 10 minutes
3. Let it pre-heat until you hear a beep
4. Transfer patties to cooking basket and let them cook for 5 minutes, flip and cook for 5 minutes more
5. Serve and enjoy once done!

Nutrition:
- Calories: 177
- Fat: 13 g
- Saturated Fat: 2 g
- Carbohydrates: 2.5 g
- Fiber: 0 g
- Sodium: 358 mg
- Protein: 11 g

5-10 Mins

10 Mins

4

Spicy Grilled Shrimps

 INGREDIENTS

- 1 teaspoon garlic salt
- ½ teaspoon black pepper
- 1 tablespoon paprika
- 1 tablespoon garlic powder
- 2 tablespoons olive oil
- 1-pound jumbo shrimps, peeled and deveined
- 2 tablespoons brown sugar

 directions:

1. Take a mixing bowl and add the listed ingredients to mix well
2. Let it chill and marinate for 30-60 minutes
3. Pre-heat Ninja Foodi by pressing the "GRILL" option and setting it to "MED" and timer to 6 minutes
4. Let it pre-heat until you hear a beep
5. Arrange prepared shrimps over grill grate, lock lid and cook for 3 minutes, flip and cook for 3 minutes more
6. Serve and enjoy!

Nutrition:
- Calories: 370
- Fat: 27 g
- Saturated Fat: 3 g
- Carbohydrates: 23 g
- Fiber: 8 g
- Sodium: 182 mg
- Protein: 6 g

5-10 Mins

6 Mins

4

INGREDIENTS

- ¼ teaspoon salt
- ¾ cup breadcrumbs
- ¼ cup parmesan cheese, grated
- ¼ teaspoon ground dried thyme
- ¼ cup butter, melted
- 1-pound haddock fillets
- ¾ cup milk

Baked Parmesan Fish

directions

1. Coat fish fillets in milk, season with salt and keep it on the side
2. Take a mixing bowl and add breadcrumbs, parmesan, cheese, thyme and combine well
3. Coat fillets in bread crumb mixture
4. Pre-heat Ninja Foodi by pressing the "BAKE" option and setting it to "325 ° F" and timer to 13 minutes
5. Let it pre-heat until you hear a beep
6. Arrange fish fillets directly over Grill Grate, lock lid and cook for 8 minutes, flip and cook for the remaining time
7. Serve and enjoy!

Nutrition:
- Calories: 450
- Fat: 27 g
- Saturated Fat: 12 g
- Carbohydrates: 16 g
- Fiber: 22 g
- Sodium: 1056 mg
- Protein: 44 g

5-10 Mins

13 Mins

3

INGREDIENTS

- 3 tablespoons chipotle in adobo sauce, minced
- ¼ teaspoon salt
- ¼ cup BBQ sauce
- ½ orange, juiced
- ½ pound large shrimps

Roast BBQ Shrimp

 directions

1. Take a mixing bowl and add all the ingredients, mix well
2. Keep it on the side
3. Pre-heat Ninja Foodi by pressing the "ROAST" option and setting it to "400 °F" and timer to 7 minutes
4. Let it pre-heat until you hear a beep
5. Arrange shrimps over Grill Grate and lock lid, cook until the timer runs out
6. Serve and enjoy!

Nutrition:
- Calories: 173
- Fat: 2 g
- Saturated Fat: 0.5 g
- Carbohydrates: 21 g
- Fiber: 2 g
- Sodium: 1143 mg
- Protein: 17 g

5-10 Mins

7 Mins

2

Vegetarian

INGREDIENTS

- 2 heads cauliflower, sliced into florets
- 3 tablespoons olive oil
- Salt and pepper to taste

Sauce
- 1 tablespoon soy sauce
- 1/4 cup olive oil
- 1 tablespoon chili paste
- 3 tablespoons honey
- 2 tablespoons rice wine vinegar
- 1/4 cup roasted peanuts, chopped
- 1 tablespoon cilantro, chopped

Roasted Cauliflower

 Method

1. Add air fry basket to your Ninja Foodi Grill.
2. Choose the air fry function.
3. Set it to 390 °F for 20 minutes.
4. Press "start" to preheat.
5. In a bowl, toss cauliflower in oil.
6. Season with salt and pepper.
7. Add cauliflower to the air fry basket.
8. Seal the hood.
9. Cook for 10 minutes.
10. Stir and cook for another 8 minutes.
11. While waiting, combine all the ingredients for the sauce.
12. Toss the roasted cauliflower in a sauce before serving.

Serving Suggestions: Garnish with sesame seeds.
Preparation / Cooking Tips: Use different colored cauliflower for a vibrant result.

 30 Mins

 20 Mins

 4

INGREDIENTS

- 2 tablespoons butter, melted
- 1 tablespoon honey
- Salt to taste
- 6 carrots, sliced
- 1 tablespoon parsley, chopped

Honey Carrots

Method

15 Mins

10 Mins

4

1. Add grill grate to your Ninja Foodi Grill.
2. Set it to grill.
3. Press max temperature and set it to 10 minutes.
4. Choose start to preheat.
5. While preheating, combine butter, honey, and salt.
6. Coat the carrots with the honey mixture.
7. Add carrots to the grill.
8. Seal the hood. Cook for 4 to 5 minutes.
9. Flip and cook for another 5 minutes.
10. Sprinkle with parsley and serve.

Serving Suggestions: Serve as a side dish to a grilled meat dish.

Preparation / Cooking Tips: You can also add honey mixture after cooking.

INGREDIENTS

- 4 ears corn
- 2 tablespoons oil
- Salt and pepper to taste
- 1/4 cup mayonnaise
- 1 cup Cotija cheese, crumbled
- 2 tablespoons lime juice
- 1/4 cup sour cream
- 1 teaspoon onion powder
- 1 teaspoon garlic powder

15 Mins

10 Mins

4

Mexican Corn

Method

1. Install grill grate to your Ninja Foodi Grill.
2. Select the grill function.
3. Set it to the max for 12 minutes.
4. Press start to preheat.
5. Coat corn with oil.
6. Sprinkle all sides with salt and pepper.
7. Add corn to the grill.
8. Grill for 5 to 6 minutes.
9. Turn and cook for another 5 minutes.
10. Combine the remaining ingredients in a bowl.
11. Coat the corn with the mixture and serve.

Serving Suggestions: Garnish with chopped cilantro.

Preparation / Cooking Tips: Use light mayonnaise and reduced-fat sour cream.

INGREDIENTS

- 1 pizza dough
- 1 tablespoon olive oil, divided
- 1/2 cup pizza sauce
- 1 cup mozzarella cheese, shredded
- 1/2 cup ricotta cheese
- 2 tomatoes, sliced
- 5 basil leaves, sliced

20 Mins

15 Mins

2

Vegetarian Pizza

Method

1. Add grill grate to the Ninja Foodi Grill.
2. Press the grill setting.
3. Set it to the max for 6 minutes.
4. Press start to preheat.
5. Roll out the dough on your kitchen table.
6. Brush top with oil.
7. Add dough to the grill.
8. Cook for 5 minutes.
9. Flip and cook for another 5 minutes.
10. Spread pizza sauce on top of the dough.
11. Sprinkle it with mozzarella cheese and then with ricotta.
12. Add tomatoes and basil on top.
13. Grill pizza for 3 to 5 minutes or until cheese has melted.

Serving Suggestions: Sprinkle with dried oregano before serving

Preparation / Cooking Tips: Poke the dough with a fork before spreading with oil.

INGREDIENTS

- 1 lb. Brussels sprouts, sliced in half
- 1 tablespoon olive oil
- Salt and pepper to taste
- 2 teaspoons garlic powder

Garlic Brussels Sprouts

Method

1. Toss Brussels sprouts in oil.
2. Season with salt, pepper, and garlic powder.
3. Add crisper plate in the air fryer basket.
4. Add the basket to the Ninja Foodi Grill.
5. Select air fry. Set it to 390 °F for 3 minutes.
6. Press start to preheat.
7. Add Brussels sprouts to the crisper plate.
8. Cook for 20 minutes.
9. Stir and cook for another 15 minutes.

Serving Suggestions: Sprinkle with minced garlic on top if desired.

Preparation / Cooking Tips: Do not overcrowd the crisper plate to ensure even cooking

15 Mins

35 Mins

4

Roasted Spicy Potatoes

INGREDIENTS

- 1 lb. baby potatoes, sliced into wedges
- 2 tablespoons olive oil
- Salt to taste
- 1 tablespoon garlic powder
- 1 tablespoon paprika
- 1/2 cup mayonnaise
- 2 tablespoons white wine vinegar
- 2 tablespoons tomato paste
- 1 teaspoon chili powder

 15 Mins

 25 Mins

 4

Method

1. Toss potatoes in oil.
2. Sprinkle with salt, garlic powder, and paprika.
3. Add crisper plate to the air fryer basket.
4. Add a basket to the Ninja Foodi Grill.
5. Set it to air fry.
6. Set it to 360 °F for 30 minutes.
7. Press start to preheat.
8. Put the potatoes on the crisper plate after 3 minutes.
9. Cook for 25 minutes.
10. While waiting, mix the remaining ingredients.
11. Toss potatoes in spicy mayo mixture and serve.

Serving Suggestions: Sprinkle with chopped parsley before serving.
Preparation / Cooking Tips: Poke potatoes with a fork before roasting.

INGREDIENTS

- 2 cauliflower steaks
- 1/4 cup vegetable oil, divided
- Salt and pepper to taste
- 1 onion, chopped
- 3 cloves garlic, minced
- 1/2 cup roasted red bell peppers, chopped
- 1/4 cup Kalamata olives, chopped
- 1 tablespoon fresh parsley, chopped
- 1 tablespoon fresh oregano, chopped
- 1/2 lb. feta cheese, crumbled
- 1 tablespoon lemon juice
- 1/4 cup walnuts, chopped

Grilled Cauliflower Steak

Method

1. Add grill grate to your Ninja Foodi Grill.
2. Choose the grill setting.
3. Set it to the max for 17 minutes.
4. Press start to preheat.
5. Brush both sides of cauliflower steaks with oil.
6. Season with salt and pepper.
7. Grill for 10 minutes per side.
8. Mix the remaining ingredients in a bowl.
9. Spread mixture on top of the steaks and cook for another 2 minutes.

Serving Suggestions: Serve as a vegetarian main dish.

Preparation / Cooking Tips: Use ricotta cheese in place of feta if not available.

30 Mins

25 Mins

2

153

INGREDIENTS

- 1 zucchini, sliced
- 8 oz. mushrooms, sliced
- 2 tablespoons olive oil
- 1 tablespoon garlic, minced
- 1 teaspoon onion powder
- 1 teaspoon garlic powder
- Salt and pepper to taste

Roasted Mixed Veggies

Method

1. Choose the air fry setting in your Ninja Foodi Grill.
2. Insert the air fryer basket.
3. Preheat it to 390 °F.
4. Toss zucchini and mushrooms in oil.
5. Sprinkle with garlic.
6. Season with onion powder, garlic powder, salt and pepper.
7. Place in the basket.
8. Cook for 10 minutes.
9. Stir and cook for another 5 minutes.

Serving Suggestions: Serve as a side dish to the main course.

Preparation / Cooking Tips: Do not overcrowd the basket with veggies.

15 Mins

15 Mins

4

INGREDIENTS

- 1 zucchini, sliced
- 2 tomatoes, sliced in half
- 1 red bell pepper, sliced
- 1 orange bell pepper, sliced
- 1 yellow bell pepper, sliced
- 3 oz. black olives
- 1 tablespoon olive oil
- 1 teaspoon dried parsley
- 1 teaspoon dried oregano
- 1 teaspoon dried basil leaves
- Salt and pepper to taste
- 6 cloves garlic, minced

Mediterranean Veggies

Method

1. Combine all the ingredients in a large bowl.
2. Transfer to the air fryer basket.
3. Insert an air fryer basket into your Ninja Foodi Grill.
4. Select air fry setting.
5. Cook at 390 degrees F for 10 minutes.
6. Stir and cook for another 10 minutes.

Serving Suggestions: Serve with crumbled feta cheese.
Preparation / Cooking Tips: Add other colorful veggies to this recipe.

30 Mins

20 Mins

6

30 Mins

45 Mins

8

Veggie Lasagna

Method

1. Combine all the ingredients except cheese, cream, and pasta sheets.
2. In another bowl, mix cheese and cream.
3. Spread some of the tomato sauce and veggie mixture on the bottom of the pot.
4. Top with the pasta sheets.
5. Spread another layer of the tomato sauce mixture, and then the cheese mixture.
6. Top with another layer of pasta sheets.
7. Repeat layers until all the ingredients have been used.
8. Cover the top layer with foil.
9. Choose the bake setting.
10. Cook at 350 °F for 45 minutes.

Serving Suggestions: Sprinkle with Parmesan and basil before serving.

Preparation / Cooking Tips: You can also pre-boil the lasagna sheets and vegetables to reduce cooking time in the Ninja Foodi Grill.

INGREDIENTS

- 6 cups tomato sauce
- 2 tablespoons olive oil
- 2 cloves garlic, minced
- 1 teaspoon dried basil
- 1 teaspoon dried oregano
- Salt and pepper to taste
- 1 red bell pepper, chopped
- 1 green bell pepper, chopped
- 1 cup mushrooms, diced
- 1 cup broccoli, diced
- 1 eggplant, diced
- 4 cups mozzarella cheese
- 4 cups cream
- 1 pack lasagna pasta sheets

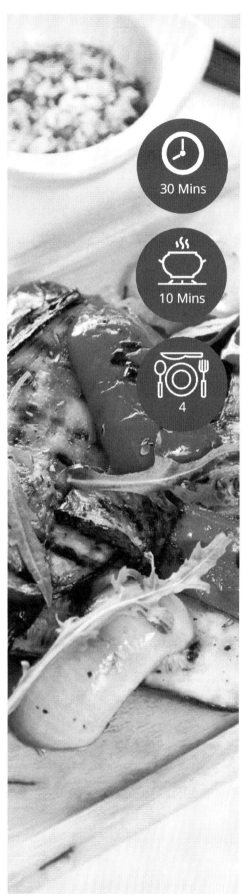

Grilled Veggies

30 Mins

10 Mins

4

 **Method**

1. Install grill grate to your Ninja Foodi Grill.

2. Select the grill setting.
3. Preheat it to medium for 10 minutes.

4. Toss the veggies in olive oil and season with salt and pepper.

5. Add to the grill grate.

6. Grill for 10 minutes.

Serving Suggestions: Sprinkle with dried herbs before serving.
Preparation / Cooking Tips: It's better to serve this dish at room temperature.

INGREDIENTS

- 1 onion, sliced

- 1 red bell pepper, sliced

- 1 cup button mushrooms, sliced

- 1 zucchini, sliced

- 1 eggplant, sliced

- 1 cup asparagus, trimmed and sliced

- 1 squash, sliced

- 2 tablespoons olive oil

- Salt and pepper to taste

Tofu Omelette

20 Mins

25 Mins

4

Method

1. Select the air fry setting in your Ninja Foodi Grill.
2. Spray tofu cubes with oil.
3. Add tofu cubes to the air fryer basket.
4. Cook at 390 °F for 10 to 15 minutes or until crispy.
5. Transfer to a plate.
6. Toss veggies in a bowl.
7. Spray with oil and season with garlic salt.
8. Cook at 390 degrees F for 10 minutes, shaking the basket half-way through
9. Add brown rice to serving bowls.
10. Top with crispy tofu and vegetables.

Serving Suggestions: Sprinkle with chopped scallions before serving.

Preparation / Cooking Tips: You can also use meat instead of tofu for this recipe if you prefer.

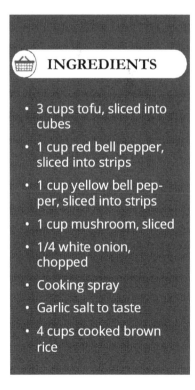

INGREDIENTS

- 3 cups tofu, sliced into cubes
- 1 cup red bell pepper, sliced into strips
- 1 cup yellow bell pepper, sliced into strips
- 1 cup mushroom, sliced
- 1/4 white onion, chopped
- Cooking spray
- Garlic salt to taste
- 4 cups cooked brown rice

20 Mins

20 Mins

4

Mixed Air Fried Veggies

 INGREDIENTS

- 1 white onion, sliced into wedges
- 1 red bell pepper, sliced
- 4 oz. mushroom buttons, sliced in half
- 1 zucchini, sliced
- 1 squash, sliced into cubes
- 1 tablespoon olive oil
- Salt and pepper to taste

 **Method**

1. Select the air fry setting in your Ninja Foodi Grill.
2. Add air fryer basket.
3. Toss veggies in oil and season with salt and pepper.
4. Add veggies to the basket.
5. Cook for 10 minutes.
6. Shake and cook for another 10 minutes.

Serving Suggestions: Serve as a side dish to the main course.

Preparation / Cooking Tips: You can also try using other vegetables for this recipe like potatoes or carrots.

INGREDIENTS

- 4 cups bok choy
- 2 tablespoons peanut oil
- 1 tablespoon oyster sauce
- 2 teaspoons garlic, minced
- Salt to taste

Asian Bok Choy

Method

1. Coat bok choy with oil and oyster sauce.
2. Sprinkle with minced garlic and salt.
3. Add grill grate to your Ninja Foodi Grill.
4. Add bok choy on top of the grill.
5. Select the grill setting. Set it to medium.
6. Grill for 10 minutes.

Serving Suggestions: Serve with peanut sauce on the side.
Preparation / Cooking Tips: You can also use Chinese cabbage for this recipe.

10 Mins   10 Mins

4

INGREDIENTS

- 1 lb. asparagus, trimmed
- 2 teaspoons olive oil
- Salt and pepper to taste

Crispy Asparagus

Method

1. Coat asparagus with oil.
2. Sprinkle with salt and pepper.
3. Choose the air fry setting in your Ninja Foodi Grill.
4. Set it to 390 °F.
5. Cook asparagus in the air fryer basket for 7 to 10 minutes, shaking halfway through.

Serving Suggestions: Sprinkle with Parmesan cheese on top before serving.

Preparation / Cooking Tips: Dry asparagus before seasoning.

10 Mins

10 Mins

4

INGREDIENTS

- 1 red onion, peeled, cut in quarters
- 1 jalapeño pepper, cut in half, seeds removed
- 5 Roma tomatoes, cut in half lengthwise
- 1 tablespoon kosher salt
- 2 teaspoons ground black pepper
- 2 tablespoons canola oil
- 1 bunch cilantro, stems trimmed
- Juice and zest of 3 limes
- 3 cloves garlic, peeled
- 2 tablespoons ground cumin

5-10 Mins

10 Mins

4

Tomato Salsa

directions

1. In a blending bowl, join the onion, tomatoes, jalapeño pepper, salt, dark pepper, and canola oil.
2. Take Ninja Foodi Grill, mastermind it over your kitchen stage, and open the top. Mastermind the barbecue mesh and close the top cover.
3. Press "Barbecue" and select the "Maximum" flame broil work. Change the clock to 10 minutes and afterward press "START/STOP." Ninja Foodi will begin preheating.
4. Ninja Foodi is preheated and prepared to cook when it begins to blare. After you hear a signal, open the top cover.
5. Arrange the vegetables over the grill grate.
6. Close the top lid and cook for 5 minutes. Now open the top lid, flip the vegetables.
7. Close the top lid and cook for five more minutes.
8. Blend the mixture in a blender and serve as needed.

Nutrition:
- Calories: 169
- Fat: 9g
- Saturated Fat: 2g
- Trans Fat: 0g
- Carbohydrates: 12g
- Fiber: 3g
- Sodium: 321mg
- Protein: 2.5g

INGREDIENTS

- 2 cups cherry tomatoes
- 2 cups cremini, button, or other small mushrooms
- 1/4 cup of vinegar (Sherry) or 1/4 cup of red wine
- 2 garlic cloves, finely chopped
- 1/2 cup extra-virgin olive oil
- 3 tablespoons chopped thyme
- Pinch of crushed red pepper flakes
- 1 teaspoon kosher salt
- 1/2 teaspoon black pepper
- 6 scallions, cut crosswise into 2-inch pieces

10 Mins

15 Mins

4

Mushroom Tomato Roast

directions

1. Take a zip-lock bag, add black pepper, salt, red pepper flakes, thyme, vinegar, oil, and garlic. Add mushrooms, tomatoes, and scallions.
2. Shake well and refrigerate for 30-40 minutes to marinate.
3. Take Ninja Foodi Grill, orchestrate it over your kitchen stage, and open the top.
4. Press "Prepare" and alter the temperature to 400°F. Modify the clock to 12 minutes and afterward press "START/STOP." Ninja Foodi will begin preheating.
5. Ninja Foodi is preheated and prepared to cook when it begins to blare. After you hear a blare, open the top.
6. Arrange the mushroom mixture directly inside the pot.
7. Close the top lid and allow it to cook until the timer reads zero.
8. Serve warm.

Nutrition:
- Calories: 253
- Fat: 24g
- Saturated Fat: 4g
- Trans Fat: 0g
- Carbohydrates: 7g
- Fiber: 2g
- Sodium: 546mg
- Protein: 1g

INGREDIENTS

- ½ teaspoon garlic powder
- ½ teaspoon paprika
- Ocean salt and ground dark pepper to taste
- 1 head cauliflower, stemmed and leaves removed
- 1 cup Cheddar cheese, shredded
- Ranch dressing, for garnish
- ¼ cup canola oil or vegetable oil
- 2 tablespoons chopped chives
- 4 slices bacon, cooked and crumbled

5-10 Mins

15 Mins

2

Cheddar Cauliflower Meal

directions

1. Cut the cauliflower into 2-inch pieces.
2. In the blending bowl, include the oil, garlic powder, and paprika. Season with salt and ground dark pepper; join well. Coat the florets with the blend.
3. Take Ninja Foodi Grill, mastermind it over your kitchen stage, and open the top cover.
4. Mastermind the flame broil mesh and close the top cover.
5. Press "Flame broil" and select the "Maximum" barbecue work. Change the clock to 15 minutes and afterward press "START/STOP." Ninja Foodi will begin preheating.
6. Ninja Foodi is preheated and prepared to cook when it begins to signal. After you hear a blare, open the top.
7. Organize the pieces over the flame broil grind.
8. Close the top lid and cook for 10 minutes. Now open the top lid, flip the pieces and top with the cheese.
9. Close the top lid and cook for 5 more minutes. Serve warm with the chives and ranch dressing on top.

Nutrition:
- Calories: 534
- Fat: 34g
- Saturated Fat: 13g
- Trans Fat: 0g
- Carbohydrates: 14.5g
- Fiber: 4g
- Sodium: 1359mg
- Protein: 31g

INGREDIENTS

- 2/3 cup Kalamata olives, halved and pitted
- 1 and ½ cups feta cheese, grated
- 4 tablespoons butter
- 2 pounds spinach, chopped and boiled
- Pepper and salt to taste
- 4 teaspoons lemon zest, grated

Buttery Spinach Meal

directions

1. Take a mixing bowl and add spinach, butter, salt, pepper and mix well
2. Pre-heat Ninja Foodi by pressing the "AIR CRISP" option and setting it to "340 °F" and timer to 15 minutes
3. Let it pre-heat until you hear a beep
4. Arrange a reversible trivet in the Grill Pan, arrange spinach mixture in a basket, and place the basket in the trivet
5. Let them roast until the timer runs out
6. Serve and enjoy!

Nutrition:
- Calories: 250
- Fat: 18 g
- Saturated Fat: 6 g
- Carbohydrates: 8 g
- Fiber: 3 g
- Sodium: 309 mg
- Protein: 10 g

10 Mins

15 Mins

4

INGREDIENTS

- 2 tablespoons Dijon mustard
- 1 teaspoon salt
- ¼ teaspoon black pepper
- ½ cup avocado oil
- ½ olive oil
- ½ cup red wine vinegar
- 2 tablespoons honey

Veggies:
- 4 sweet onions, quartered
- 4 yellow squash, cut in half
- 4 red peppers, seeded and halved
- 4 zucchinis, halved
- 2 bunches green onions, trimmed

10 Mins

30-40 Mins

Mustard Green Veggie Meal

directions

1. Take a small bowl and whisk mustard, pepper, honey, vinegar, and salt
2. Add oil to make a smooth mixture
3. Mastermind the flame broil mesh and close the top cover
4. Pre-heat Ninja Foodi by pressing the "GRILL" option and setting it to "MED" and timer to 10 minutes
5. Let it pre-heat until you hear a beep
6. Arrange the onion quarters over the grill grate, lock the lid and cook for 5 minutes
7. Flip the peppers and cook for 5 minutes more
8. Grill the other vegetables in the same manner with 7 minutes on each side for zucchini, pepper, and squash and 1 minute for onion
9. Prepare the vinaigrette by mixing all the ingredients under vinaigrette in a bowl
10. Serve the grilled veggies with vinaigrette on top
11. Enjoy!

Nutrition:
- Calories: 326
- Fat: 4.5 g
- Saturated Fat: 1 g
- Carbohydrates: 35 g
- Fiber: 4 g
- Sodium: 543 mg
- Protein: 8 g

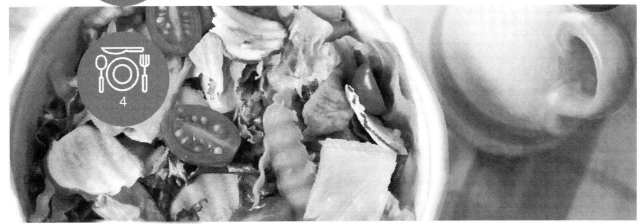

INGREDIENTS

- 2 heads broccoli, trimmed into florets
- 4 cups arugula, torn
- 2 tablespoons parmesan cheese, grated
- 1 tablespoon lemon juice
- 1 teaspoon honey
- 1 teaspoon Dijon mustard
- 1 garlic clove, minced
- ½ red onion, sliced
- 1 tablespoon canola oil
- 2 tablespoons extra-virgin olive oil
- Red pepper flakes
- ¼ teaspoon of sea salt
- Black pepper, freshly grounded

10 Mins

12 Mins

Broccoli and Arugula Salad

directions

1. Supplement the flame broil mesh and close the hood
2. Pre-heat Ninja Foodi by pressing the "GRILL" option and setting it to "MAX" and the timer to 12 minutes
3. Take a large bowl and combine the broccoli, sliced onions, canola oil
4. Toss until coated
5. Once it pre-heat until you hear a beep
6. Arrange the vegetables over the grill grate, lock the lid and cook for 8 to 12 minutes
7. Take a medium bowl and whisk together lemon juice, mustard, olive oil, honey, garlic, red pepper flakes, salt, and pepper
8. Once cooked, combine the roasted vegetables and arugula in a large serving bowl
9. Drizzle with the vinaigrette to taste and sprinkle with parmesan cheese
10. Serve and enjoy!

Nutrition:
- Calories: 168
- Fat: 12 g
- Saturated Fat: 3 g
- Carbohydrates: 13 g
- Fiber: 1 g
- Sodium: 392 mg
- Protein: 6 g

Mustard Green Veggies

directions

1. In a little bowl, whisk the vinegar, mustard, nectar, pepper, and salt. Include the oils and consolidate them to make a smooth blend.
2. Take Ninja Foodi Grill, organize it over your kitchen stage, and open the top.
3. Organize the barbecue mesh and close the top cover.
4. Press "Flame broil" and select the "Drug" barbecue work. Alter the clock to 10 minutes and afterward press "START/STOP." Ninja Foodi will begin pre-warming.
5. Ninja Foodi is preheated and prepared to cook when it begins to blare. After you hear a signal, open the top.
6. Arrange the onion quarters over the grill grate.
7. Close the top lid and cook for 5 minutes. Now open the top lid, flip the onions.
8. Close the top lid and cook for 5 more minutes.
9. Grill the other vegetables in the same manner with 7 minutes per side for the zucchini, peppers, and squash. And 1 minute per side for the green onions.
10. Serve the grilled veggies with the vinaigrette on top.

Nutrition:
- Calories: 326
- Fat: 4.5g
- Saturated Fat: 0.5g
- Trans Fat: 0g
- Carbohydrates: 35.5g
- Fiber: 2g
- Sodium: 524mg
- Protein: 8g

INGREDIENTS

- 2 tablespoon Dijon mustard
- 1/2 cup red wine vinegar
- 2 tablespoon honey
- 1 teaspoon salt
- 1/4 teaspoon black pepper
- 1/2 cup avocado oil
- 1/2 cup olive oil

Veggies:
- 4 zucchinis, halved
- 4 sweet onions, quartered
- 4 red peppers, seeded and halved
- 2 bunches green onions, trimmed
- 4 yellow squash, cut in half

5-10 Mins

30-40 Mins

7-8

Creamy Corn Potatoes

 directions

1. Drain the potatoes and rub them with oil.
2. Take Ninja Foodi Grill, mastermind it over your kitchen stage, and open the top cover.
3. Mastermind the flame broil mesh and close the top cover.
4. Press "Flame broil" and select the "Drug" barbecue work. Modify the clock to 10 minutes and afterward press "START/STOP." Ninja Foodi will begin pre-warming.
5. Ninja Foodi is preheated and prepared to cook when it begins to blare. After you hear a signal, open the top cover.
6. Arrange the poblano peppers over the grill grate.
7. Close the top lid and cook for 5 minutes. Now open the top lid, flip the peppers.
8. Close the top lid and cook for 5 more minutes.
9. Grill the other vegetables in the same manner with 7 minutes per side for the potatoes and corn.
10. Whisk the remaining ingredients in another bowl.
11. Peel the grilled pepper and chop them. Divide corn ears into smaller pieces and cut the potatoes as well.
12. Serve the grilled veggies with the vinaigrette on top.

Nutrition:
- Calories: 322
- Fat: 4.5g
- Saturated Fat: 1g
- Trans Fat: 0g
- Carbohydrates: 51.5g
- Fiber: 3g
- Sodium: 600mg
- Protein: 5g

 INGREDIENTS

- 1 1/2-pound red potatoes, quartered and boiled
- 3 tablespoons olive oil
- 1 tablespoon cilantro, minced
- 2 sweet corn ears, without husks
- 1/4 teaspoon cayenne pepper
- 2 poblano peppers
- 1/2 cup milk
- 1 teaspoon ground cumin
- 1 tablespoon lime juice
- 1 jalapeno pepper, seeded and minced
- 1/2 cup sour cream
- 1 ½ teaspoons garlic salt

5-10 Mins

30-40 Mins

4

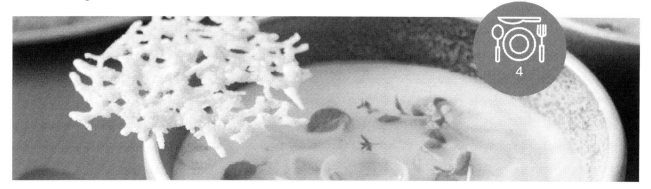

169

Classic Bruschetta

directions

1. In a mixing bowl, add the tomato mixture ingredients.

   Combine the ingredients to mix well with each other. Cover and refrigerate for 30-60 minutes.
2. In another bowl, combine the mayonnaise, mustard, onion, garlic, and oregano.
3. Take Ninja Foodi Grill, mastermind it over your kitchen stage, and open the top cover. Orchestrate the flame broil mesh and close the top.
4. Press "Flame broil" and select the "Drug" barbecue work. Modify the clock to 4 minutes and afterward press "START/STOP." Ninja Foodi will begin preheating.
5. Ninja Foodi is preheated and prepared to cook when it begins to signal. After you hear a signal, open the top cover.
6. Arrange the bread slices over the grill grate. Close the top lid and cook for 2 minutes. Now open the top lid, flip the slices and spread with the mayo mixture. Close the top lid and cook for 2 more minutes. Serve warm with the tomato mixture on top.

INGREDIENTS

Tomato mixture:
- 1-pound plum tomatoes, seeded and chopped
- 1 cup chopped celery or fennel bulb
- 1/4 cup minced basil
- 3 tablespoons balsamic vinegar
- 3 tablespoons olive oil
- 3 tablespoons Dijon mustard
- 1/2 teaspoon salt
- 2 garlic cloves, minced
- Mayonnaise Spread:
- 3/4 teaspoon dried oregano
- 1/4 cup Dijon mustard
- 1/2 cup mayonnaise
- 1 garlic clove, minced
- 1 tablespoon finely chopped green onion
- 1 loaf (1 pound) French bread, cut into 1/2-inch slices

Nutrition:
- Calories: 241
- Fat: 15.5g
- Saturated Fat: 3g
- Trans Fat: 0g
- Carbohydrates: 24.5g
- Fiber: 4g
- Sodium: 526mg
- Protein: 8g

5-10 Mins

4 Mins

8

Meatless Recipes

Rice & Bean Meal

directions

1. Take Ninja Foodi multi-cooker, arrange it over a cooking platform, and open the top lid.

2. In the pot, add the oil; Select "SEAR/SAUTÉ" mode and select "MD: HI" pressure level. Press "STOP/START." After about 4-5 minutes, the oil will start simmering.

3. Add the onions, garlic, jalapeno, and cook (while stirring) until they become softened for 2 minutes.

4. Mix the rice, salsa, tomato sauce, vegetable stock/water, seasoning, pinto beans, and salt.

5. Seal the multi-cooker by locking it with the pressure lid; ensure to keep the pressure release valve locked/sealed.

6. Select "PRESSURE" mode and select the "HI" pressure level. Then, set the timer to 6 minutes and press "STOP/START"; it

   will start the cooking process by building up inside pressure, when the timer goes off, naturally release inside pressure for about 8-10 minutes, then, quick-release pressure by adjusting the pressure valve to the VENT.

INGREDIENTS

- 2 large garlic cloves, minced
- 1 jalapeño pepper, seeded and chopped
- 3 tablespoons olive oil
- 1 small onion, chopped (about ²/₃cup)
- 1 cup long-grain white rice, thoroughly rinsed
- 1 (16-ounce) can pinto beans, depleted and flushed
- ¹/₃ cup red salsa
- ¼ cup tomato sauce
- ½ cup vegetable stock or broth
- 1 teaspoon Mexican seasoning mix
- 1 teaspoon kosher salt
- 1 tablespoon chopped fresh cilantro (optional)

Nutrition:
- Calories: 366
- Fat: 11g
- Saturated Fat: 2g
- Trans Fat: 0g
- Carbohydrates: 48.5g
- Fiber: 6.5g
- Sodium: 951mg
- Protein: 11g

5-10 Mins

8 Mins

4

Bacon Potato Soup

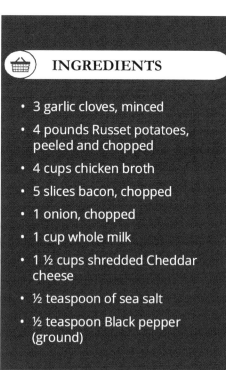

- 3 garlic cloves, minced
- 4 pounds Russet potatoes, peeled and chopped
- 4 cups chicken broth
- 5 slices bacon, chopped
- 1 onion, chopped
- 1 cup whole milk
- 1 ½ cups shredded Cheddar cheese
- ½ teaspoon of sea salt
- ½ teaspoon Black pepper (ground)

5-10 Mins

20 Mins

5-6

directions

1. Take Ninja Foodi multi-cooker, arrange it over a cooking platform, and open the top lid.
2. In the pot, add the oil, select "SEAR/SAUTÉ" mode and select "MD: HI" pressure level. Press "STOP/START." After about 4-5 minutes, the oil will start simmering.
3. Add the onions, bacon, garlic, and cook (while stirring) until they become softened and translucent for 4-5 minutes.
4. Add the potatoes and chicken broth.
5. Seal the multi-cooker by locking it with the pressure lid, ensure to keep the pressure release valve locked/sealed.
6. Select "PRESSURE" mode and select the "HI" pressure level. Then, set the timer to 10 minutes and press "STOP/START," it will start the cooking process by building up inside pressure.
7. When the timer goes off, quickly release pressure by adjusting the pressure valve to the VENT. After pressure gets released, open the pressure lid.
8. Add the milk and mash the ingredients, season with paper, and salt. Add the cheese on top.
9. Seal the multi-cooker by locking it with the Crisping Lid, ensure to keep the pressure release valve locked/sealed.
10. Select "BROIL" mode and select the "HI" pressure level. Then, set the timer to 5 minutes and press "STOP/START," it will start the cooking process by building up inside pressure.
11. When the timer goes off, quickly release pressure by adjusting the pressure valve to the VENT, after pressure gets released, open the Crisping Lid.

Nutrition:
- Calories: 433
- Fat: 17.5g
- Saturated Fat: 7g
- Trans Fat: 0g
- Carbohydrates: 46g
- Fiber: 7g
- Sodium: 941mg
- Protein: 22.5g

Pasta Squash Soup

1. Take Ninja Foodi multi-cooker, arrange it over a cooking platform, and open the top lid.
2. Select "SEAR/SAUTÉ" mode and select "MD: HI" pressure level. Press "STOP/START".
3. Add the bacon and cook (while stirring) until it becomes crisp for 4-5 minutes, and fat is rendered. Set aside the bacon and place it over paper towels.
4. Keep the fat in the pot, add the butternut squash, apple, salt, and pepper, stir cook for about 5 minutes. Mix in the stock, oregano, and bacon.
5. Set "SEAR/SAUTÉ" mode to "HI" and boil the mixture for 10 minutes. Mix in the pasta and stir cook for about 8 minutes.

 INGREDIENTS

- 1 green apple, cut into small cubes
- 4 slices uncooked bacon, cut into ½ -inch pieces
- 12 ounces butternut squash, peeled and cubed
- 1 tablespoon minced oregano
- 2 quarts chicken stock
- Kosher salt and black pepper (ground) to taste
- 1 cup orzo

Nutrition :
- Calories: 253
- Fat: 6.5g
- Saturated Fat: 2g
- Trans Fat: 0g
- Carbohydrates: 32g
- Fiber: 3.5g
- Sodium: 533mg
- Protein: 12g

5-10 Mins

30 Mins

7-8

Mustard Green Veggies

INGREDIENTS

Vinaigrette:
- 2 tablespoon Dijon mustard
- 1/2 cup red wine vinegar
- 2 tablespoon honey
- 1 teaspoon salt
- 1/4 teaspoon black pepper
- 1/2 cup avocado oil
- 1/2 cup olive oil

Veggies :
- 4 zucchinis, halved
- 4 sweet onions, quartered
- 4 red peppers, seeded and halved
- 2 bunches green onions, trimmed
- 4 yellow squash, cut in half

directions

1. In a little bowl, whisk the vinegar, mustard, nectar, pepper, and salt. Include the oils and join them to make a smooth blend.
2. Take Ninja Foodi Grill, organize it over your kitchen stage, and open the top.
3. Organize the flame broil mesh and close the top cover.
4. Press "Flame broil" and select the "Drug" barbecue work. Modify the clock to 10 minutes and afterward press "START/STOP." Ninja Foodi will begin pre-warming.
5. Ninja Foodi is preheated and prepared to cook when it begins to blare. After you hear a blare, open the top.
6. Arrange the onion quarters over the grill grate.
7. Close the top lid and cook for 5 minutes. Now open the top lid, flip the onions.
8. Close the top lid and cook for 5 more minutes.
9. Grill the other vegetables in the same manner with 7 minutes per side for the zucchini, peppers, and squash, and 1 minute per side for the green onions.
10. Serve the grilled veggies with the vinaigrette on top.

Nutrition:
- Calories: 326
- Fat: 4.5g
- Saturated Fat: 0.5g
- Trans Fat: 0g
- Carbohydrates: 35.5g
- Fiber: 2g
- Sodium: 524mg
- Protein: 8g

30-40 Mins

5-10 Mins

7-8

INGREDIENTS

- 1 1/2-pound red potatoes, quartered and boiled
- 3 tablespoons olive oil
- 1 tablespoon cilantro, minced
- 2 sweet corn ears, without husks
- 1/4 teaspoon cayenne pepper
- 2 poblano peppers
- 1/2 cup milk
- 1 teaspoon ground cumin
- 1 tablespoon lime juice
- 1 jalapeno pepper, seeded and minced
- 1/2 cup sour cream
- 1 ½ teaspoons garlic salt

5-10 Mins

30-40 Mins

4

Creamy Corn Potatoes

directions

1. Drain the potatoes and rub them with oil.
2. Take Ninja Foodi Grill, orchestrate it over your kitchen stage, and open the top cover.
3. Orchestrate the flame broil mesh and close the top.
4. Press "Barbecue" and select the "MED" flame broil work. Change the clock to 10 minutes and afterward press "START/STOP." Ninja Foodi will begin pre-warming.
5. Ninja Foodi is preheated and prepared to cook when it begins to blare. After you hear a blare, open the top cover.
6. Arrange the poblano peppers over the grill grate.
7. Close the top lid and cook for 5 minutes. Now open the top lid, flip the peppers.
8. Close the top lid and cook for 5 more minutes.
9. Grill the other vegetables in the same manner with 7 minutes per side for the potatoes and corn.
10. Whisk the remaining ingredients in another bowl.
11. Peel the grilled pepper and chop them. Divide corn ears into smaller pieces and cut the potatoes as well.
12. Serve the grilled veggies with the vinaigrette on top.

Nutrition:
- Calories: 322
- Fat: 4.5g
- Saturated Fat: 1g
- Trans Fat: 0g
- Carbohydrates: 51.5g
- Fiber: 3g
- Sodium: 600mg
- Protein: 5g

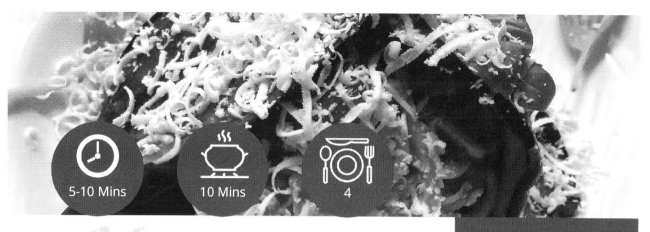

5-10 Mins	10 Mins	4

Eggplant Pasta Delight

directions

1. Take Ninja Foodi multi-cooker, arrange it over a cooking platform, and open the top lid.
2. In the pot, add the oil, select "SEAR/SAUTÉ" mode and select "MD: HI" pressure level. Press "STOP/START." After about 4-5 minutes, the oil will start simmering.
3. Add the onions, capers, garlic, and cook (while stirring) until they become softened and translucent for 2 minutes.
4. Add the eggplant and bell peppers, stir-cook for 1 minute. Mix in the pasta, tomatoes, broth, tomato paste, rosemary, thyme, and pepper.
5. Seal the multi-cooker by locking it with the pressure lid, ensure to keep the pressure release valve locked/sealed.
6. Select "PRESSURE" mode and select the "HI" pressure level. Then, set timer to 8 minutes and press "STOP/START," it will start the cooking process by building up inside pressure.
7. When the timer goes off, quickly release pressure by adjusting the pressure valve to the VENT. After pressure gets released, open the pressure lid.

Nutrition:
- Calories: 278
- Fat: 8g
- Saturated Fat: 1g
- Trans Fat: 0g
- Carbohydrates: 44g
- Fiber: 4g
- Sodium: 754mg
- Protein: 8.5g

INGREDIENTS

- 1 tablespoon capers, drained and rinsed, minced
- 1 tablespoon minced garlic
- 8-ounces dried whole wheat ziti
- 1 small red onion, chopped
- 1-pound eggplant, stemmed and diced
- 1 (28-ounce) can diced tomatoes about 3 ½ cups
- 1 ¼ cups vegetable broth
- 2 tablespoons canned tomato paste
- 2 medium yellow bell peppers, stemmed, cored and chopped
- 2 tablespoons olive oil
- 2 teaspoons dried rosemary
- 1 teaspoon dried thyme
- 1/2 teaspoon ground black pepper

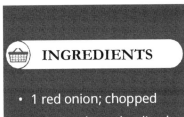

INGREDIENTS

- 1 red onion; chopped
- 1/2 cup almonds; sliced
- 2 broccoli heads; florets chopped
- 2 carrots; shredded
- 1 tablespoon olive oil
- 3 tablespoons apple cider vinegar
- 1/2 cup cranberries; dried
- Black pepper (finely ground) and salt to the taste

Healthy Broccoli Salad

 **directions**

1. Take Ninja Foodi multi-cooker, arrange it over a cooking platform, and open the top lid.
2. In the pot, add the ingredients one by one. Stir gently.
3. Seal the multi-cooker by locking it with the pressure lid; ensure to keep the pressure release valve locked/sealed.
4. Select "PRESSURE" mode and select the "HI" pressure level. Then, set the timer to 15 minutes and press "STOP/START"; it will start the cooking process by building up inside pressure.
5. When the timer goes off, quickly release pressure by adjusting the pressure valve to the VENT. After pressure gets released, open the pressure lid.

Nutrition:
- Calories: 165
- Fat: 5g
- Saturated Fat: 1g
- Trans Fat: 0g
- Carbohydrates: 21.5g
- Fiber: 5g
- Sodium: 87mg
- Protein: 3g

5-10 Mins

15 Mins

4

5-10 Mins | 30 Mins | 5-6

Veggie Rice Soup

 **directions**

1. Take Ninja Foodi multi-cooker, arrange it over a cooking platform, and open the top lid.
2. In the pot, add the ingredients one by one. Stir gently.
3. Seal the multi-cooker by locking it with the pressure lid; ensure to keep the pressure release valve locked/sealed.
4. Select "PRESSURE" mode and select the "HI" pressure level. Then, set the timer to 30 minutes and press "STOP/START"; it will start the cooking process by building up inside pressure.
5. When the timer goes off, quickly release pressure by adjusting the pressure valve to the VENT. After pressure gets released, open the pressure lid.

INGREDIENTS

- 1 onion, chopped
- 3 garlic cloves, minced
- 5 medium carrots, chopped
- 5 celery stalks, chopped
- 1 cup wild rice
- 1 teaspoon kosher salt
- 1 teaspoon poultry seasoning
- ½ teaspoon dried thyme
- 8 ounces mushrooms, sliced
- 6 cups vegetable broth

Nutrition:
- Calories: 198
- Fat: 3.5g
- Saturated Fat: 0.5g
- Trans Fat: 0g
- Carbohydrates: 26.5g
- Fiber: 3.5g
- Sodium: 654mg
- Protein: 11g

179

Dessert

INGREDIENTS

- 1 cup butter
- ¼ cup heavy cream
- 2 ounces unsweetened chocolate
- ¼ cup peanut butter, separated
- 4 packets stevia

Peanut Butter Cups

1. Melt the peanut butter and butter in a bowl and stir well with unsweetened chocolate, stevia, and cream.
2. Mix well and pour the mixture into a baking mold.
3. Put the baking mold in the Ninja Foodi and press "Bake/Roast."
4. Set the timer for 30 minutes at 360 °F and dish out to serve.

Nutrition:
- Calories 479
- Total Fat 51.5 g
- Saturated Fat 29.7 g
- Cholesterol 106 mg
- Sodium 69 mg
- Total Carbs 7.7 g
- Fiber 2.7 g
- Sugar 1.4 g
- Protein 5.2 g

15 Mins

30 Mins

3

| 15 Mins | 32 Mins | 4 |

Chocolate Brownies

- 3 eggs
- ½ cup butter
- ½ cup sugar-free chocolate chips
- 2 scoops stevia
- 1 teaspoon vanilla extract

 **directions**

1. Take a bowl and mix eggs, stevia, and vanilla extract.
2. Pour this mixture into the blender and blend until smooth.
3. Put the butter and chocolate in the pot of Ninja Foodi and press sauté.
4. Sauté for 2 minutes until the chocolate is melted.
5. Add the melted chocolate into the egg mixture.
6. Pour the mixture into the baking mold and place it in the Ninja Foodi.
7. Press "Bake/Roast" and set the timer for about 30 minutes at 360 °F.
8. Bake for about 30 minutes, cut into pieces and serve.

Nutrition:
- Calories 266
- Total Fat 26.9 g
- Saturated Fat 15.8 g
- Cholesterol 184 mg
- Sodium 218 mg
- Total Carbs 2.5 g
- Fiber 0 g
- Sugar 0.4 g
- Protein 4.5 g

INGREDIENTS

- 1½ teaspoons Splenda
- 3 organic eggs
- 3 tablespoons coconut flour
- ½ cup heavy cream
- 3 tablespoons coconut oil, melted and divided
- Salt to taste

Cream Crepes

directions

1. Take a bowl and mix 1½ tablespoons of coconut oil, Splenda, eggs, and salt.
2. Add the coconut flour and continuously stir.
3. Add the heavy cream and stir continuously until smooth.
4. Press sauté on Ninja Foodi and pour about ¼ of the mixture in the pot.
5. Sauté for 2 minutes on each side and dish out.
6. Repeat until the mixture ends and serve.

Nutrition:
- Calories 145
- Total Fat 13.1 g
- Saturated Fat 9.1 g
- Cholesterol 96 mg,
- Sodium 35 mg
- Total Carbs 4 g
- Fiber 1.5 g
- Sugar 1.2 g
- Protein 3.5 g

15 Mins

16 Mins

6

INGREDIENTS

- 4 teaspoons coconut oil, melted
- 1 cup pecans, halved
- 2 cups of water
- 2 tablespoons stevia
- 1 cup cashew nuts, raw and unsalted

Nut Porridge

 **directions**

1. Put the cashew nuts and pecans in the precision processor and blend till they are in chunks.
2. Put this mixture into the pot of Ninja Foodi and stir in water, coconut oil, and stevia.
3. Select sauté on Ninja Foodi and cook for 15 minutes.
4. Serve and enjoy.

Nutrition:
- Calories 260,
- Total Fat 22.9 g,
- Saturated Fat 7.3 g,
- Cholesterol 0 mg,
- Sodium 9 mg,
- Total Carbs 12.7 g,
- Fiber 1.4 g,
- Sugar 1.8 g,
- Protein 5.6 g

15 Mins

10 Mins

4

184

15 Mins

12 Mins

2

Lemon Mousse

directions

1. Take a bowl and mix cream cheese, heavy cream, lemon juice, salt, and stevia.
2. Pour this mixture into the ramekins and transfer the ramekins in the pot of Ninja Foodi.
3. Select "Bake/Roast" and bake for 12 minutes at 350 °F.
4. Pour into the serving glasses and refrigerate for at least 3 hours.

Nutrition:
- Calories 305,
- Total Fat 31 g,
- Saturated Fat 19.5 g,
- Cholesterol 103 mg,
- Sodium 299 mg,
- Total Carbs 2.7 g,
- Fiber 0.1 g,
- Sugar 0.5 g,
- Protein 5 g

INGREDIENTS

- 4 ounces cream cheese softened
- ½ cup heavy cream
- 1/8 cup fresh lemon juice
- ½ teaspoon lemon liquid stevia
- 2 pinches salt

Chocolate Cheesecake

directions

1. Add eggs, cocoa powder, vanilla extract, swerve, cream cheese in an immersion blender and blend until smooth.
2. Pour the mixture evenly to mason jars.
3. Put the mason jars in the insert of Ninja Foodi and close the lid.
4. Select "Bake/Roast" and bake for 15 minutes at 360 °F.
5. Refrigerate for at least 2 hours.

Nutrition:
- Calories 244,
- Total Fat 24.8 g,
- Saturated Fat 15.6 g,
- Cholesterol 32 mg,
- Sodium 204 mg,
- Total Carbs 2.1 g,
- Fiber 0.1 g,
- Sugar 0.4 g,
- Protein 4 g

15 Mins | **15 Mins** | **6**

INGREDIENTS

- 2 cups cream cheese, softened
- 2 eggs
- 2 tablespoons cocoa powder
- 1 teaspoon pure vanilla extract
- ½ cup Swerve

Vanilla Yogurt

INGREDIENTS

- ½ cup full-fat milk
- ¼ cup yogurt starter
- 1 cup heavy cream
- ½ tablespoon pure vanilla extract
- 2 scoops stevia

directions

1. Add milk, heavy cream, vanilla extract, and stevia in Ninja Foodi.
2. Let yogurt sit and press "slow cooker" and set the timer to 4 hours on "low."
3. Add yogurt starter in 1 cup of milk.
4. Return this mixture to the pot.
5. Close the lid and wrap the Ninja Foodi in small towels.
6. Let yogurt sit for about 9 hours.
7. Dish out, refrigerate and then serve.

Nutrition:
- Calories 292,
- Total Fat 26.2 g,
- Saturated Fat 16.3 g,
- Cholesterol 100 mg,
- Sodium 86 mg,
- Total Carbs 8.2 g,
- Fiber 0 g,
- Sugar 6.6 g,
- Protein 5.2 g

15 Mins

3 Hour

2

INGREDIENTS

- 4 ounces mascarpone cream cheese
- 1 teaspoon espresso powder
- ¼ cup unsalted butter
- 4 large organic eggs, whites and yolks separated
- 1 tablespoon water
- ¼ teaspoon cream of tartar
- ½ teaspoon liquid stevia
- ¼ teaspoon monk fruit extract drops

Coffee Custard

directions

1. Select sauté and "Lo: Md" on Ninja Foodi and add butter and cream cheese, sauté for 3 minutes and mix in espresso powder, egg yolks, and water.
2. Select "low" and cook for 4 minutes.
3. Take a bowl and whisk together egg whites, fruit drops, stevia, and cream of tartar.
4. Pour in the egg white mixture in the mixture present in Ninja Foodi and cook for 3 minutes.
5. Pour it into serving glasses and refrigerate it for 3 hours.

Nutrition:
- Calories 292,
- Total Fat 26.2 g,
- Saturated Fat 16.3 g,
- Cholesterol 100 mg,
- Sodium 86 mg,
- Total Carbs 8.2 g,
- Fiber 0 g,
- Sugar 6.6 g,
- Protein 5.2 g

15 Mins

10 Mins

4

15 Mins | 6 Hour | 24

Chocolate Fudge

directions

1. Select sauté and "Md: Hi" on Ninja Foodi and add vanilla and heavy cream, sauté for 5 minutes at "low."
2. Sauté for 10 minutes and add butter and chocolate.
3. Sauté for 2 minutes and pour this mixture into a serving dish.
4. Refrigerate it for some hours and serve.

Nutrition:
- Calories 292,
- Total Fat 26.2 g,
- Saturated Fat 16.3 g,
- Cholesterol 100 mg,
- Sodium 86 mg,
- Total Carbs 8.2 g,
- Fiber 0 g,
- Sugar 6.6 g,
- Protein 5.2 g

Lime Cheesecake

 **directions**

1. In a bowl, add ¼ cup of Erythritol and the remaining ingredients except for eggs and sour cream, and with a hand mixer beat on high speed until smooth.

2. Add the eggs and beat on low speed until well combined.

3. Transfer the mixture into a 6-inch greased springform pan evenly.

4. With a piece of foil, cover the pan.

5. In the pot of Ninja Foodi, place 2 cups of water.

6. Arrange a "Reversible Rack" in the pot of Ninja Foodi.

7. Place the springform pan over the "Reversible Rack".

8. Close the Ninja Foodi with a pressure lid and place the pressure valve in the "Seal" position.

9. Select "Pressure" and set it to "High" for 30 minutes.

10. Press "Start/Stop" to begin cooking.

11. Switch the valve to "Vent" and do a "Natural" release.

12. Place the pan onto a wire rack to cool slightly.

13. Meanwhile, in a small bowl, add the sour cream and remaining Truvia and beat until well combined.

14. Spread the cream mixture on the warm cake evenly.

15. Refrigerate for about 6-8 hours before serving.

INGREDIENTS

- ¼ cup plus 1 teaspoon Erythritol
- 8 ounces cream cheese, softened
- 1/3 cup Ricotta cheese
- 1 teaspoon fresh lime zest, grated
- 2 tablespoons fresh lime juice
- ½ teaspoon organic vanilla extract
- 2 organic eggs
- 2 tablespoons sour cream

Nutrition:

- Calories: 182,
- Fats: 16.6g,
- Net Carbs: 2.1g,
- Carbs: 2.1g,
- Fiber: 0g,
- Sugar: 0.3g,
- Proteins: 6.4g,
- Sodium: 152mg

INGREDIENTS

- 1½ cups almond flour
- 4 tablespoons butter, melted
- 3 tablespoons sugar-free peanut butter
- 3 tablespoons Erythritol
- 1 large organic egg, beaten

For Filling:
- 1 cup ricotta cheese
- 24 ounces cream cheese, softened
- 1½ cups Erythritol
- 2 teaspoons liquid stevia
- 1/3 cup heavy cream
- 2 large organic eggs
- 3 large organic egg yolks
- 1 tablespoon fresh lemon juice
- 1 tablespoon organic vanilla extract

15 Mins

4 Hour

12

Lemon Cheesecake

 directions

1. Grease the pot of Ninja Foodi.
2. For the crust: in a bowl, add all the ingredients and mix until well com-bined.
3. In the pot prepared by Ninja Foodi, place the crust mixture and press to smooth the top surface.
4. With a fork, prick the crust at many places.
5. For the filling: in a food processor, add the ricotta cheese and blend until smooth.
6. In a large bowl, add the ricotta, cream cheese, Erythritol and stevia and with an electric mixer, beat over medium speed until smooth.
7. In another bowl, add the heavy cream, eggs, egg yolks, lemon juice and vanilla extract and beat until well combined.
8. Add the egg mixture into cream cheese mixture and beat over medium speed until just combined.
9. Place the filling mixture over the crust evenly.
10. Close the Ninja Foodi with a crisping lid and select "Slow Cooker".
11. Set on "Low" for 3-4 hours.
12. Press "Start/Stop" to begin cooking.
13. Place the pan onto a wire rack to cool.
14. Refrigerate to chill for at least 6-8 hours before serving.

Nutrition :
- Calories: 410,
- Fats: 37.9g,
- Net Carbs: 5.1g,
- Carbs: 6.9g,
- Fiber: 1.8g,
- Sugar: 1.3g,
- Proteins: 13g,
- Sodium: 260mg

INGREDIENTS

- 1 cup almond flour
- 2 tablespoons butter, melted
- 8-10 drops liquid stevia
- 3-4 cups fresh strawberries, hulled and sliced
- 1 tablespoon butter, chopped

15 Mins

2 Hour

5

Strawberry Crumble

directions

1. Lightly, grease the pot of Ninja Foodi.
2. In a bowl, add the flour, melted butter and stevia and mix until a crumbly mixture forms.
3. In the pot of the prepared Ninja Foodi, place the strawberry slices and dot with chopped butter.
4. Spread the flour mixture on top evenly
5. Close the Ninja Foodi with a crisping lid and select "Slow Cooker".
6. Set on "Low" for 2 hours.
7. Press "Start/Stop" to begin cooking.
8. Place the pan onto a wire rack to cool slightly.

Nutrition:
- Calories: 233g
- Fats: 19.2g
- Net Carbs: 6.6g
- Carbs: 10.7g
- Fiber: 4.1g
- Sugar: 5g
- Proteins: 0.7g
- Sodium: 50mg

18 Mins   **10 Mins**   **10**

Cashew Cream

 **directions**

1. Combine the cashews with the chicken stock in the Multicooker.

2. Add salt and close the Multicooker lid. Cook the dish in the" Pressure" mode for 10 minutes.

3. Remove the cashews from the Multicooker and drain the nuts from the water. Transfer the cashews to a blender and add the ricotta cheese and butter.

4. Blend the mixture until it is smooth. When you get the texture you want, remove it from a blender. Serve it immediately or keep the cashew butter in the refrigerator.

Nutrition :
- calories 252
- fat 20.6g
- carbs 13.8g
- protein 6.8g

INGREDIENTS

- 3 cups cashew
- 2 cups chicken stock
- 1 teaspoon salt
- 1 tablespoon butter
- 2 tablespoons ricotta cheese

35 Mins | 25 Mins | 4

Blackberry Cake

 directions

2. Then add baking powder, almond flour, and Erythritol.
3. Stir the mixture until smooth.
4. Add blackberries and stir the batter gently with the help of the spoon.
5. Take the non-sticky springform pan and transfer the batter inside.
6. Place the springform pan in the pot and lower the air fryer lid.
7. Cook the cake for 20 minutes at 365 F.
8. When the time is over – check the doneness of the cake with the help of the toothpick and cook for 5 minutes more if needed.
9. Chill it little and serve!

Nutrition:
- Calories: 173
- Fat: 16.7g
- Carbohydrates: 2.2g
- Protein: 4.2g

INGREDIENTS

- 4 tablespoons butter
- 3 tablespoon Erythritol
- 2 eggs, whisked
- ½ teaspoon vanilla extract
- 1 oz blackberries
- 1 cup almond flour
- ½ teaspoon baking powder

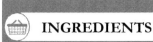

INGREDIENTS

- 6 egg yolks
- 2 cups heavy whip cream
- 1/3 cup cocoa powder
- 1 tablespoon pure vanilla extract
- ½ teaspoon liquid stevia
- Whipped coconut cream as needed for garnish
- Shaved dark chocolate, for garnish

30 Mins

12 Mins

4

The Original Pot-De-Crème

directions

1. Take a medium bowl and whisk in yolks, heavy cream, cocoa powder, vanilla, and stevia
2. Pour the mixture into a 1 and ½ quart baking dish and place the dish in your multi-cooker insert
3. Add enough water to reach about halfway up the sides of the baking dish
4. Lock the lid and cook on HIGH pressure for 12 minutes
5. Quickly release pressure once the cycle is complete
6. Remove baking dish from the insert and let it cool
7. Chill the dessert in the refrigerator and serve with a garnish of whipped coconut cream and shaved dark chocolate

Nutrition

- Calories: 275
- Fat: 18g
- Carbohydrates: 3g
- Protein: 5g

25 Mins | 15 Mins | 8

Cinnamon Bun

directions

1. Mix up together the almond flour, baking powder, vanilla extract, egg, salt, and almond milk.
2. Knead the soft and non-sticky dough.
3. Roll up the dough with the help of the rolling pin
4. Sprinkle dough with butter, cinnamon, and Erythritol.
5. Roll the dough into the log.
6. Cut the roll into 7 pieces.
7. Spray a multi-cooker basket with the cooking spray.
8. Place the cinnamon buns in the basket and close the lid.
9. Set the Bake mode and cook the buns for 15 minutes at 355 °F
10. Check if the buns are cooked with the help of the toothpick.
11. Chill the buns well and serve!

Nutrition:
- Calories: 292
- Fat: 26g
- Carbohydrates: 8g
- Protein: 5g

INGREDIENTS

- 1 cup almond flour
- ½ teaspoon baking powder
- 3 tablespoon Erythritol
- 2 tablespoon ground cinnamon
- ½ teaspoon vanilla extract
- 1 tablespoon butter
- 1 egg, whisked
- ¾ teaspoon salt
- ¼ cup almond milk

INGREDIENTS

- 1/2 cup all-purpose flour
- Pinch salt
- 1/4 cup cocoa powder
- 2 eggs
- 1/2 cup brown sugar
- 1/2 cup white sugar
- 1 tablespoon vanilla extract
- 1 tablespoon water
- 3/4 cup butter, melted
- 6 oz. chocolate chips, melted

Fudge Brownies

 Method

1. Combine flour, salt and cocoa powder in a bowl.
2. Beat eggs in another bowl.
3. Stir in sugars, vanilla and water.
4. Add butter and chocolate chips to the mixture.
5. Slowly add dry ingredients to this mixture.
6. Mix well.
7. Spray a small baking pan with oil.
8. Pour batter into the pan.
9. Add crisper plate to the air fry basket in the Ninja Foodi Grill.
10. Choose the air fry setting.
11. Preheat at 300 °F for 3 minutes.
12. Add a small baking pan to the crisper plate.
13. Cook for 1 hour.

Serving Suggestions: Serve with milk.

Preparation / Cooking Tips: Use unsweetened cocoa powder.

20 Mins

1 Hour

6

15 Mins

45

4

Baked Apples

 **Method**

1. Add crisper plate to the air fryer basket inside the Ninja Foodi Grill.
2. Choose air fry function.
3. Preheat it to 325 °F for 3 minutes.
4. Add apples to the crisper plate.
5. Drizzle with lemon juice and sprinkle with brown sugar.
6. Place butter cubes on top.
7. Air fry for 45 minutes

Serving Suggestions: Top with caramel syrup or crushed graham crackers.

Preparation / Cooking Tips: Poke apples with a fork before cooking.

INGREDIENTS

- 2 apples, sliced in half
- 1 tablespoon lemon juice
- 4 teaspoons brown sugar
- 1/4 cup butter, sliced into small cubes

198

INGREDIENTS

- 1 pack white cake mix
- 2 cups strawberries, sliced in half
- 2 tablespoons honey
- 1/4 cup sugar
- Cooking spray

Strawberry & Cake Kebabs

 Method

1. Cook cake mix according to the directions in the box.
2. Insert the grill grate in the Ninja Foodi Grill.
3. Choose the grill setting.
4. Preheat at 325 °F for 15 minutes.
5. While waiting, slice the cake into cubes.
6. Toss strawberries in honey and sugar.
7. Thread cake cubes and strawberries alternately onto skewers.
8. Grill for 3 minutes per side.

    Serving Suggestions: Serve with vanilla ice cream.

    Preparation / Cooking Tips: When preparing a cake mix, you can replace water with pudding to make the cake thicker.

15 Mins

6 Mins

5

Grilled Donuts

INGREDIENTS

- 1/4 cup milk
- 1 teaspoon vanilla extract
- 2 cups powdered sugar
- 16 oz. prepared biscuit dough
- Cooking spray

Method

1. In a bowl, mix milk, vanilla and sugar.
2. Cut rings from the prepared dough.
3. Refrigerate for 5 minutes.
4. Add grill grate to the Ninja Foodi Grill.
5. Choose the grill setting.
6. Set it to medium
7. Preheat for 6 minutes.
8. Spray round dough with oil.
9. Add to the grill and cook for 4 minutes.
10. Dip in the milk mixture and grill for another 4 minutes.

Serving Suggestions: Sprinkle with cinnamon sugar or chocolate sprinkles before serving.

15 Mins

10 Mins

8

INGREDIENTS

- 8 cups cold water
- 1 tablespoon lemon juice
- 8 apples, diced
- 1/2 cup brown sugar
- 1/2 teaspoon ground cinnamon
- 1/2 teaspoon ground ginger
- 3 tablespoons all-purpose flour
- 1/2 cup applesauce
- 1 frozen pie crust

30 Mins

30 Mins

8

Method

1. In a bowl, mix water, lemon juice and apples.
2. Let sit for 10 minutes.
3. Drain and pat dry.
4. Add grill grate to Ninja Foodi Grill.
5. Press the grill setting.
6. Set it to the max and preheat for 8 minutes.
7. Coat apples with sugar.
8. Grill for 8 minutes without flipping.
9. In a bowl, combine the remaining ingredients.
10. Stir in grilled apples.
11. Pour the mixture into a small baking pan.
12. Top with the pie crust.
13. Select the bake setting.
14. Cook pie at 350 °F for 20 minutes.

Serving Suggestions: Serve with vanilla ice cream.
Preparation / Cooking Tips: Defrost pie crust before using.

Peanut Butter Cups

INGREDIENTS

- 4 graham crackers
- 4 peanut butter cups
- 4 marshmallows

Method

1. Add a crisper plate to the air fryer basket of your Ninja Foodi Grill.
2. Choose the air fry function.
3. Preheat at 360 °F for 3 minutes.
4. Break the crackers in half.
5. Add crackers to the crisper plate.
6. Top with the peanut butter cups.
7. Cook for 2 minutes.
8. Sprinkle mushrooms on top and cook for another 1 minute.
9. Top with the remaining crackers and serve.

Serving Suggestions: Serve with warm milk.

Preparation / Cooking Tips: You can also use chocolate spread in place of peanut butter cups if you like.

5 Mins

5 Mins

4

Cookies

INGREDIENTS

- 4 oz. cookie dough

10 Mins

10 Mins

2

Method

1. Choose the air fry setting in your Ninja Foodi Grill.
2. Set it to 350 °F.
3. Preheat it for 1 minute.
4. Line air fryer basket with parchment paper.
5. Create 6 cookies from the dough.
6. Add these to the air fryer basket.
7. Place air fryer basket inside the unit.
8. Cook for 8 to 10 minutes.

Serving Suggestions: Serve with warm milk.
Preparation / Cooking Tips: Make sure there is enough space between the cookies.

10 Mins

5 Mins

8

INGREDIENTS

- 8 oz. crescent rolls (refrigerated)
- 16 Oreos
- 3 tablespoons peanut butter

Fried Oreos

Method

1. Spread dough onto a working surface.
2. Slice into 8 rectangles.
3. Slice each rectangle into 2.
4. Add cookie on top of the dough.
5. Spread with peanut butter.
6. Wrap the dough around the Oreos.
7. Place these in the air fryer basket inside the Ninja Foodi Grill.
8. Choose the air fry setting.
9. Air fry at 320 °F for 5 minutes.

Serving Suggestions: Dust with powdered sugar before serving.
Preparation / Cooking Tips: You can also use this recipe for other sandwich cookies.

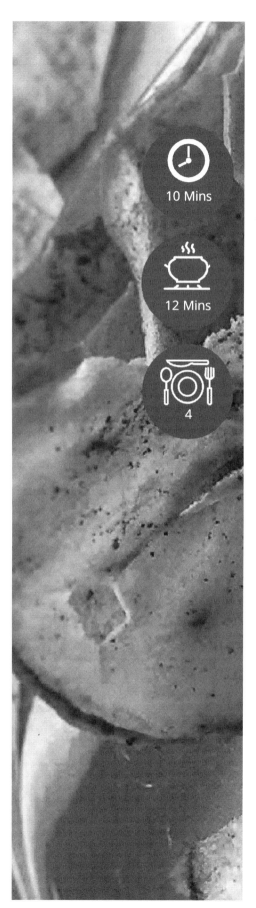

Cinnamon Apple Chips

10 Mins

12 Mins

4

Method

1. Coat the apple slices in oil and sprinkle with cinnamon.
2. Spray the air fryer basket with oil.
3. Choose the air fry setting in the Ninja Foodi Grill.
4. Air fry the apples at 375 °F for 12 minutes, flipping once or twice.

Serving Suggestions: Serve with almond yogurt dip.
Preparation / Cooking Tips: Use a mandolin to slice the apples very thinly.

INGREDIENTS

- 1 apple, sliced thinly
- 2 teaspoons vegetable oil
- 1 teaspoon ground cinnamon
- Cooking spray

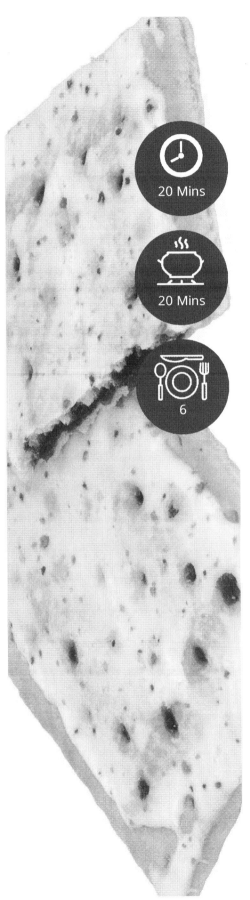

Strawberry Pop Tarts

20 Mins

20 Mins

6

 Method

1. Combine strawberries and sugar in a pan over medium heat.
2. Cook while stirring for 10 minutes.
3. Let it cool.
4. Spread pie crust on your kitchen table.
5. Slice into rectangles.
6. Add strawberries on top of the rectangles.
7. Brush edges with water.
8. Wrap and seal.
9. Spray tarts with oil.
10. Add tarts to the air fryer basket.
11. Choose the air fry setting in your Ninja Foodi Grill.
12. Air fry at 350 °F for 10 minutes.
13. Let it cool before serving.

Serving Suggestions: Sprinkle with colorful candy sprinkles before serving.

Preparation / Cooking Tips: You can also use other berries for this recipe.

 **INGREDIENTS**

- 8 oz. strawberries
- 1/4 cup granulated sugar
- 1 refrigerated pie crust
- Cooking spray

Chapter 10

30-Day

Meal Plan

Day 1

Breakfast: Spicy sausage and mushroom casserole

Lunch: Sugar glazed chicken

Dinner: Grilled herbed steak

Day 2

Breakfast: Honey carrots

Lunch: Tenderloin steak with bacon

Dinner: Grilled citrus fish

Day 3

Breakfast: Breakfast potatoes

Lunch: Lemon garlic chicken

Dinner: Paprika pork chops

Day 4

Breakfast: Mexican corn

Lunch: Shrimp bang bang

Dinner: Roasted chicken

Day 5

Breakfast: French toast

Lunch: Ranch pork chops

Dinner: Roasted cauliflower

Day 6

Breakfast: Eggs and avocado

Lunch: Chicken, potatoes and cabbage

Dinner: Herbed salmon

Day 7

Breakfast: Breakfast omelet

Lunch: Teriyaki salmon

Dinner: Roast beef and grilled potatoes

Day 8

Breakfast: Ham and cheese casserole

Lunch: Roasted mixed veggies

Dinner: Shrimp fajitas

Day 9

Breakfast: Breakfast casserole

Lunch: Barbeque chicken breast

Dinner: Cuban pork chops

Day 10

Breakfast: Garlic Brussels sprouts

Lunch: Crispy fish fillet

Dinner: Vegetarian pizza

Day 11

Breakfast: Breakfast bell peppers

Lunch: Chicken and zucchini

Dinner: Steak kebab

Day 12

Breakfast: Mediterranean veggies and quinoa

Lunch: Grilled ranch chicken

Dinner: Herbed salmon

Day 13

Breakfast: Breakfast burrito

Lunch: Crispy fish sandwich

Dinner: Grilled pork chops

Day 14

Breakfast: Eggs and avocado

Lunch: Crumbed flounder fillet

Dinner: Roasted beef with garlic

Day 15

Breakfast: Roasted spicy potatoes

Lunch: Chicken quesadilla

Dinner: Grilled lemon pepper shrimp

Day 16

Breakfast: French toast sticks

Lunch: Roast beef with garlic

Dinner: Veggie lasagna

Day 17

Breakfast: Roasted breakfast potatoes

Lunch: Grilled cauliflower steak

Dinner: Salmon with coconut aminos

Day 18

Breakfast: Eggs and avocado

Lunch: Beer battered cod

Dinner: Coffee ribeye

Day 19

Breakfast: Mixed air-fried veggies
Lunch: Sausage and pepper
Dinner: Buffalo chicken wings

Day 20

Breakfast: Crispy garlic potatoes
Lunch: Grilled paprika salmon
Dinner: Grilled herbed steak

Day 21

Breakfast: Bacon
Lunch: Vegetarian bowl
Dinner: Grilled steak and potatoes

Day 22

Breakfast: Spicy sausage and mushroom casserole
Lunch: Fried chicken
Dinner: Honey garlic shrimp

Day 23

Breakfast: Sausage casserole
Lunch: Grilled shrimp
Dinner: Grilled balsamic chicken breast

Day 24

Breakfast: Breakfast burrito
Lunch: Steak with asparagus
Dinner: Mustard chicken

Day 25

Breakfast: French toast sticks
Lunch: Grilled garlic chicken
Dinner: Asian bok choy

Day 26

Breakfast: Breakfast casserole
Lunch: Crispy fish sandwich
Dinner: Ribeye steak with onions and peppers

Day 27

Breakfast: Eggs and avocado
Lunch: Cheeseburger
Dinner: Cuban pork chops

Day 28

Breakfast: Mediterranean veggies and quinoa
Lunch: Honey and rosemary chicken
Dinner: Herbed salmon

Day 29

Breakfast: Mexican corn
Lunch: Shrimp boil
Dinner: Steak kebab

Day 30

Breakfast: Hash browns
Lunch: Grilled chicken with veggies
Dinner: Coffee ribeye

Chapter 10

Recipes of Sweets and Desserts

The following Chapter contains sweets and dessert recipes that will serve as amazing guilty free pleasures.

Peach Pie

(Ready in about 45 mins | Servings 4 | Normal)

Ingredients:

One Pie dough

- 2 and 1/4 pounds of peaches pitted and sliced
- 2 tablespoons of cornstarch
- 1/2 cups of sugar
- 2 tablespoons of flour
- A shot of nutmeg, ground
- 1 tablespoon of dark rum
- 1 tablespoon of lemon juice
- 2 tablespoon of butter, molten

Directions:

1. Pull the pastry dough into a saucepan that suits the fryer, and pressure well.
2. Balance the peaches in a bowl with the cornstarch, sugar, flour, nutmeg, rum lemon. Mix in milk, butter, and blend well.
3. Pour it into a pie pan, position the fryer, and cook for 35 minutes 350° F.
4. Serve hot or cold.

Enjoy!

Nutrition: Calories: 231,Fat: 6g, Fiber: 7g, Carbohydrates 9g, Protein: 5g.

Cheesecake with Sweet Potato

(Ready in about 15 min | Servings 4 | Normal)

Ingredients:

- Four tablespoons of butter, molten
- Six ounces of mascarpone, mild
- Eight ounces of fluffy cream cheese
- 2/3 cup of graham
- 3/4 cup of milk
- 1 vanilla flavor extraction
- Puree with 2/3 cup sweet potato
- 1/4 tablespoons of ground cinnamon

Directions:

1. Combine butter and crumbled crackers in a pan, stir well and press the bottom of the cake pan, which suits your fridge and holds it in the fridge.
2. Blend the cream cheese and mascarpone in another container, sweet potato puree, milk, espresso, and cinnamon and whisk very nicely.
3. Place over crust, placed in an AirFryer, cook at 300 °F. Hold in the fridge for four minutes, a few hours before serving, and enjoy!

Nutrition: Calories: 172, Fat: 4g, Fiber: 6g, Carbohydrates 8g, Protein: 3g.

Cookies with Brown Butter

(Ready in about 20 mins | Servings 6 | Normal)

Ingredients:

- 1 and 1/2 cup of butter
- 2 cups of brown sugar
- Two whisked eggs
- Three cups of flour
- 2/3 cup of diced pecans
- Two vanilla tablespoons extract
- 1 teaspoon of baking soda
- 1/2 teaspoon of baked powder

Directions:

1. Heat a saucepan over a moderate flame with the butter, whisk till it melts, add brown sugar and whisk until it decomposes.

2. In a cup, add pecan flour, vanilla extract, baking soda, baking, eggs, and flour, then mix well.

3. Apply brown butter, mix well and put a spoonful of this mixture on a lined sheet pan that perfectly fits your fryer.

4. Stir in the fryer and cook for 10 minutes at 340° F.

5. Cookies should be left to cool off and serve.

Enjoy!

Nutrition: Calories: 144, Fat: 5g, Fiber: 6g, Carbohydrates 19g, Protein: 2g

Bar Cashew

(Ready in about 25 mins | Servings 6 | Normal)

Ingredients:

- 1/3 cup of honey
- 1/4 cup of almond meal
- 1 tablespoon of almond butter
- 1 and 1/2 cups of cashews
- 4 dates, sliced
- 3/4 cup of crushed coconut
- 1 spoonful of chia seeds

Directions:

1. Combine honey and almond butter in a cup, then mix well.

2. Insert cashews, coconut, chia seeds, and dates, and mix well again.

3. Place this on a rimmed baking sheet that works well with your AirFryer and press.

4. Stir in the fryer and cook for fifteen min at 300 °F.

5. Leave the mixture to cool, cut to medium bars, and serve.

Enjoy it!

Nutrition: Calories:121, Fat: 4g, Fiber: 7g, Carbohydrates 5g, Protein: 6g.

Tasty Orange Cookies

(Ready in about 22 mins | Servings 8 | Normal)

Ingredients:

- 2 cups of flour
- 1 teaspoon of baking powder
- ½ cup of butter, soft
- ¾ cup of sugar
- 1 egg, whisked
- 1 teaspoon of vanilla extract
- 1 tablespoon of orange zest, grated

For the filling:

- 4 ounces of cream cheese, soft
- ½ cup of butter
- 2 cups of powdered sugar

Directions:

1. In a bowl, mix cream cheese with ½ cup butter and 2 cups powdered sugar, stir well using your mixer and leave aside for now.

2. In another bowl, mix flour with baking powder.

3. In a third bowl, mix ½ cup butter with ¾ cup sugar, egg, vanilla extract, and orange zest and whisk well.

4. Combine flour with the orange mix, stir well and scoop one tablespoon of the mix on a lined baking sheet that fits your AirFryer.

5. Repeat with the rest of the orange batter, introduce in the fryer, and cook at 340° F for 12 minutes.

6. Leave cookies to cool down, spread cream filling on half of the top with the other cookies, and serve.

Enjoy!

Nutrition: Calories: 124, Fat: 5g, Fiber: 6g, Carbs: 8g, Protein: 4g.

Currant and Plum Tart

(Ready in about 1hrs 5 mins | Servings 6 | Difficult)

Ingredients:

For crumbling:

- 1/4 cup of almond flour
- One and a half cup of millet flour
- 1 cup of brown rice flour
- 1/2 cup of sugar cane
- 10 tablespoons of butter, mild
- Three tablespoons of milk

Filling for:

- 1 lb. of small, pitted, and halved plums
- 1 cup of white currant
- 2 tablespoons of cornstarch
- Three spoonfuls of sugar
- 1/2 teaspoon of strawberry extract
- 1/2 teaspoon of ground cinnamon
- 1/4 teaspoon of ground ginger
- 1 teaspoon of lime juice

Directions:

1. Mix the brown rice flour in a dish with 1/2 cup butter, millet meal, and almond flour, butter, and milk, then mix until you have a dough-like layer.

2. Put aside 1/4 of the dough, press the remaining dough into a tart pan to match. Fry the air and keep it in the refrigerator for 30 minutes.

3. Meanwhile, blend the plums and currants in a cup, 3 tablespoons of sugar, cornstarch, vanilla extract, cinnamon, lime juice, and ginger, then mix well.

4. Pour over tart crust, crumble over reserved bread, put in your freeze air, and simmer for 35 minutes at 350° F.

5. Leave the tart to cool, cut, and slice.

Enjoy!

Nutrition: Calories: 200, Fat: 5g, Fiber: 4g, Carbohydrates 8g, Protein: 6g.

Plum Bars

(Ready in about 26 min | Servings 8 | Normal)

Ingredients:

- 2 cups of dry plums
- 6 tablespoons of water
- 2 cups of rolling oats
- 1 cup of brown sugar
- 1/2 teaspoon of baking soda
- 1 teaspoon of cinnamon powder
- 2 tablespoon of butter, melted
- 1 whisked egg
- Cooking spray

Directions:

1. Combine the plums with water in your mixing bowl and mix before you have a sticky stretch.
2. Mash oats and cinnamon in a tub, baking soda, sugar, egg, and butter, and whisk very strong.
3. Place half the oats in a baking saucepan, which matches your sprayed AirFryer, combine the plums with the frying oil, and finish with the remaining half of the oats. Shake it up.
4. Stir in your AirFryer and cook for 16 minutes at 350° F.
5. Set the mixture aside to cool down, break into medium bars, and serve.

Enjoy it!

Nutrition: Calories: 111, Fat: 5g, Fiber: 6g, Carbohydrates 12g, Protein: 6g.

SweetSquares

(Ready in about 40 min | Servings 6 | Normal)

Ingredients:

- 1 cup of flour
- Butter: 1/2 cup, mild
- 1 cup of sugar
- One and a half cup of powdered sugar
- Two spoons of lemon, rubbed
- Two tablespoons of lemon juice
- Twowhisked eggs
- 1/2 teaspoon of powder

Directions:

1. Mix the flour with the ground sugar and butter in a tub, mix well, press the bottom of the saucepan that suits your fryer, put in the fryer, and bake for fourteen minutes at 350°F .
2. Combine sugar with lemon juice, lemon peel, eggs, and baking in another cup. Stir with the mixer, then sprinkle over the baked crust.
3. Bake for 15 minutes, allow to cool, cut into medium squares, and cool served.

Enjoy!
Nutrition: Calories: 100, Fat:s 4g, Fiber: 1g,Carbohydrates 12g, Protein: 1g.

Poppyseed Cake

(Ready in about 40 mins | Servings 6 | Normal)
Ingredients:
- 1 and a half cups of flour
- 1 teaspoon of powder baking
- 3⁄4 cups of sugar:
- Onetablespoon of rubbed orange zest
- Two lime zest, rubbed
- Butter: 1⁄2 cup, mild
- 2 whisked eggs,
- 1⁄2 teaspoon of vanilla extract
- 2 tablespoons of poppy seeds
- 1 cup of milk

To the cream:
- 1 cup of sugar
- 1⁄2 cup of passion fruitpuree
- Three tablespoons of butter, melted
- 4 yolks of eggs

Directions:
1. Mix the flour and baking powder in a tub, 3⁄4 cup sugar, orange zest, and zest lime, then mix.
2. Add 1⁄2 cup butter, eggs, poppy seeds, vanilla, and milk and blend with your blender load into an air-fried cake pan and cook at 350° F for thirty minutes.
3. In the meantime, fire up a pan over medium heat with three tablespoons of butter. Mix and add sugar till it decomposes.
4. Strip from heat, steadily add the passion fruit puree and egg yolks and whisk well.
5. Remove the cake from the fryer, cool it down a little, and horizontally break into halves.
6. Pour over 1⁄4 of the passion fruit cream, finish with the other half of the cake and finish with 1⁄4 of the cream.
7. Serve fresh.
Enjoy!
Nutrition: Calories: 211, Fat: 6g, Fiber: 7g, Carbohydrates 12g, Protein: 6g.

Pears and Espresso

(Ready in about 40 mins | Servings 4 | Normal)

Ingredients:

- 4 half pears, and hulled
- 2 tablespoons of lemon juice
- 1 tablespoon of sugar
- 2 tablespoons of water
- 2 tablespoons of butter

For the creme:

- 1 cup of ice cream
- One cup of mascarpone
- 1/3 cups of sugar
- 2 tablespoons of espresso, cool

Directions:

1. Combine pears half with lemon juice, 1 tablespoon of sugar, and butter in a bowl, including water, stir well, switch to the AirFryer, and cook at 360° F for 30 minutes.
2. In the meantime, blend whipped cream and mascarpone in a tub, 1/3 cup. Whisk sugar and espresso very well and hold in the refrigerator until the pears are prepared.
3. Split pears into bowls, cover with and serve with espresso cream.
Enjoy!

Nutrition: Calories: 211, Fat: 5g, Fiber: 7g, Carbohydrates 8g, Protein: 7g.

Bars of Lemon

(Ready in about 35 mins | Servings 6 | Normal)

Ingredients:

- Four eggs
- 2 and 1⁄4 cups of flour
- 2 lemon juice
- 1 cup of soft butter
- 2 cups of sugar

Directions:

1. Combine butter in a dish of 1⁄2 cup of sugar and 2 cups of flour, mix well and push in the fryer and position on the bottom of the pan that suits your AirFryer. Cook for 10 minutes, at 350° F.
2. Combine the rest of the sugar in yet another container with the rest of the flour, the eggs, and lemon juice, whisk well, scatter all over the crust.
3. Put in the fryer at 350° F for another 15 minutes, set aside the cut bars, cool off, and

serve.
Enjoy! **Nutrition:** Calories: 125, Fat: 4g, carbohydrate 16g, Protein: 2g.

Figs and Butter Blend with Coconut

(Ready in about 10 min | Servings 3 | Normal)

Ingredients:
- Two tablespoons of coconut butter
- 12 half-figs
- One and a half cup of sugar
- 1 cup of almonds, fried and chopped

Directions:
1. Put butter in a saucepan that suits your fryer and melt over medium-strong temperature.
2. Include figs, sugar, and almonds, toss, put in your frying pan, and cook 4 minutes at 300° F.
3. Serve cool and split into cups.
Enjoy!
Nutrition: Calories: 170, Fat: 4g, Fiber: 5g, Carbohydrates 7g, Protein: 9g.

Pumpkin Cookies

(Ready in about 25 mins | Servings 24 | Normal)

Ingredients:
- Two and a half cups of rice
- 1/2 teaspoon of baking soda
- 1 tablespoon of flaxseed
- 3 tablespoon of water
- 1/2 cup of pumpkin squash, mashed
- 1/4 cups of honey
- 2 cups of butter
- 1 teaspoon of vanilla extract
- 1/2 cup of dark chocolate chips

Directions:
1. Combine flax seed with water in a tub, swirl, and set aside for a couple of minutes.
2. Mix the flour with the salt and baking soda in another dish.
3. Match the honey and the pumpkin puree, butter, and spice in a separate dish extract and field flax.

4. Combine the flour and the chocolate chips with the honey mixture and whisk.

5. Scoop 1 pound of cookie dough on a rimmed baking sheet. Put in your AirFryer, repeat for the rest of the dough, bring them in the AirFryer, and cook for fifteen minutes at 350° F.

6. Cookies should be left to cool off and serve.

Enjoy!

Nutrition: Calories: 140, Fat: 2g, Carbohydrates 7g, Protein: 10g.

Air Fried Apples

(Ready in about 37 min | Servings 4 | Normal)

Ingredients:

- Four big, cored apples
- Just a couple of raisins
- 1 tablespoon of cinnamon, ground
- Honey to satisfy

Directions:

1. Fill the apple with raisins, sprinkle cinnamon, chop honey, place in and cook them in the AirFryer and simmer for 17 minutes at 367° F.

2. Let them cool off and then serve.

Enjoy!

Nutrition: Calories: 220, Fat: 3g, Fiber: 3g, Carbohydrates 6g, Protein: 10g.

Fruit Pudding withPassion

(Ready in about 50 mins | Servings 6 | Normal)

Ingredients:

- 1 cup of passion fruit curd
- 4 passion fruits pulp and seeds
- 3 and one-half ounces of maple syrup
- 3 eggs
- 2 glee ounces, melted
- 3 and one-half ounces of almond milk
- half cup of almond flour
- 1/2 teaspoon of baking powder

Directions:

1. Blend half the fruit curd in a dish with the passion fruit seeds and mix, pulp, and split into six heat-proof ramekins.

2. Whisked eggs in a tub, with maple syrup, ghee, the rest of the mix excellently: curd,

baking powder, milk, and flour.

3. Also, split this into the ramekins, put it in the fryer, and cook for 40 minutes at 200°F.

4. Leave the puddings and prepare to cool down!

Enjoy!

Nutrition: Calories: 430, Fat: 22g, Fiber: 3g, Carbohydrates 7g, Protein: 8g.

Mixed Berries

(Ready in about 11 mins | Servings 6 | Normal)

Ingredients:
- 2tablespoons of lemon juice
- 1 and 1⁄2 tablespoons of maple syrup
- 1 and 1⁄2 spoonful of champagne vinegar
- 1 tablespoon of olive oil
- 1 lb. of strawberries, half cut
- 1 and 1⁄2 cups of blueberries
- 1⁄4 cup of basil leaves

Directions:

1. Combine lemon juice with maple syrup in a saucepan that suits your AirFryer. Stir in vinegar, bring to a simmer over a moderate flame, and add oil. Stir, put the blueberries and strawberries in your AirFryer, and cook 6 minutes, at 310° F.

2. Sprinkle over the basil and serve!

Enjoy!

Nutrition: Calories: 163, Fat: 4g, Carbohydrates 4g, Carbohydrates 10g, Protein: 2.1g.

Cake Tomato

(Ready in about 40 mins | Servings 4 | Normal)

Ingredients:
- 1 and a half cups of flour
- 1 tsp. of powder of cinnamon
- 1 tsp. of powder for baking
- 1 tsp. of baking soda
- Three and a half cup maple syrup
- 1 cup of sliced tomatoes
- Olive oil: 1⁄2 cup
- 2 teaspoons of cider apple vinegar

Directions:
1. Layer flour and baking powder, baking soda, cinnamon in a dish, and mix well with maple syrup.
2. Combine tomatoes with olive oil and vinegar in another bowl and pour in well.
3. Integrate and blend well and pour into a round pan that suits your fryer, stir in the fryer, and cook at 360° F for 30 minutes.
4. Leave the cake to cool, cut, and serve.
Enjoy!
Nutrition: Calories:153, Fat: 2g, Fiber: 1g, Carbohydrates 25g, Protein: 4g.

Chocolate andPomegranate Bars

(Ready in about 2hrs 10 mins | Servings 6 | Difficult)
Ingredients:
- 1⁄2 cup of milk
- 1 teaspoon of vanilla flavor extract
- 1 and 1⁄2 cups of dark chocolate
- 1⁄2 cup of sliced almonds
- 1⁄2 cup of pomegranate seed

Directions:
1. Warm a saucepan over moderately low heat with milk, add chocolate, whisk. Take off the heat for five minutes and incorporate vanilla extract, half of the pomegranate seeds, and half nuts and mix
2. Load into a lined baking casserole, scatter, and sprinkle a teaspoon of salt, the rest from the arils and nuts of the pomegranate, put in your AirFryer, and cook for4 minutes at 300° F.
3. Keep 2 hours in the fridge before serving.
Enjoy!
Nutrition: Calories:68, Fat: 1g, Fiber: 4g, Carbohydrates 6g, Protein: 1g.

Chocolate and Almond Bars

(Ready in about 34 mins | Servings 6 | Normal)
Ingredients:
- 1⁄4 cup of cocoa nibs
- 1 cup of almonds, soaked and drained
- 2 teaspoons of powdered cocoa
- 1⁄4 cup of seeds from the hemp
- 1⁄4 cup of gobi berries

- 1/4 cup of shredded coconut
- Eight dates, bruised and drenched

Directions:

1. Put almonds in the mixing bowl, combine, add hemp seeds, cacao nibs, ground chocolate, goji, coconut, and blend.

2. Add dates, mix well, and spread over a rimmed baking sheet which suits your fryer and simmers for four minutes at 320° F.

3. Break into equal parts and keep in the refrigerator for 30 minutes beforehand. Serve. Enjoy!

Nutrition: Calories: 140,Fat: 6g,Fiber: 3g, Carbohydrates7g,Protein:19g.

Blueberry Pudding

(Ready in about 35 mins | Servings 6 | Normal)

Ingredients:

- Two cups of flour
- 2 cups of rolled oats
- Eight cups of blueberries
- 1 butter stick, melted
- 1 cup of walnuts, chopped
- 3 spoonful of maple syrup
- 2 rosemary spoons, chopped

Directions:

1. Cover the blueberries and set them aside in a greased baking tray.

2. Mix the dried oats with rice, walnuts, sugar, and maple in your mixing bowl syrup and rosemary, combine well, pour over blueberries, whisk in and fry it all in your AirFryerand simmer for 25 minutes at 350°F.

3. Leave the dessert to cool, cut, and serve. Enjoy!

Nutrition: Calories:150, Fat:3g,Carbohydrates 7g, Protein:4 g.

Tangerine Cake

(Ready in about 30 mins | Servings | Normal)

Ingredients:

- 3/4 cup of sugar
- 2 cups of flour
- Olive oil: 1/4 cup

- 1/2 cup of milk
- 1 cider vinegar teaspoon
- 1/2 teaspoon of vanilla extract
- 2 lemon juice and zest
- 1 tangerine juice and zest
- 2 parts of mandarin, for serving

Directions:

1. Blend the flour and sugar in a dish, then whisk.
2. Combine the oil with the sugar, vinegar, vanilla extract, and lemon juice in another cup, and tangerine and zest, and swirl very well.
3. Add flour, stir well and spill it into a cake saucepan that suits your fryer. Stir in the fryer, and cook for 20 minutes at 360° F.
4. Serve right up with slices of tangerine on top.

Enjoy!

Nutrition: Calories: 190, Fat: 1g, carbohydrate 4g, Protein: 4g.

Lemon Cake with Ricotta

(Ready in about 1hr 20 mins | Servings 4 | Normal)

Ingredients:

- 8whisked eggs
- 3 lbs. of ricotta cheese
- 1/2 cup of sugar
- 1 lemon zest, grated
- 1 orange zest, grated
- Butter for saucepan

Directions:

1. Combine the eggs in a dish with the sugar, cheese, lemon, and orange peel and mix well.
2. Lubricate a baking pan that matches your fryer with a batter and spread it out the mixture of ricotta, introduce in the fryer at 390° F and cook for 30 minutes.
3. Reduce heat to 380° F and bake for another 40 minutes.
4. Take the cake out of the oven to cool off and eat!

Enjoy it!

Nutrition: Calories:110, Fat: 3g, Fiber:2g, Carbohydrates 3g, Protein: 4g.

Sponge Cake

(Ready in about 30 mins | Servings 12 | Normal)

Ingredients:

- Three cups of flour
- Three spoons of baking powder
- 1/2 cup of corn starch
- 1 tsp. of baking soda
- 1 cup of olive oil
- 1 and 1/2 cup of milk
- 1 cup and 2/3 of sugar
- Two cups of water
- 1/4 cup juice of a lemon
- 2 teaspoons of vanilla extract

Directions:

1. In a dish, blend flour and cornstarch, baking powder, baking soda, and sugar and swirl away.
2. Balance oil with milk, sugar, vanilla, lemon juice in another tub, and whisk.
3. Merge the best mixtures, stir and pour into a grated baking dish. Stir in the fryer, and cook at 350° F for 20 minutes
4. Leave the cake to cool, cut, and serve.

Enjoy it!

Nutrition: Calories:246, Fat: 3g, Carbohydrates 6g, Protein: 2g.

Strawberry Shortcakes

(Ready in about 1hr 5 mins | Servings 6 | Normal)

Ingredients:

- Cooking spray
- 1/4 cup of sugar + 4 tablespoons
- 1 and 1/2 cup of flour
- 1 teaspoon of baking powder
- 1/4 teaspoon of baking soda
- 1/3 cup of butter
- 1 cup of buttermilk
- One whisked egg
- 2 cups cut strawberries
- 1 tablespoon of rum
- One spoonful of mint, minced
- 1 lime zest in a mortar, rubbed
- 1/2 cup of cream with whipping

Directions:

1. Mix the flour and 1/4 cup butter, baking powder, baking soda in a dish, and then swirl.
2. Combine buttermilk and egg in another cup, whisk, add to flour mixture and whisk.

3. Spoon this baking dough into six jars greased with oil, cover with tin foil them in your AirFryer, cook for 45 minutes at 360° F.

4. In the meantime, combine strawberries with three tablespoons of sugar in a cup, rum, zest, mint, and lime, in a cold place, mix, and set aside.

5. Mix the whipped cream with 1 tablespoon of sugar in another dish, then whisk.

6. Let the jars out, split the strawberry mix on top, and serve with the whipped cream. Enjoy!

Nutrition: Calories:164, Fat: 2g, Fiber: 5g, carbohydrate 3g, Protein: 2g.

Pudding Mandarins

(Ready in about 1hr | Servings 8 | Difficult)
Ingredients:
- 1 Mandarin, sliced, trimmed
- Two mandarin Juice
- Two spoonfuls of brown sugar
- Four ounces of butter, mild
- Two whisked eggs
- Cup sugar: 3⁄4
- 3⁄4 cup of white flour
- 3⁄4 cup of almonds, ground
- Honey to serve

Directions:
1. Lubricate a saucepan with a little butter, add brown sugar on the bottom, and prepare for mandarin slices.

2. Combine butter and honey, eggs, almonds, flour, and mandarin juice in a cup, and stir, spill this over the slices of mandarin, put the pan in your fryer, and cook for 40 minutes, at 360° F.

3. Switch pudding to a plate and pour over with honey. Enjoy!

Nutrition: Calories:162, Fat: 3g, Carbohydrates 3g, Protein: 6g.

Lemon Tart

(Ready in about 1hr 35 mins | Servings 6 | Normal)
Ingredients:
To the crust:
- 2 spoonful of sugar
- 2 cups of white flour

- A pinch of salt
- 3 tablespoons of ice water
- 12 tablespoons of fresh butter

To fill out:
- 2whisked eggs
- 1 and 1⁄4 cup of sugar
- Ten tablespoons of butter melted and chilled
- Lemon juice
- Two lemon zest rubbed

Directions:

1. Mix 2 cups of flour with a touch of salt and 2 tablespoons of sugar in a dish, and just brush.

2. Add 12 spoonfuls of butter and water, knead before dough is obtained, shape the ball, seal it in foil and keep for 1 hour in the fridge.

3. Move the dough to a baking sheet and flatten it. Pinch with a fork the tart, hold in the refrigerator for 20 minutes, and place in AirFryer at 360° F for fifteen minutes.

4. Mix 1 and 1⁄4 cup of sugar with milk, ten spoons of honey, and lemon in a dish. Add the zest, the juice, and the sugar, then whisk well.

5. Pour it into a pie crust, spread it evenly, put in the fryer, and cook for20 minutes at 360° F.

6. Cut it and serve.

Enjoy!

Nutrition: Calories:182, Fat: 4g, Carbohydrates 1g, Protein: 3g.

Rhubarb Pie

(Ready in about 1hr 15 mins | Servings 6 | Difficult)

Ingredients:
- 1 and 1⁄4 tablespoon of almond flour
- Eight tablespoons of butter
- Five tablespoons of ice water
- 1 tsp. of sugar

To fill out:
- 3 cups of rhubarb, hackled
- 3 tablespoons of flour
- 1and 1⁄2 cup sugar
- 2 Eggs
- Nutmeg 1⁄2 tsp., ground
- 1 tablespoon of butter
- 2 low-Fat: milk spoons

Directions:

1. Mix 1 and 1⁄4 cups of flour with 1 teaspoon of sugar in a dish, 8 table tsp. Mix and knead the butter and the cold water until you have the dough.

2. Move the dough to a vibrant working surface, form a circle, flatten, wrap it, hold it in the refrigerator for about 30 minutes, turn it over and press onto the plastic pie pan at the bottom that suits your AirFryer.

3. Mix the rhubarb in a dish of 1 and 1⁄2 cups of water, musk, 3 tablespoons of corn, and flour.

4. In another cup, whisk the milk into the shells, add to the rhubarb mixture, pour in the pie crust, bring in the AirFryer and cook at 390° F for 45 minutes.

5. Cut to cold and serve.

Enjoy!

Nutrition: Calories:200, Fat: 2g, Fiber: 1g, Carbohydrates6g, Protein: 3g.

Maple Cupcakes

(Ready in about 30 mins | Servings 4 | Normal)

Ingredients:

- Four tablespoons of butter
- Four eggs
- 1⁄2 cup of apple puree
- Two cinnamon powder teaspoons
- 1 teaspoon of vanilla extract
- Apple 1⁄2, cored and chopped
- 4 tablespoons of maple syrup
- 3⁄4 cup of white flour
- 1⁄2 teaspoon of baking powder

Directions:

1. Burn up a pan over medium heat with the butter, add applesauce, vanilla. Whisk, switch off the heat and set the eggs and maple syrup aside to cool off.

2. Add rice, sugar, baking powder, apples, and comb. Stir, introduce in your AirFryer in 350° F AirFryer and bake for 20 minutes.

3. Leave the cupcakes to cool, pass them to a plate, and serve them.

Nutrition: Calories:150, Fats 3g, Carbohydrates 5g, Protein: 4g.

Lentils and Brownie Dates

(Ready in about 25 mins | Servings 8 | Normal)

Ingredients:

- 28 Rinsed and drained ounces of canned lentils
- Twelve dates
- 1 tablespoon of honey
- 1 banana, chopped and peeled
- 1/2 teaspoon of baking soda
- 4 tablespoon of almond butter
- 2 teaspoons of cocoa

Directions:
1. Mix the lentils with butter, pineapple, cocoa, and bake in your mixing bowl. Add soda and sugar, and mix well.
2. Insert dates, pulse a couple more times, pour in a grated pan to match. Place the AirFryer uniformly, put 360° F in the fryer, and bake for fifteen minutes.
3. Mix brownies out of the microwave, cut, place, and serve on a platter. Enjoy!
Nutrition: Calories: 162,Fat: 4g, Fiber: 2g, Carbohydrates3g, Protein:4g.

Cookies Lentils

(Ready in about 35 mins | Servings 36 | Normal)
Ingredients:
- 1 cup of drinking water
- 1 cup of dried, drained, and mashed lentils
- 1 cup of white flour
- 1 teaspoon powder of cinnamon
- 1 cup of whole wheat flour
- 1 teaspoon of baking powder
- Nutmeg 1/2 tsp., ground
- 1 cup of soft butter
- 1/2 cup of brown sugar
- One and a half cup white sugar
- 1 egg
- 2 teaspoons of almond extract
- 1 teaspoon of raisins
- 1 cup of rolling oats
- 1 cup of coconut, without flavoring and shredded

Directions:
1. Place the white and whole wheat meal in a bowl of salt, cinnamon, baking nutmeg, and flour, then stir.
2. Combine butter with brown and white sugar in a dish and whisk with your kitchen mixer.
3. Connect milk, almond extract, lentils, flour mixture, oats, raisins, and coconut, and all

swirl well.

5. Squeeze dough spoons on a rimmed baking sheet that suits your AirFryer and cook at 350° F for 15 minutes.

6. Arrange cookies and put them on a baking platter.

Enjoy!

Nutrition: Calories:154, Fat: 2g, Fiber: 2g, Carbohydrates: 4g,Protein: 7g.

Black Teacake

(Ready in about 45 mins | Servings 12 | Normal)

Ingredients:

- Six tablespoons of ground black tea
- 2 cups of milk
- One and a half cup of butter
- 2 cups of sugar
- 4 eggs
- 2 vanilla teaspoons
- Olive oil: 1/2 cup
- 3 and 1/2 cups of flour
- 1 teaspoon of baking soda
- 3 spoons of dried powder

For the cream:

- Six honey spoons
- Four cups of sugar
- 1 cup of soft butter

Directions:

1. Put the milk in a saucepan, fire over a moderate flame, introduce tea and stir well. Take off the heat, and leave to cool.

2. Mix 1/2 cup butter and 2 cups of sugar, eggs, vegetable oil in a dish, vanilla powder, baking soda, and 3 and 1/2 cup flour, and just stir it all well.

3. Put it into 2 lubricated round pans, then put it into the fryer. Bake for 25 minutes and 330° F.

4. Place 1 cup of butter with honey and 4 cups of sugar in a dish and stir well.

5. Arrange one cake on a plate, pour the cream over it, and keep the other cake in the refrigerator before you serve.

Enjoy!

Nutrition: Calories: 200, Fat: 4g, carbohydrate 6g, Protein: 2g.

Strawberry Cobbler

(Ready in about 35 mins | Servings 6 | Normal)
Ingredients:
- 3⁄4 cup of sugar
- Six cups of strawberries, half sliced
- Baking powder: 1/8 teaspoon
- 1 tablespoon of lemon juice
- 1⁄2 cup of flour
- A sprinkle of baking soda
- 1⁄2 cup of water
- 3 and 1⁄2 tablespoon of olive oil
- Cooking spray

Directions:
1. Combine the strawberries and half of the sugar in a cup, sprinkle some flour, add lemon juice and spill it into the baking dish that suits your AirFryerand oiled Cooking spray.
2. Mix the flour with the rest of the sugar, baking powder, and soda and stir well.
3. Apply the olive oil and mix with your hands before the entire thing is finished.
4. Put 1⁄2 cup of water and brush on strawberries.
5. At 355° F, put in the fryer and bake for 25 minutes.
6. Place aside the cobbler to cool, slice, and serve.
Nutrition: Calories:221, Fat: 3g, Fiber: 3g, Carbohydrates 6g, Protein: 9g.

Easy Granola

(Ready in about 45 mins | Servings 4 | Normal)
Ingredients:
- 1 cup of shredded coconut
- Half cup of almonds
- 1⁄2 cup of chopped pecans
- 2 tablespoon of sugar
- 1⁄2 cup of pumpkin seeds
- Sunflower seeds: 1⁄2 cup
- 2 tablespoons of sunflower oil
- 1 teaspoon of nutmeg, ground
- 1 tsp. of the spicy apple pie mixture

Directions:
1. Combine the almonds and pecans in a dish with the pumpkin seeds and the sunflower. Sprinkle with seeds, coconut, and nutmeg, and apple pie spice and mix well.
2. Heat a saucepan over a moderate flame with the oil, add sugar and stir well.
3. Place over a mixture of nuts and coconut, then blend well.

4. Place this on a smooth baking sheet that suits your AirFryer, heat at 300° F in an AirFryer, and bake for 25 minutes.
5. Leave the granola to cool, cut, and serve.
Enjoy!
Nutrition: Calories:322, Fat:7g, Fiber:8g, Carbohydrates: 12g, Protein: 7g.

Cheesecake Lime

(Ready in about 4hr 14 mins | Servings 10 | Normal)
Ingredients:
- Two tablespoons butter, warmed
- Two sugar teaspoons
- Four ounces flour
- 1/4 cup, shredded coconut

To fill out:
- 1 pound cream cheese
- One lime zest, grated
- 1 lime juice
- 2 cups of warm water
- 2 sachets lime jelly

Directions:
1. Combine the coconut with flour, butter, and sugar in a bowl, mix well. Press this on the bottom of the saucepan, which suits your fryer.
2. In the meantime, place the warm water in a bowl, add sachets of jelly, and stir before they dissolve.
3. In a cup, place the cream cheese, add the jelly, lime juice, and zest and whisk strong.
4. Apply this over the crust, spread, place, and cook in the AirFryer for 4 minutes at 300°F.
5. Hold 4 hours in the fridge before serving.
Enjoy!
Nutrition: Calories:260, Fat: 2g3, Fiber: 2g,Carbohydrates 5g,Protein: 7g.

Macaroons

(Ready in about 18 mins | Servings 20 | Normal)
Ingredients:
- 2 spoonful of sugar
- 4 white Eggs
- 2 cups of shredded coconut

- 1 teaspoon of vanilla extract

Directions:

1. Place egg whites with stevia in a tub, and use your mixer to pound.
2. Add coconut and vanilla extract, whisk, form small balls. Place these in your AirFryer and cook at 340° F for 8 minutes.
3. Serve cold macaroons.

Enjoy!

Nutrition: Calories: 55, Fat: 6g, Fiber: 1g, Carbohydrates 2g, Protein: 1g.

Tasteful Orange Cake

(Ready in about 42 mins | Servings 12 Normal)

Ingredients:

- Six eggs
- 1 orange, peeled and quarter-cut
- 1 teaspoon of vanillaextract
- 1 teaspoon of baking powder
- Nine ounces of flour
- Two ounces of sugar + 2 tablespoons
- Two spoonfuls of orange zest
- Four ounces of cream cheese
- 4 ounces of yogurt

Directions:

1. Blend orange very well into your mixing bowl.
2. Add flour, Two tablespoons of sugar, eggs, baking powder, and vanilla extract again and blend well.
3. Move this to 2 spring pans, put each one in your fryer and cook 16 minutes at 330°F.
4. In the meantime, mix cream cheese with orange zest, yogurt in a dish, and the remaining butter, then blend well.
5. Place one layer of cake on a platter, add half the cream cheese mixture, add another layer of cake and finish with the leftover cream cheese.
6. Nice spread, slice, and serve.

Enjoy!

Nutrition: Calories: 200, Fat:13g,Fiber: 2g,Carbohydrates 9g, Protein:8g.

ChocolateCookies

(Ready in about 35 mins | Servings 12 | Normal)

Ingredients:
- 1 teaspoon of vanilla extract
- Half cup of butter
- 1 egg
- Four spoonfuls of sugar
- 2 cups of flour
- 1/2 cup of unsweetened chocolate chips

Directions:
1. Heat butter in a saucepan over medium pressure, stir and cook for 1 minute.
2. Combine egg and vanilla extract with sugar in a cup, then mix well.
3. Stir in butter, flour, and half of the chocolate chips and stir all.
4. Move this to a saucepan that suits your fryer and disperse the rest of the chocolate chips on top, introduce it in the fryer at 330° F. Bake for another 25 minutes.
5. Slice when cold, and then serve.
Enjoy it!
Nutrition: Calories:230, Fat:12g, Fiber: 2g, Carbohydrates 4g, Protein: 5g.

Scones Blueberry

(Ready in about 20 mins | Servings 10 |
Normal) **Ingredients:**
- 1 cup of white flour
- 1 cup of blackberries
- 2eggs
- 1/2 cup milk, heavy
- One and a half cup butter
- 5 spoonful of sugar
- 2 vanilla teaspoons extract
- 2 spoons of baking powder

Directions:
1. Mix the rice, salt, baking powder, and blueberries in a bowl and mix.
2. Mix the heavy cream with butter and vanilla extract in another dish. Add sugar and milk, and sprinkle well.
3. Integrate the two blends, knead until the dough is full, shape from this mix triangles, put them on a rimmed baking sheet that suits the AirFryer to cook them for ten minutes at 320° F.
4. Serve them cold
Enjoy!
Nutrition: Calories:130, Fat: 2g, Fiber: 2g, Carbohydrates 4g, Protein: 3g.

Special Brownies

(Ready in about 27 mins | Servings 4 | Normal)

Ingredients:

- 1 egg
- 1/3 cup of powdered cocoa
- 1/3 cups of sugar
- 7 tablespoons of butter
- 1/2 teaspoon of vanilla
- 1/4 cup of white flour
- 1/4 cup of walnuts
- 1/2 teaspoon of baking powder
- 1 tablespoon of peanut butter

Directions:

1. Heat a pan over medium with six spoons butter and sugar. Heat, stir, cook for 5 minutes, put this in a bowl, and add salt, vanilla paste, powdered cocoa, egg, baking powder, walnuts, and whisk the entire lot well and pour it into a saucepan that fits in your fryer well.

2. Mix 1 spoonful of butter and peanut butter in a tub, heat up in a few seconds on your oven, swirl well and drizzle it over mixed brownies.

3. Put in the AirFryer, bake at 320° F, and bake only for 17 minutes.

4. Let brownies cool, cut, and serve.

Enjoy!

Nutrition: Calories: 223, Fat:32g, Fiber: 1g, Carbohydrates 3g, Protein: 6g.

Cocoa Cookies

(Ready in about 24 mins | Servings 12 | Normal)

Ingredients:

- 6 ounces of coconut oil,
- six eggs
- 3 ounces of ground cocoa
- 2 vanilla teaspoons
- 1/2 teaspoon of baking powder
- 4 ounces of cream cheese
- 5 spoonful of sugar

Directions:

1. Combine eggs with coconut oil, cocoa powder, and bake in a blender brush, vanilla, cream cheese, and swerve with a whisk using the mixer.
2. Pour this into a flavored baking dish that suits your fryer, insert in the fryer for 320° F and bake for fifteen minutes.
3. Slice a tray of cookies into rectangles and serve.
Enjoy it!
Nutrition: Calories: 178, Fat:14g, Carbohydrates: 2g, Fiber:3g,Protein:5g.

Coffee Cheesecakes

(Ready in about 30 mins | Servings 6 | Normal)
Ingredients:
For cheesecake:

- 2 tablespoons of butter
- Eight ounces of cream cheese
- 3 tablespoons of coffee
- 3 eggs
- 1/3 cups of sugar
- 1 tablespoon of caramel syrup

For frost:

- Three spoons of caramel syrup
- Three tablespoons of butter
- 8 ounces of cheese with mascarpone, mild
- 2 spoonful of sugar

Directions:
1. Combine the cream cheese with the eggs in your mixer, two tablespoons butter, coffee, 1 tablespoon caramel syrup, 1/3 cup sugar, and blend well. Put it in a cupcake saucepan that suits your fryer. Stir in the frying pan and cook at 320° F and cook for 20 minutes.
2. Set aside to cool off, and instead keep for 3 hours in the fridge.
3. In the meantime, blend 3 spoons of butter with 3 spoonfuls of caramel syrup, sugar, and mascarpone two tablespoons spoons, combine well and serve.
Enjoy it!
Nutrition: Calories:254,Fat: 23g, Fiber: 21g, Carbohydrates21g, Protein: 5g.

Strawberry Pie

(Ready in about 30 mins | Servings 12 | Normal)
Ingredients:

For the crust:
- 1 cup of crushed coconut
- One cup of sunflower seeds
- One and a quarter cup of butter

To fill out:
- 1 gelatin teaspoon
- Eight ounces of cream cheese
- Four ounces of strawberries
- 2 tablespoons of water
- 1/2 tablespoon of lemon juice
- 1/4 stevia teaspoon
- 1/2 cup of milk, heavy
- Eight ounces of strawberries to serve

Directions:

1. Combine the sunflower seeds with coconut in your mixing bowl, a pinch of salt, and butter. Place it on the bottom of a cake pan that's good for your AirFryer.
2. Heat a saucepan over medium heat with water, add gelatin, stirring. Set aside for cooling before it disperses; add this to your food, combine with 4 ounces of strawberries, cream cheese, and lemon juice, and stevia, whisk together well.
3. Whisk well, apply heavy cream, and spread over crust.
4. Cover with 8 ounces of strawberries, put in the AirFryer and Cook for 15 minutes, at 330° F.
5. Hold in the freezer before serving.
Enjoy!
Nutrition: Calories:234,Fat: 23g, Fiber: 2g,Carbohydrates 6g, Protein:7g.

Cheesecake with Ginger

(Ready in about 2hr 30 mins | Servings 6 | Normal)
Ingredients:
- Two butter teaspoons, warmed
- 1/2 cup of ginger cookies
- 16 ounces of soft cream cheese
- 2 eggs
- 1/2 cups of sugar
- 1 teaspoon of rum
- 1/2 teaspoon of vanilla
- Nutmeg 1/2 tsp., ground

Directions:

1. Lubricate a saucepan with the butter and scatter the crumbs over the bottom.
2. Shake nutmeg, vanilla, rum, and eggs on cream cheese in a cup, stir well and sprinkle the crumbs over the cookie.
3. Put in the AirFryer and cook at 340° F for 20 minutes.
4. Drop the cheesecake to cool and hold in the refrigerator for 2 hours before you slice and then serve.
Enjoy!
Nutrition: Calories:412, Fat:12g,Fiber: 6g, Carbohydrates20g,Protein: 6g.

Carrot Cake

(Ready in about 55 mins | Servings 6 | Normal)
Ingredients:
- Five ounces of flour
- 3⁄4 teaspoon of baking powder
- 1⁄2 teaspoon of baking soda
- 1⁄2 teaspoon of ground cinnamon
- Nutmeg 1⁄4 tsp., ground
- 1⁄2 allspice teaspoon
- 1 egg
- Three yogurt spoons
- 1⁄2 cups of sugar
- 1⁄4 cup of pineapple juice
- Four spoonfuls of sunflower oil
- 1/3 cup of carrots, ground together
- 1/3 cup of pecans, diced and toasted
- 1/3 cup of crushed coconut flakes
- Cooking spray

Directions:
1. Mix the flour in a cup of baking soda and powder, salt and allspice, nutmeg, and cinnamon, then combine.
2. Put the egg and yogurt, sugar, pineapple juice, oil, carrots in another dish. Mix well and pecans and cocoa powder.
3. Merge the best mixtures and blend properly; pour into a spring pan that suits your fryer with cooking spray, which you grated with. Switch to your AirFryer and bake for 45 minutes at 320° F.
4. Let the cake cool off, then cut it down and serving it.
Enjoy!
Nutrition: Calories:200,Fat: 6g, Fiber:20g,Carbohydrates 22g,Protein: 4g.

Crispy Apple

(Ready in about 20 mins | Servings 4 | Normal)
Ingredients:

- Two teaspoons of cinnamon powder
- Five apples, sliced and diced
- 1/2 cubit musk powder
- 1 tablespoon of maple syrup
- 1/2 cup of water
- Four tablespoons of butter
- 1/4 cup of flour
- 3/4 cup of old dried style oats
- 1/4 cup of brown sugar

Directions:
1. Place the apples in a saucepan that suits your fryer, add the cinnamon, nutmeg, water, and maple syrup.
2. Combine butter and oats, sugar, salt, and flour in a cup, whisk and drop. Introduce a spoonful of this mixture on top of apples in your AirFryer. Cook for ten minutes, at 350°F.
3. Serve hot.
Enjoy!
Nutrition: Calories:200, Fat: 6g, Fiber: 8g, Carbohydrates29g, Protein:12g.

Tiny LavaCake

(Ready in about 30 mins | Servings 3 | Normal)
Ingredients:

- 1 egg
- Four spoonfuls of sugar
- Two tablespoons of olive oil
- Four tablespoons of milk
- Four teaspoons of flour
- 1 tablespoon of cocoa powder
- 1/2 teaspoon of baking powder
- 1/2 teaspoon of orange zest

Directions:
1. Blend the egg in a bowl with the sugar, oil, milk, flour, salt, coconut powder, baking

powder, and orange zest; blend well and sprinkle in small ramekins.

2. Add ramekins to your fryer and cook for 20 minutes at 320° F

3. Serve molten lava cake.

Enjoy!

Nutrition: Calories:201,Fat: 7g, Fiber:8g,Carbohydrates 23g, Protein:4g.

Banana bread

(Ready in about 40 mins | Servings 6 | Normal)

Ingredients:

- 3⁄4 cups of sugar
- One-third cup of butter
- 1teaspoon of vanilla extract
- 1 egg
- Two mashed bananas
- 1 tsp. of baking powder
- 1 and 1⁄2 cups of flour
- Baking soda, 1⁄2 teaspoons
- 1/3 tablespoon of milk
- 1 and 1⁄2 tablespoons of tartar cream
- Cooking spray

Directions:

1. Combine the milk in a bowl of tartar cream, sugar, butter, egg and vanilla, and the bananas, and mix everything

2. Mix the flour with the baking powder and baking soda in another dish.

3. Integrate the 2 mixtures, mix well and pour into a lubricated cake tray. Place the fryer in your air with some cooking spray and cook for 40 minutes at 320° F.

4. Take out the bread, set it aside to cool, slice, and serve.

Enjoy it!

Nutrition: Calories:292,Fat: 7g, Fiber:8g, Carbohydrates: 28g,Protein: 4g.

Apple Cup

(Ready in about 50 mins | Servings 6 | Normal)

Ingredients:

- 3 cups of apples, roasted and cubed
- 1 cup of sugar
- 1 tablespoon of vanilla

- 2 eggs

- 1 tablespoon of apple pie seasoning
- Two cups of white flour
- 1 tablespoon of baking powder
- 1 butter Stick
- 1 cup of drinking water

Directions:
1. Place the egg and 1 butter stick, the apple pie spice, and the sugar in a cup. Whisk with the mixer.
2. Insert apples and mix well again.
3. Add baking powder and flour to another dish, then whisk.
4. Integrate the 2 mixtures, swirl, and pour into a pan creating a spring.
5. Place spring pan in the AirFryer and cook for 320° F for forty minutes
6. Cut and serve.
Enjoy!
Nutrition: Calories: 192, Fat:6g, Fiber:7g,Carbohydrates 14g, Protein:7g.

Chocolate Cocoa

(Ready in about 40 mins | Servings 12 | Normal
Ingredients:
- 3⁄4 cup of white flour
- 3⁄4 cup of wheat flour
- 1 teaspoon of baking soda
- 3⁄4 teaspoon of pumpkin pie powder
- 3⁄4 cup of sugar
- 1 mashed banana
- 1⁄2 teaspoon of baking powder
- Two spoonfuls of canola oil
- One-half cup of greek yogurt
- 8 ounces of pumpkin canned puree
- Cooking spray
- 1 egg
- 1⁄2 teaspoon vanilla extract
- 2/3 cup of chocolate chips

Directions:
1. Mix white flour and whole wheat flour, salt and baking in a dish, pulverized soda and pumpkin spice, and swirl.
2. Combine the sugar with the oil, banana, yogurt, and pumpkin in another bowl puree, vanilla, and milk, blend with mixer, and swirl.

3. Integrate the 2 mixtures, add the chocolate chips, whisk and pour into agrated bundt pan, which suits your AirFryer.
4. Put in the AirFryer and cook at 330° F for 30 minutes.
5. Leave the cake to cool, then cut and serve.
Enjoy!
Nutrition: Calories:232, Fat:7g, Fiber:7g, Carbohydrates:29g, Protein:4g.

Cacao Cake

(Ready in about 27 mins | Servings 6 | Normal)
Ingredients:

- 3.5 ounces of butter, melted
- Three eggs
- Three ounces of sugar
- 1 teaspoon of powdered cocoa
- Three ounces of flour
- 1/2 teaspoon of lemon juice

Directions:
1. Mix 1 spoonful of butter with cocoa powder and swirl in a cup.
2. Combine the remaining butter and sugar, eggs, and flour in another cup, and lemon juice, whisk well and spill half into an appropriate cake pan, which fits your fryer.
3. Bring half the cocoa mixture, spread, add the remaining layer of butter, and finish with the cocoa.
4. Put in the AirFryer and cook at 360° F for 17 minutes.
5. Before cutting and serving, cool off the cake.
Enjoy!
Nutrition: Calories:340, Fat:11g,Fiber: 3g,Carbohydrates 25g,Protein: 5g.

Bananas

(Ready in about 25 mins | Servings 4 | Normal)
Ingredients:

- Three tablespoons of butter
- 2eggs
- Eight bananas, peeled and sliced into half
- 1/2 cup of cornflour
- Three spoons of cinnamon sugar
- 1 cup of Panko

Directions:

1. Warm the butter in a saucepan over moderate pressure, insert panko. Adjust and simmer for 4 minutes, then transfer to a cup.
2. Roll each into flour, eggs, and panko mixture, place in the air basket fryer, cinnamon sugar, and cook at 280° F for10 minutes.
3. Serve immediately.
Enjoy!
Nutrition: Calories:164, Fat: 1g, Fiber:4g,Carbohydrates: 32g,Protein: 4g.

Strawberry Donuts

(Ready in about 25 mins | Servings 4 | Normal)
Ingredients:
- 8 ounces Flour
- 1 tablespoon brown sugar
- 1 tablespoon of white sugar
- 1 egg
- 2 and 1/2 spoonful of butter
- Four ounces of full milk
- 1 teaspoon of baking powder

For strawberries icing:
- 2 tablespoons of butter
- 3.5 ounces of iced sugar
- 1/2 teaspoon of rose coloring
- 1/4 tablespoon of strawberries, sliced
- 1 liter of whipped cream

Directions:
1. Combine butter in a cup, 1 tsp of brown sugar, 1 tablespoon. Stir in both white sugar and flour.
2. Combine the egg with 1 and 1/2 tablespoon butter and milk in a second dish and then stir well.
3. Mix the two mixtures, whisk, shape the donuts, and place them. Cook them in the basket of your AirFryer, 360° F for 15 minutes.
4. Put 1 spoonful of butter, icing sugar, coloring powder, whipped cream, puree the strawberry, and whisk well.
5. Place donuts on a platter and cover it with strawberry icing.
Enjoy!
Nutrition: Calories:250, Fats: 12g,Fiber: 1g,Carbohydrates 32g,Protein: 4g.

Pears Wrapped

(Ready in about 25 mins | Servings 4 | Normal)

Ingredients:

- Four puffer pastry sheets
- 14 ounces of custard of vanilla
- 2 half pears
- 1 whisked egg
- 1/2 teaspoon of ground cinnamon
- 2 spoonful of sugar

Directions:

1. Put slices of puff pastry on a working board, insert a spoonful of vanilla custard in the center of each, pear halves top and close.
2. Scatter the pears with the egg, spray the sugar and the cinnamon, and bring them in the basket of your AirFryer and cook for fifteen minutes at 320° F.
3. Divide parcels and serve.

Enjoy!

Nutrition: Calories:200, Fat: 2g, Fiber: 1g,Carbohydrates 14g, Protein: 3g.

Cinnamon Rolls and Cheese Dip

(Ready in about 2hrs 15 mins | Servings 8 | Normal)

Ingredients:

- 1 pound of bread dough
- 3/4 cup of brown sugar
- 1 and 1/2 cinnamon spoons, ground
- 1/4 cup of melted butter

For Dip cream cheese:

- 2 tablespoons of butter
- 4 ounces of cream cheese
- 1 and 1/4 cup of sugar
- 1/2 tablespoon of vanilla extract

Directions:

1. Roll the dough on a floured board, form a rectangle, and a 1/4 cup butter brush.
2. Combine the cinnamon and the sugar in a cup, stir, and scatter over the dough, in a log roll dough, seal tightly, and cut into eight bits.
3. Let the rolls rise for 2 hours, put them in the basket of your AirFryer, heat for five minutes at 350° F, turn over, heat for four minutes, and then switch to a bowl.

4. Mix the cream cheese in a bowl of butter, sugar, vanilla, and whisk very strongly.
5. Serve this cream cheese sauce on your cinnamon rolls.
Enjoy!
Nutrition: Calories: 200, Fat: 1g, Fiber: 0g, Carbohydrates5g,Protein: 6g.

Dessert with Bread Dough and Amaretto

(Ready in about 22 mins | Servings 12 | Normal)
Ingredients:

- 1 lb. of bread dough
- 1 cup of sugar
- 1/2 cup of butter, molten,
- 1 cup of cream, heavy
- 12 ounces of Chocolate Chips
- 2 spoonful of amaretto

Directions:liqueur
1. Roll bread, cut into 20 strips, and then halve per slice.
2. Put the dough pieces in butter, sprinkle the honey, and place them in your bowl; after you have brushed some butter, cook in the AirFryer's basket at 350° F for five minutes. Flip them, cook for 3 minutes, then put them on a platter.
3. Heat a saucepan over a moderate flame with heavy cream, add chocolate chips, then mix until molten.
4. Stir in liqueur, switch to a bowl, and serve bread dippers and with the sauce.
Enjoy!
Nutrition: Calories: 200Fat: 1g, Fiber: 0g, Carbohydrates: 6g, Protein: 6g.

Pudding Bread

(Ready in about 1hr 10 mins | Servings 4 | Normal)
Ingredients:

- Six glazed, crumbled doughnuts
- 1 cup of cherries
- Four yolks of eggs
- 1 and 1/2 cups of milk to whip
- 1/2 cup of raisins
- One-fourth cup of sugar
- Half cup of chocolate chips

Directions:

1. Combine the egg yolks and the whipped cream in a cup and stir well.
2. Mix the raisins in another bowl with the sugar, chocolate chips, and mix doughnuts.
3. Combine the Two blends, shift both to a grated pan that suits the AirFryer to cook for 1 hour at 310° F.
4. Before cutting, chill the pudding and serve.
Enjoy!
Nutrition: Calories: 302, Fat: 8g, Fiber: 2g, sugars 23g,Protein: 10g.

Simple Cheesecake

(Ready in about 25 mins | Servings 15 | Normal)
Ingredients:
- 1 lb. of cream cheese
- 1/2 teaspoon of strawberryextract
- 2 eggs
- 4 spoonful of sugar
- 1 cup of crumbled graham crackers
- 2 tablespoons of butter

Directions:
1. Combine the crackers and the butter in a tub.
2. Match crackers on the bottom of a lined cake tray, bring in the AirFryer for four minutes at 350° F.
3. In the meantime, blend the sugar in a dish with cream cheese, eggs, vanilla, and whisk nicely.
4. Cover the crust over the crackers and cook the cheesecake in your AirFryer for fifteen minutes, at 310° F.
5. Keep the cake in the freezer for 3 hours, slice, and serve.
Enjoy!
Nutrition: Calories:245, Fat:12g, sugars 1g, Carbohydrates20g, Protein: 3g.

Tasty Banana Cake

(Ready in about 40 mins | Servings 4 | Normal)
Ingredients:
- 1 tablespoon of butter, mild
- 1 egg
- One-third cup of brown sugar
- 2 tablespoons of honey
- 1 banana, mashed and peeled

- 1 cup of white flour
- 1 teaspoon of baking powder
- 1/2 teaspoon of ground cinnamon
- Cooking spray

Directions:
1. Sprinkle a cooking spray on a baking pan and set aside.
2. Mix the butter in a bowl with the sugar, banana, honey, egg, cinnamon, flour, and baking powder and whisk
3. Load this into a spray-filled cake pan, stir in, and heat the AirFryer for thirty min at 350°F.
4. Leave the cake to cool, slice, and serve.
Enjoy it!
Nutrition: Calories:232, Fat: 4g, Fiber: 1g, Carbohydrates: 34g, Protein: 4g.

Sweet Breakfast Casserole

(Ready in about 40 mins | Servings 4 | Normal)
Ingredients:
- Three tablespoons of brown sugar
- Four tablespoons of butter
- 2 tablespoons of white sugar
- 1/2 teaspoon of ground cinnamon
- 1/2 cup of flour

For the Pottery:
- 2 eggs
- 2 tablespoons of white sugar
- 2 and a half cups of white flour
- 1 teaspoon of baking soda
- 1 teaspoon of baking powder
- 2 eggs
- 1/2 cup of dairy
- 2 buttermilk cups
- 4 tablespoons of butter
- 1 lemon zest, grated
- 1 cup of blueberries

Directions:
1. Mix the eggs in a dish of 2 spoons of white sugar, 2 and 1/2 cups of white sugar, flour, baking powder, soda, 2 eggs, milk, buttermilk, 4 spoonfuls. Stir in butter, lemon zest, and blueberries and pour into a frying pan that suits your need.
2. Mix 3 spoonful of brown sugar with 2 teaspoons in another dish. Mix in white sugar, 4

spoonfuls of butter, 1/2 cup of flour, and cinnamon, have a combination of crumble and blueberries scattered over.

3. Put in hot oven AirFryer and bake for thirty min at 300° F.

4. Serve for breakfast and split between dishes.

Enjoy!

Nutrition: Calories: 214, Fat: 5g, fruit 8, sugars 12g, Protein:5g.

Casserole Oatmeal

(Ready in about 30 mins | Servings 8 | Normal)

Ingredients:

- 2 cups of rolled oat
- 1 teaspoon of baking powder
- One-third cup of brown sugar
- 1 teaspoon powder of cinnamon
- Halfcup of chocolate chips
- Blueberries: 2/3 cup
- 1 banana, smashed and sliced
- 2 cups of butter
- 1 egg
- 2 tablespoons of butter
- 1 tablespoon of vanillaextract
- Cooking spray

Directions:

1. Place the sugar and baking powder, salt, chocolate chips in a bowl. Add banana and blueberries, then mix.

2. Combine eggs with vanilla extract and butter in a different dish, then whisk.

3. Heat your AirFryer to 320° F, grease with spray, and cook. Add oats underneath.

4. Add the combination of cinnamon and the eggs, swirl, and simmer for 20 minutes.

5. Split into bowls and enjoy breakfast once more.

Enjoy!

Nutrition: Calories: 300, Fat:4g, fruit 7,Carbohydrates: 12g.

LimePudding

(Ready in about 25 mins | Servings 3 | Normal)

Ingredients:

- Two cups of pulp lime

- Two tablespoons of zest lime
- 2 cups of milk
- 2 tablespoons of custard
- 3 tbsp. of glazed sugar
- 3 tbsp. of utter unsalted

Directions:

1. In a saucepan, boil the milk and the sugar, incorporate the custard powder, and whisk the pear pulp until you have a nice mixture. Preheat the fryer to 300 Fahrenheit. For 5 minutes.

2. Place the platter in the pan basket and cool down to 250 °F. Cook 10 minutes and prepare to cool down.

Nutrition: Calories: 100kcl.

Cherry Pancakes

(Ready in about 15 mins | Servings 2 | Normal)

Ingredients:

- 2 tabsof cherries sliced into pieces
- 1 1/2 tablespoon of almond flour
- Three eggs
- 2 tsp of dry basil
- 2 tsp of dried parsley
- Salt and pepper to the taste
- Three tbsp. of butter

Directions:

1. The AirFryer is preheated to 250 °F.Stir the mixture together in such a tiny dish. Be certain that the mixture is well smooth and stable.

2. Take a mound from a pancake and sprinkle it with sugar. Place the batter in the mold, and put it in the basket of an AirFryer. Cook until all sides of the pancake have golden-brown. Use maple syrup to finish.

Nutrition: Calories:100,Fat: 4g,Carbohydrates 12g,Protein: 5g.

Pie Cantaloupe

(Ready in about 15 mins | Servings 3 | Normal)

Ingredients:

- 1 cup of flour
- 1 tbsp. of butter unsalted

- 4 tbsp. of glazed sugar
- 2 cups of cold milk

For filling with honey and nut:

- 3 tbsp. of honey
- 2 cups of cantaloupe pungent

Directions:

1. Combine the ingredients to create a mushy mixture. Knead the sauce cold with the milk and cover it in. Shape out the dough into two wide circles and push the dough into a pie tin and prick with a fork on the bottom.
2. Heat the ingredients on low heat for filling and spill over the pot. Cover the second round of pie foil for Preheat the Fryer for five minutes at 300 °F.Take a basket pan, then cover it.
3. You'll need to take the tin off and let it cool. Divide into slices and offer with a chocolate dollop.

Nutrition: Calories: 13 Fat: 12g,Protein: 5g.

Peach muffins

(Ready in about 30 mins | Servings 5 | Normal)

Ingredients:

- 2 cups of usable flour
- 1 1/2 cups of milk
- 1/2 tsp. of baking powder
- 1/2 tsp. of baking soda
- 2 tbsp. of butter
- 1 cup of sugar
- 3 tsp. of vinegar
- 1 cup of poached sliced peach
- Cups of muffin or paper cups of butter

Directions:

1. Combine all the ingredients and use your fingers to create a crumbly combination. Apply the baking soda and vinegar to the milk and finish blending. Add this milk into the mixture and produces a batter that you need to cup of muffins.
2. Five minutes to heat the fryer to 300 °F. You ought to blend in and cover the muffin cups in the basket. Heat the muffins for 15 Minutes to verify whether the muffins are baked using a toothpick or not.
3. Remove the tassels and serve sweet.

Nutrition: Calories:100, Fat: 4g, Protein: 2g.

Rhubarb Pie

(Ready in about 15 mins | Servings 5 | Normal)
Ingredients:

- 1 cup of flour
- 1 tbsp. of butter unsalted
- 4 tsp. of glazed sugar
- 2 cups of fresh milk

For filling apple:

- 1 cup of rhubarb cut
- 1/2 tsp of cinnamon
- 2 tsp. of citrus extract

Directions:
1. Combine the ingredients to create a crumbly combination. Knead the sauce with the cold milk and cover it in. Roll out the dough into two wide circles and push the dough into a pie tin and prick with a fork on the bottom.
2. Heat the ingredients on low heat for filling and spill over the pot. Cover the second round of pie foil.
3. Preheat the Fryer for five minutes to 300 °F. Take a basket pan, then cover it. If the pastry is golden brown, take the tin off and let it cool. Divide into slices and serve with a chocolate dollop.
Nutrition: Calories: 230, Carbohydrates 10g, Protein: 5g.

Tangerine Cake

(Ready in about 15 mins | Servings 4 |
Normal) **Ingredients:**

- 1 tbsp of butter, unsalted
- 2 tbsps of freshwater
- 2 cups of all-purpose beef
- One and a half cup of condensed milk
- 1 cup of sliced tangerine

Directions:
1. Put the products together, whisk before the mixture becomes smooth. Start preparing a jar of butter, greasing it. The liquid is moved into the container.
2. Preheat the Fryer for five minutes to 300 °F. Take a basket pan, then cover it. Check if there were brownies cooked with a knife or a toothpick, then cut the pan. When brownies cooled, diced, and serve with ice cream dollop.

Nutrition: Calories: 67, Fat: 8g, Protein: 1g.

Pancakes of Rhubarb

(Ready in about 10 mins | Servings 3 |
Normal) **Ingredients:**
- 1 cup of rhubarb shredded
- 1 1/2 tablespoon of almond flour
- Three eggs
- 2 tsp.of dry basil
- 2 Tsp of dried parsley
- Salt and pepper to the taste
- 3 tbsps of butter

Directions:
1. The AirFryer is preheated to 250 °F. Combine all the ingredients in such a small dish. Be certain the mixture is smooth and stable.
2. Take a mound from a pancake and sprinkle it with sugar. Add the batter to the mold, and put it in the basket of an AirFryer.
3. Cook until all sides of the pancake have browned. Use maple syrup to serve.
Nutrition: Calories: 30, Fat: 5g, Protein: 17g.

Pudding with Mulberry

(Ready in about 30 mins | Servings 6 | Normal)
Ingredients:
- 2 cups of almond flour
- 1 cup of milk
- 2 tbsp of custard
- Three tbsp of glazed sugar
- 1 cup of mulberries juice
- Three tbsp of butter, unsalted

Directions:
1. In a saucepan, heat the milk and the sugar and incorporate the custard powder. Whisk in the almond flour and the mulberry juice until the mixture is thick.
2. Preheat the Fryer for five minutes to 300 °F. Place the platter in the pan basket and cool down to 250 °F. Cook 10 minutes, and set to cool down.
Nutrition: Calories: 34, Fat: 7g, Protein: 9g.

Pudding Cauliflower

(Ready in about 22 mins | Servings 4 |
Normal) **Ingredients:**
- 1 cup of flowering cauliflower
- 2 cups of milk
- Two tbsp. of mine custard
- Three tbsp. of glazed sugar
- Three tbsp. of butter, unsalted

Directions:
1. Parboil the flowering cauliflower and put it on a plate. In a saucepan, heat the milk and sugar and introduce the custard powder and whisk until you get a thickness variation. Pour the blend over the florets.
2. Preheat the Fryer for five minutes to 300 °F. Place the platter in the pan basket and cool down to 250 °F. Heat 10 minutes and cool down. **Nutrition:**Calories: 34, Fat: 6g, Protein: 10g.

Key Lime Pie

(Ready in about 15 mins | Servings 3 |
Normal) **Ingredients:**
- One and a half cup of plain flour
- 1 cup of almond meal
- 3 tbsp. of butter, unsalted
- Two tbsp. of glazed sugar
- 2 cups of warm water

For the filling:
- 2 cups of lime key
- 1 cup of fresh cream
- 3 tbsp of butter

Directions:
1. Use milk to knead all the ingredients together, fluffy bread. Stretch out the dough, then cut it into two pieces. Squeeze the dough into the tins using a fork to press both ends.
2. Place ingredients into a bowl for filling. Sure it's a little bit solid. Cover the second round of pie foil. . Preheat the Fryer for five minutes to 300 °F. You ought to blend in, take a basket pan, then cover it. If the pastry is golden brown, take the tin off and let it cool. Divide into slices and serve with a chocolate dollop.
Nutrition: Calories: 45 Fat: 7g, Protein: 8g.

Peanut Butter and Jam Muffins

(Ready in about 30 mins | Servings 5 | Normal)

Ingredients:

- 1 cup + 2 tbsp. of glazed sugar
- 1 1/2 + 2 tbsp of all-purpose flour
- 1 tbsp. of baking powder
- 1/2 tbsp. of baking sauce
- 2 tbsp. of marmalade
- 2 tbsp. of peanuts butter
- 1tbsp of butter, unsalted
- 2cups of buttermilk
- Parchment paper

Directions:

1. Add the flour and the buttermilk to a dish. Fold the mixture with the aid of a sparkling spatula. Insert the jelly and swirl the ingredients to make sure the jelly comes with it. Add the rest components to the bowl and finish mixing materials. Don't over-mix.

2. Grease the muffin cups and use the parchment paper to fill them in. Transfer the mix to the cups, then set them aside.

3. Preheat the Fryer for five minutes to 300 °F. Set the muffin cups in order in the basket and lower to 250 °F. Cool in the Air Basket and serve.

Nutrition: Calories: 34, Fat: 6g, Protein: 7g.

Cookie Multigrain

(Ready in about 16 mins | Servings 5 | Normal)

Ingredients:

- 1 all-purpose cup of flour
- 1 tablespoon of flour
- 1 tsp. of baking powder
- 1tbsp of glucose, liquid
- 1 cup of blended kernels
- 1/2 cup of dairy
- 1 tbsp. of butter, unsalted
- 2 tsp. of honey

Directions:

1. In a large tub, mix the dry ingredients and steam the glucose with limited water. Place the glucose, honey, and butter in the dish, then the milk.You'll need to use a pin to shape

the dough. Make cookies, and put them on a ready cookie sheet.

2. Preheat the Fryer for five minutes to 300 °F. Place in the baking tray in the basket and lower to 250 °F. Turn off when cookies are placed in the tray.Place them in an airtight jar when the cookies have cooled

Nutrition: Calories: 56, Fat: 2g, Protein: 7g.

Dry Fruit Muffins

(Ready in about 30 mins | Servings 5 | Normal)

Ingredients:
- 2 cups of usable flour
- 1 1⁄2 cups of milk
- 1⁄2 tsp. of baking powder
- 1⁄2 tsp. of baking sauce
- 2 tbsp. of butter
- 1 cup of blended nuts
- 1 cup of sugar
- 1 cup of oats
- Cups of muffin or paper cups of butter

Directions:

1. Mix the ingredients and use the fingers to create a crumbly combination. Split the milk into 2 parts, and introduce one part to the milk and baking powder. Shake the milk mixture now and add it mushy and start whisking the ingredients quickly.

3. Unless a smooth batter is obtained, the mixture must be transferred into a muffin cup and set aside. Five minutes to heat the fryer to 300 °F. You ought to blend in muffin cups and fill the pot. Heat the quince muffins for fifteen minutes to verify whether the muffins are baked using a toothpick or not.

4. Remove the tassels and serve hot.

Nutrition: Calories: 100, Fat: 12g, Protein: 6g.

Pear Pudding

(Ready in about 25 mins | Servings 5 | Normal)

Ingredients:
- 2 cups of pear pulp
- 2 cups of milk
- Two tbsp. of mine custard
- Three tbsp. of glazed sugar
- Three tbsp. of butter, unsalted

Directions:

1. In a saucepan, heat the milk and the sugar and add the custard powder. Then whisk the pear pulp until you have an ethnic mixture.
2. Preheat the Fryer for five minutes to 300 °F. Place the platter in the pan basket and cool down to 250 °F. Heat 10 minutes and then cold down.
Nutrition: Calories: 90, Fat: 10g, Protein: 7g.

Pistachio Pancakes

(Ready in about 16 mins | Servings 4 | Normal)
Ingredients:
- 2 tbsp. of cut pistachio
- 1 1/2 tablespoon of almond flour
- Three eggs
- 2 tsp. of dry basil
- 2 tsp. of dried parsley
- Salt and pepper for taste
- Three tbsp. of butter

Directions:
1. The AirFryer is preheated to 250 °F. Mix all the ingredients in a tiny dish. Make sure the mixture is smooth and balanced.
2. Take a mound from a pancake and sprinkle it with butter. Place the batter in the mound, and put it in the basket of an AirFryer. Cook until all sides of the pancake have browned. Use maple syrup to serve.
Nutrition: Calories: 56, Fat: 5g, Protein: 6g.

Papaya Pancakes

(Ready in about 15 mins | Servings 4 | Normal)
Ingredients:
- 1 cup of grated papaya
- 1 1/2 tablespoon of almond flour
- Three eggs
- 2 tsp. of dry basil
- 2 tsp. of dried parsley
- Salt and pepper to the taste
- 3 tbsp. of butter

Directions:
1. The AirFryer is preheated to 250 °F. Mix all the ingredients in a small container.

Make sure the mixture is smooth and balanced. Take a mound from a pancake and sprinkle it with sugar. Place the batter in the mound, and put it in the basket of an AirFryer.

2. Cook until all sides of the pancake have browned. Use maple syrup to serve.

Nutrition: Calories: 156, Fat: 7g, Protein: 11g.

SpongyBanana Cake

(Ready in about 29 mins | Servings 5 | Normal)

Ingredients:
- Half cup of condensed milk
- 1 cup of all-purpose flour
- 2 cups of banana mashed
- 1⁄2 tsp. of baking sauce
- 1⁄2 tsp. of baking powder
- 1⁄2 cup of gas
- 3 tbsp. of glazed sugar
- 1⁄2 cup of baking soda
- Parchment or butter paperto line the tin

Directions:
1. Bring the products together just to form a smooth and thick batter. Lubricate a buttered cake pan and then cover it with parchment or butter paper. Put the batter into the pan.
2. Preheat the Fryer for five minutes to 300 °F. Take a basket pan, then cover it. Fifteen minutes to prepare the cake and check whether the cake is baked using a toothpick or not. Remove tin, slice the cake, and serve.

Nutrition: Calories: 100, Fat: 12g, Protein: 6g.

Nannyberry cake

(Ready in about 17 mins | Servings 4 | Normal)

Ingredients:
- 1 tbsp. of butter, unsalted
- Two tbsp of freshwater
- 1 cup of pulp nannyberry
- 1 all-purpose cup of flour
- One and a half cup of condensed milk

Directions:
1. Put the ingredients together and stir until a smooth combination is obtained. Prepare a

jar of butter, greasing it. The mixture is transferred into the container.

2. Preheat the Fryer for five minutes to 300 °F. Take a basket pan, then cover it. Test if the cake is baked using a toothpick or a knife. Serve with a dollop of ice cream.

Nutrition: Calories: 45, Fat: 8g, Protein: 4g.

Key Custard in the Lime

(Ready in about 20 mins | Servings 5 | Normal)

Ingredients:

- 2 cups of usable flour
- 1 1/2 cups of milk
- 1/2 tsp. of baking powder
- 1/2 tsp. of baking sauce
- 2 tbsp. of brown sugar
- 1 cup of sugar
- 1 cup of lime key juice
- Cups for muffin or cloth cups of butter

Directions:

1. Mix all the ingredients and use the fingers to create a crumbly combination. Apply the baking soda to the milk and continue mixing. Stir in this milk, and mix and make a paste, to be passed to the muffin cups.

2. Preheat the Fryer for five minutes to 300 °F. You ought to blend in and cover the muffin cups in the box. Heat the muffins for fifteen minutes to verify whether the muffins are baked using a toothpick or not. Remove the tassels and serve hot.

Nutrition: Calories: 45, Fat: 7g, Protein: 2g.

Rambutan Cakes

(Ready in about 21 mins | Servings 5 | Normal)

Ingredients:

- 2 cups of usable flour
- 1 1/2 cups of milk
- 1/2 tsp. of baking powder
- 1/2 tsp. of baking sauce
- Two tbsp. of butter
- 1 cup of sugar
- 1 cup of sliced rambutan
- Two tsp. of vinegar

- Cups of muffin or paper cups of butter

Directions:

1. Mix all the ingredients and use the fingers to create a crumbly combination. Apply the baking soda and vinegar to the milk and finish blending. Add this milk into the mixture and produces a batter that you need to pass to cups of muffins.

2. Preheat the Fryer for five minutes to 300 °F. Cover the muffin cups in the basket. Heat the muffins for fifteen minutes to verify whether the muffins are baked using a toothpick or not.

3. Remove the tassels and serve hot.

Nutrition: Calories: 47 Fat: 9g, Protein: 4g.

Grapefruit and Honey Pudding

(Ready in about 20 mins | Servings 4 | Normal)

Ingredients:

- 2 cups of grapefruit, cubed
- 2 cups of milk
- 1 cup of honey
- 2 tbsp. of custard powder
- 3 tbsp. of butter unsalted

Directions:

1. In a saucepan, boil the milk and the sugar and add the custard powder. Stir in the sugar and grapefruit until the paste is thick.

2. Preheat the heat for 5 minutes to 300 °F. Place the dish in the pan and switch temperature down to 250 °F. Cook 10 minutes, then set aside to cool down.

Nutrition: Calories: 56, Fat: 8g, Protein: 10g.

Grapefruit Flakes

(Ready in about 15 mins | Servings 4 | Normal)

Ingredients:

- One and a half cup of plain flour
- Half cup of almond flour
- 3 tbsp. of butter unsalted
- 2 tbsp. of glazed sugar
- 2 cups of cold water
- 1 tbsp. of shredded cashew

Filling with:

- 1 cup of cubed grapefruit
- 1 cup of fresh cream
- 3 tbsp. of butter

Directions:
1. Mix the rice, cocoa powder, butter, and sugar in a big bowl with your fingers. The blend should be breadcrumbs-like. Knead the dough with the cold milk and allow it to cool for 10 minutes. Roll dough out into the cake and pinch the pie sides.
2. Place ingredients into a tub for filling. Sure it's a little bit thick—Preheat the Fryer for five minutes to 300 °F.
3. Take a basket pan, then cover it. If the pastry is golden brown, take the tin off and let it cool. Divide into pieces and serve with a chocolate dollop.
Nutrition: Calories: 100, Fat: 10g, Protein: 12g.

AsparagusPancakes

(Ready in about 15 mins | Servings 4 | Normal)
Ingredients:
- 1 (shredded asparagus)
- 1 1⁄2 cups of almond flour
- Three eggs
- Two tsp. of dry basil
- Two tsp. of dried parsley
- Salt and pepper to the taste
- 3 tbsp. of butter

Directions:
1. The AirFryer is preheated to 250 °F. Mix all the ingredients in a tiny bowl. Make sure the mixture is smooth and seamless. Take a mound from a pancake and sprinkle it with butter. Place the batter in the mold and put it in the basket of an AirFryer.
2. Cook until both sides of the pancake have browned. Use maple syrup for serving.
Nutrition: Calories: 50, Fat: 12g, Protein: 11g.

Pudding of Guava

(Ready in about 18 mins | Servings 3 | Normal)
Ingredients:
- 2 cups of milk
- 2 cups of pulp guava
- 2 cups of almond flour
- 2 tbsp. of mine custard

- 3 tbsp. of glazed sugar
- 3 tbsp. of butter, unsalted

Directions:

1. In a saucepan, simmer the milk and the sugar and add the custard powder. Mix with the almond flour and bring to a boil until the mixture is thick. Blend the pulp into the guava. Add the combination and stir until the pigment is fully spread.

2. Preheat the Fryer for five minutes to 300 °F. Place the platter in the pan basket and cool down to 250 °F. Fry 10 minutes, and place to cool apart.

Nutrition: Calories: 45, Fat: 3g, Protein: 6g.

Waffles with PoachedPear

(Ready in about 23 mins | Servings 3 | Normal)

Ingredients:

- 3 cups of all-in-one powder
- Three eggs
- 3 tbsp.of butter
- 1 cup of poached pear, diced

Directions:

1. The AirFryer is preheated to 250 °F. Combine the ingredients in a shallow bowl, except for the poached pear.

2. Make sure the blend is consistent and well balanced. Take a buttered waffle mold, then grate it. Apply the mound to the batter and place it in the basket of an AirFryer. Cook until both sides tan. Trying to create a cavity and add the poached pears, or garnish them.

Nutrition: Calories: 56, Fat: 8g, Protein: 8g.

PuddingGrapes

(Ready in about 15 mins | Servings 4 | Normal)

Ingredients:

- 2 cups of milk
- 2 cups of almond flour
- Three tbsp. of grapefruit juice
- Two tbsp. of custard powder
- 3 tbsp. of glazed sugar
- 3 tbsp. of butter unsalted

Directions:

1. In a saucepan, boil the milk and the sugar and add the custard powder. Whisk with the almond flour and grape juice until the solution becomes thick.

2. Preheat the Fryer for five minutes to 300 °F. Place the platter in the pan basket and cool down to 250 °F. Cook 10 minutes, and set to cool off.
Nutrition: Calories: 5, Fat: 10g, Protein: 9g.

Semolina Pancakes

(Ready in about 15 mins | Servings 2 | Normal)
Ingredients:

- 2 cups of pudding with semolina
- 1 1/2 cup of almond flour
- 3 eggs
- Two tsp. of dry basil
- 2 tsp. of dried parsley
- Salt and pepper
- 3 tbsp.of butter

Directions:
1. The AirFryer is preheated to 250 °F. Mix all the ingredients in such a tiny dish. Make sure the mixture is perfectly smooth and balanced.
2. Take a mound from a pancake and sprinkle it with butter.Place the batter in the mound, and put it in the basket of an AirFryer. Cook before pancake on both sides browned and served with maple syrup on both sides.
Nutrition: Calories: 12, Fat: 3g, Protein: 4g.

Date Cakes

(Ready in about 15 mins | Servings 2 | Normal)
Ingredients:

- 2 cups of usable flour
- 1 1/2 cups of milk
- 2 cups of mashed and dates pureed
- 1/2 tsp. of baking powder
- 1/2 tsp. of baking soda
- 2 tbsp. of butter
- 2 tbsp. of sugar
- Muffin cup

Directions:
1. Blend the ingredients and use the fingertips to get a crumbly blend. Insert the baking

soda into the milk and keep mixing. Add this milk to the mixture and create a batter, to be passed to the muffin cups.

2. Preheat the Fryer for five minutes to 300 °F. You need to blend in and cover the muffin cups in the basket. Cook the muffins for fifteen minutes to verify whether the muffins are baked using a toothpick or not. Remove the cups and serve hot.

Nutrition: Calories: 50, Fat: 5g, Protein: 11g.

Pajamas Jiggery

(Ready in about 15 mins | Servings 2 | Normal)
Ingredients:

- 2 cups of milk
- 1 cup of jiggery melted
- 2 tbsp. of custard powder
- 3 tbsp. of glazed sugar
- 3 tbsp. of butter, unsalted

Directions:

1. In a saucepan, boil the milk and the sugar and add the custard powder through the jiggery and whisk until the mixture is thick. You need to stir well.

2. Preheat the Fryer for five minutes to 300 °F. Place the platter in the pan basket and cool down to 250 °F. Cook for ten mines and left alone to get cool down.

Nutrition: Calories: 5, Fat: 6g, Protein: 11g.

Semolina Pudding

(Ready in about 15 mins | Servings 2 | Normal)
Ingredients:

- 2 cups of milk
- 2 tbsp. of custard powder
- Three tbsp. of glazed sugar
- 2 tbsp. of semolina
- 3 tbsp. of butter, unsalted

Directions:

1. In a saucepan, boil the milk and sugar, add the custard powder and mix until prepared. Apply the semolina to the saucepan and ensure the mixture is becoming somewhat thicker.

2. Preheat the Fryer for five minutes to 300 °F. Place the platter in the pan basket and cool down to 250 °F. Heat 10 minutes and let it cool down.

Nutrition: Calories: 34, Fat: 9g, Protein: 13g.

Date Waffles

(Ready in about 18 mins | Servings 8 | Normal)

Ingredients:

- 3 cups of almond meal
- 3 eggs
- 2 tsp. of dry basil
- 2 tsp. of dried parsley
- Salt and pepper
- 3 tbsp. of butter
- 2 cups of dates, pitted and diced

Directions:

1. The AirFryer is preheated to 250 °F. Mix the ingredients, except the dates, in a shallow dish. Check it's a smooth and well-balanced blend.

2. Take a buttered waffle mold, then grate it. Apply the mound to the batter and put it in the basket of an AirFryer. Cook until all sides tan. Try to create a cavity, and fill with dates.

Nutrition: Calories: 232, Fat: 4g, Protein: 4g.

Pudding Times

(Ready in about 15 min | Servings 2 | Normal)

Ingredients:

- 2 tbsp. of powder custard
- 3 tbsp. of glazed sugar
- 3 tbsp. of butter unsalted
- 1 cup of dates pitted and diced

Directions:

1. In a saucepan, boil the milk and the sugar and add the custard powder rile up by the dates before you have a thick blend. Pour in the sliced fruits and Blend.

2. Preheat the Fryer for five minutes to 300 °F. Place the platter in the pan basket and cool down to 250 °F. Heat 10 minutes and set to cool down.

Nutrition: Calories: 60, Fat: 12g, Protein: 3g.

Mediterranean Splendor

(Ready in about 18 mins | Servings 5 | Normal)

Ingredients:

- 2 cups of milk
- 2 cups of almond flour
- 2 tbsp. of mine custard
- 3 tbsp. of glazed sugar
- 3 tbsp. of butter unsalted
- 2 cups of mix Mediterranean fruit

Directions:

1. In a saucepan, heat the milk and the sugar and add the custard powder. Combine with the almond flour and mix until the paste is thick. Add the fruit mixture to the bowl.

2. Preheat the Fryer for five minutes to 300 Fahrenheit. Place the platter in the pan basket and cool down to 250 °F. Heat 10 minutes and ready to cool down.

Nutrition: Calories: 98, Fat: 42g, Protein: 33g.

Pudding of Guava

(Ready in about 12 mins | Servings 3 | Normal)

Ingredients:

- 2 cups of butter
- 2 cups of almond flour
- Two tbsp. of mine custard
- Three tbsp. of glazed sugar
- Three tbsp. of butter unsalted
- 2 cups of pulp guava

Directions:

1. In a saucepan, heat the milk and the sugar and add the custard powder. Combine with the almond flour and whisk until the paste is thick. Mix in the guava pulp to the combination.

2. Preheat the Fryer for five minutes to 300 °F. Place the platter in the pan basket and cool down to 250 °F. Heat 10 minutes and ready to cool down.

Nutrition: Calories: 50, Fat: 34g, Protein: 12g.

Passion Fruit Pudding

(Ready in about 20 mins | Servings 4 | Normal)

Ingredients:

- 2 cups of almond flour
- 2 cups of milk
- 2 cups of passion fruit pulp
- 2 tbsp. of mine custard
- 3 tbsp. of glazed sugar
- 3 tbsp. of butter, unsalted

Directions:

1. In a saucepan, simmer the milk and the sugar and add the custard powder and flour and whisk until the mixture is thick. Finely chop the apricot and Throw it into the mix.

2. Preheat the Fryer for five minutes to 300 °F. Place the platter in the pan basket and cool down to 250 °F. Heat 10 minutes and ready to cool down. Cover the fruit over the bread and serve.

Nutrition: Calories: 50, Fat: 24g, Protein: 2g.

BlackcurrantPudding

(Ready in about 20 mins | Servings 4 | Normal)

Ingredients:

- 2 cups of milk
- 2 cups of almond flour
- 2 tbsp. of mine custard
- 3 tbsp. of glazed sugar
- 1 cup of pulp with black currant
- 3 tbsp. of butter unsalted

Directions:

1. In a saucepan, simmer the milk and the sugar and add the custard powder. Combine with the almond flour and stir until the paste is thick. Slice the figs fine and then apply it to the blend.

2. Preheat the Fryer for five minutes to 300 °F. Place the platter in the pan basket and cool down to 250 °F. Heat 10 minutes and set to cool down.

Nutrition: Calories: 43, Fat: 23g, Protein: 12g.

Plum Pancakes

(Ready in about 19 mins | Servings 2 | Normal)

Ingredients:

- 1 cup of sliced prunes

- 1 1/2 tablespoon of almond flour
- 3 eggs
- 1 tsp. of honey
- Salt and pepper
- 3 tbsp. of butter

Directions:
1. The AirFryer is preheated to 250 °F. Mix all the ingredients in a small container. Make sure the mixture is good seamless, and stable. Take a mound from a pancake and grate it with sugar.
2. Place the batter in the mound and put it in the basket of an AirFryer. Cook until all sides of the pancake have browned. Use maple syrup to serve.
Nutrition: Calories: 43, Fat: 23g, Protein: 12g.

Caramel Blueberry

(Ready in about 20 mins | Servings 4 | Normal)
Ingredients:
- 2 cups of milk
- 2 cups of dried custard
- 3 tbsp. of glazed sugar
- 1 cup of blueberry sliced
- 3 tbsp. of butter, unsalted
- Four tbsp. of caramel

Directions:
1. In a saucepan, simmer the milk and sugar, introduce the custard powder, and whisk it to get a variation in thickness. Add the slices of blueberry, and mix it.
2. Preheat the Fryer for five minutes to 300 °F. Place the platter in the pan basket and cool down to 250 °F. Heat 10 minutes and let it cool down. Cover the caramel over the platter and serve warm.
Nutrition: Calories: 23, Fat: 25g, Protein: 2g.

Pudding BarbaDine

(Ready in about 20 mins | Servings 3 | Normal)
Ingredients:
- 1 cup of barba dine pulp
- 2 cups of milk
- Two tbsp. of mine custard

- Three tbsp. of glazed sugar
- Three tbsp. of butter, unsalted
- 1 cup slices of strawberries

Directions:

1. In a saucepan, simmer the milk and the sugar and add the custard powder. Whisk with the Barba dine pulp before you achieve a thick mixture.

2. Preheat the Fryer for five minutes to 300 °F. Put the platter in the pan basket and cool down to 250 °F. Heat 10 minutes and prepare to cool down. Top with strawberry.

Nutrition: Calories: 45, Fat: 15g, Protein: 5g.

Walnut Milk

(Ready in about 18 mins | Servings 4 | Normal) **Ingredients:**

- 2 cups of powdered walnut
- 2 cups of milk
- One tsp. of gelatin
- Two tbsp. of powder custard
- Three tbsp. of glazed sugar
- Three tbsp. of butter unsalted

Directions:

1. In a saucepan, simmer the milk and the sugar and incorporate the custard powder followed by the walnut powder and whisk until the mixture is thick. Mix in gelatin and ingredients also blend well.

2. Preheat the Fryer for five minutes to 300 °F. Place the platter in the pan basket and cool down to 250 °F. Heat 10 minutes and set to cool down.

Nutrition: Calories: 30, Fat: 11g, Protein: 6g.

Plum Pudding

(Ready in about 20 mins | Servings 3 | Normal)

Ingredients:

- 1 cup of plum pulp
- 2 cups of milk
- 2 tbsp. of custard
- Three tbsp. of glazed sugar
- Three tbsp. of butter unsalted

Directions:

1. In a saucepan, simmer the milk and the sugar and add the custard powder followed by the banana juice and whisk until the paste is thick.

2. Preheat the Fryer for five minutes to 300 °F. Place the platter in the pan basket and cool down to 250 °F. Heat 10 minutes and ready to cool down.

Nutrition: Calories: 30, Fat: 5g, Protein: 4g.

Apple Pudding

(Ready in about 24 mins | Servings 3 | Normal)

Ingredients:
- 1 cup of apple pulp
- 2 cups of milk
- 2 tbsp. of powder custard
- 3 tbsp. of glazed sugar
- 3 tbsp. of butter unsalted
- 1 cup of strawberries slices

Directions:

1. In a saucepan, simmer the milk and the sugar and add the custard powder followed by apple pulp and blend until a thick mixture is obtained.

2. Preheat the Fryer for five minutes to 300 °F. Place the platter in the pan basket and cool down to 250 °F. Heat 10 minutes and prepare to cool down. Garnish with strawberry slices.

Nutrition: Calories: 20, Fat: 6g, Protein: 3g.

ChestnutTart

(Ready in about 27 mins | Servings 2 | Normal)

Ingredients:
- One and a half cup plain flour
- 3 tbsp. of butter, unsalted
- 2 tbsp.of glazed sugar
- 2 cups of cool water
- 1 tbsp.of shredded cashew

For filling:
- 2 cups of chestnut, diced
- 1 cup of fresh cream
- 3 tbsp. of butter

Directions:

1. Combine the rice, cocoa powder, butter, and sugar in a big bowl with your fingers. The combination must be breadcrumbs-like. Knead the dough with the aid of cold milk and allow it to cool for 10 minutes. Roll dough out into the pie and pinch the pie edges.

2. Place the ingredients into a container for filling. Ensure it's a little bit thick.
3. Preheat the Fryer for five minutes to 300 °F. You will need to position the tin in a basket then cover it. If the pastry is golden brown, it's ready. Divide into pieces and serve with a cream dollop.
Nutrition: Calories: 18, Fat: 5g, Protein: 5g.

Waffles with Kidney Beans

(Ready in about 25 mins | Servings 4 | Normal)
Ingredients:
- 1 1/2 tablespoon of almond flour
- 3 eggs
- 2 Tsp. of dry basil
- 2 tsp. of dried parsley
- Salt and pepper
- 3 tbsp.of butter
- 1 cup of pickled beans

Directions:
1. The AirFryer is preheated to 250 °F. Blend the ingredients, except the beans, in a separate bowl. Be sure that it's a smooth and well-balanced blend.
2. Take a buttered waffle mold, then grate it. Apply the mold to the batter and place it in the basket of an AirFryer. Cook until all sides tan. Then, make a cavity fill it with the beans, and serve.
Nutrition: Calories: 21, Fat: 7g Protein: 6g.

Mangos TeenPudding

(Ready in about 28 mins | Servings 4 | Normal)
Ingredients:
- 1 cup of teen mango pulp
- 2 cups of milk
- 2 tbsp. of maize flour
- 3 tbsp. of glazed sugar
- 3 tbsp. of butter unsalted

Directions:
1. In a saucepan, simmer the milk and the sugar, add the custard powder followed by the pulp of teen mangos, and whisk until the paste is thick.
2. Preheat the Fryer for five minutes to 300 °F. Put the platter in the pan basket and cool down to 250 °F. Heat 10 minutes and ready to cool down.
Nutrition: Calories: 18, Fat: 5g Protein: 7g.

Apple Custard Cake

(Ready in about 15 mins | Servings 2 | Normal)

Ingredients:

- 1 tbsp. of butter unsalted
- 2 tbsp. of freshwater
- 2 tsp. of vanilla extract
- 1 cup of cornflour
- 1 cup of apple custard juice
- Half cup of condensed milk

Directions:

1. Put the ingredients together and whisk before the mixture becomes smooth. Prepare a tin of butter, greasing it. Move the mixture into the pan.

2. Preheat the Fryer for five minutes to 300 °F. You ought to move the tin into a basket pan, then shield it. Check that the cake's getting upright. Cold the cake, and serve.

Nutrition: Calories: 14, Fat: 7g Protein: 9g.

Custard Mango

(Ready in about 20 mins | Servings 4 | Normal)

Ingredients:

- 2 cupsof mango slices
- 2 cups of butter
- 2 tbsp. of mine custard
- 3 tbsp. of glazed sugar
- 3 tbsp. of butter, unsalted

Directions:

1. In a saucepan, simmer the milk and the sugar and add the custard powder, followed by Slices of the mango, and whisk until the mixture is thick.

2. Preheat the Fryer for five minutes to 300 °F. Place the platter in the pan basket and cool down to 250 °F. Heat 10 minutes and ready to cool down.

Nutrition: Calories: 31, Fat: 11g, Protein: 6g.

CitrusCustard

(Ready in about 24 mins | Servings 2 | Normal)

Ingredients:

- 1 cup of Kiwis
- 1 tsp. of lemon zest

- 1 tsp. of orange peel
- 2 cups of butter
- 2 tbsp. of mine custard
- 3 tbsp. of glazed sugar
- 3 tbsp.of butter, unsalted

Directions:
1. In a saucepan, boil the milk and the sugar and add the custard powder from the fruits and whisk until the mixture is thick.
2. Preheat the Fryer for five minutes to 300 °F. Place the platter in the pan basket and cool down to 250 °F. Heat 10 minutes and ready to cool down.
Nutrition: Calories: 15, Fat: 1g, Protein: 4

Muffins Persimmons

(Ready in about 27 mins | Servings 4 | Normal)
Ingredients:
- 2 cups of corn starch
- 1 1/2 cups of milk
- Three eggs
- 2 tbsp of butter
- 2 tbsp. of sugar
- 2 cups of persimmons pulp
- 1 tsp. of vanilla pulp
- Muffin cups

Directions:
1. Mix the ingredients and use the fingers to create a crumbly combination. Apply the baking soda to the milk, and constantly blend. Stir in this milk and make a paste, to be passed to the muffin cups.
2. Preheat the Fryer for five minutes to 300 °F. You ought to blend in and cover the muffin cups in the basket. Heat the muffins for fifteen minutes to confirm if the muffins are baked; just use a toothpick. Serve hot.
Nutrition: Calories: 12, Fat: 4g, Protein: 7g.

MuffinsMango

(Ready in about 28 mins | Servings 2 | Normal)
Ingredients:
- 2 cups of usable flour

- 1 1/2 buttermilk of cup
- 1/2 tsp. of baking powder
- 1/2 tsp. of baking soda
- Two tablespoons of butter
- Two tbsp. of maple syrup
- Two cups of mango pulp
- Muffin tassels

Directions:
1. Combine all the ingredients and use your fingers to create a crumbly combination. Apply the baking soda to the milk and keep mixing. Stir in this milk and make a paste, to be passed to the muffin cups.
2. Preheat the Fryer for five minutes to 300 °F. You ought to blend in and cover the muffin cups in the basket. Heat the muffins for fifteenminutes to verify if the muffins are baked using a toothpick. Remove the cups and serve warm.

Nutrition: Calories: 23, Fat: 2g, Protein: 5g.

Vanilla Cake

(Ready in about 21 mins | Servings 2 | Normal)

Ingredients:
- 1 tbsp. of butter, unsalted
- Two tbsp. of freshwater
- Two tsp. of extract vanilla
- 1 cup of all-purpose flour
- Half cup of condensed milk

Directions:
1. Put the ingredients together and stir until the mixture becomes smooth. Start preparing a jar of butter, lubricating it. The liquid is moved into the pan.
2. Preheat the Fryer for five minutes to 300 °F. You ought to blend in. Take a basket pan, then cover it. Check that the cake's gotten up well. Cool the cakedown, and serve.

Nutrition: Calories: 7, Fat: 3g, Protein: 8g.

Jack Fruit Pudding

(Ready in about 20 mins | Servings 3 | Normal)

Ingredients:
- 2 cups of ripened jackfruit
- 2 cups of butter

- Two tbsp. of mine custard
- Three tbsp. of glazed sugar
- Three tbsp. of butter unsalted

Directions:

In a saucepan, simmer the milk and the sugar and add the custard powder. Whisk in the orange juice until the paste is thick.

2. Preheat the Fryer for five minutes to 300 °F. Place the platter in the bowl and cool down to 250 °F. Heat 10 minutes and ready to cool down.

Nutrition: Calories: 12, Fat: 4g, Protein: 7g.

Cupcake of Mixed Fruit

(Ready in about 20 mins | Servings 2 | Normal)

Ingredients:

- 1 tbsp. of butter unsalted
- 2 tbsp. of freshwater
- 2 cups of fruit added in
- 1 cup of all-purpose flour
- One and a half cup condensed milk

Directions:

1. Put the products together and stir before the mixture becomes smooth. Prepare a tin of butter, greasing it. The mixture is transferred into the pan.

2. Preheat the Fryer for five minutes to 300 °F. You ought to blend in. Take a basket tin, then shield it. Check that the cake's getting up well. Cold the cake, and serve.

Nutrition: Calories: 11, Fat: 5g, Protein: 4g.

Blueberry Cake

(Ready in about 17 mins | Servings 2 | Normal)

Ingredients:

- 1 tbsp. of unsalted butter
- 2 tbsp.of clean water
- 2 cups of sliced whey
- 1 cup of all-purpose flour
- 1/2 cup of condensed milk

Directions:

1. Put the products together and whisk before the mixture becomes smooth. Prepare a tin of butter, greasing it. The liquid is moved into the pan.

2. Preheat the Fryer for five minutes to 300 °F. You ought to fit in a basket pan, then cover it. Check that the cake's getting upright. Caramelize with chocolate chips when the cake has cooled, and offer.
Nutrition: Calories: 9, Fat: 4g, Protein: 2g.

Corn Waffles

(Ready in about 16 mins | Servings 4 | Normal)
Ingredients:
- 1 1/2 tablespoon of almond flour
- Three eggs
- Two tsp. of dried basil
- Two tsp. of dried parsley
- Salt and pepper
- 3 tbsp. of butter
- 2 cups of cooked corn and mayonnaise

Directions:
1. The AirFryer is preheated to 250 °F.
2. Mix the ingredients in a small tub, except the corn and mayonnaise integrated. Make sure the blend is consistent and well balanced.Take a buttered waffle mold, then grate it.
3. Apply the mound to the batter and place it in the basket of an AirFryer. Cook until all sides tan. Create and fill a cavity with the corn and mayonnaise, and serve.
Nutrition: Calories: 10, Fat: 3g, Protein: 4g.

Mexican Waffles

(Ready in about 17 mins | Servings 3 | Normal)
Ingredients:
- 1 1/2 cup of almond flour
- Three eggs
- Two tsp. of dried basil
- Two tsp. of dried parsley
- Salt and pepper
- Three tbsp. of butter
- 1 cup of jalapenos marinated
- 1 cup of green olives
- 1 cup of black olives
- 2 tbsp. of salsa

Directions:

1. The AirFryer is preheated to 250 Fahrenheit. Comb the ingredients in a small bowl, except the jalapenos, olives, and salsa. Ensure the blend is smooth and well balanced.

2. Take a buttered waffle mold, then grate it. Apply the mound to the batter and place it in the basket of an AirFryer. Cook until all sides tan.

3. Create a cavity and sprinkle with jalapenos, olives, and salsa.

Nutrition: Calories: 13, Fat: 4g, Protein: 5g.

Mexican Waffles

(Ready in about 21 min | Servings 3 | Normal)

Ingredients:

- 1 1/2 cup of almond flour
- Three eggs
- Two tsp. of dried basil
- Two tsp. of dried parsley
- Salt and pepper
- Three tbsp. of butter
- 1 cup of jalapenos, marinated
- 1 cup of green olives
- 1 cup of black olives
- 2 tbsp. of salsa

Directions:

The AirFryer is preheated to 250 °F. Combine the ingredients in a small bowl, except the jalapenos, olives, and the salsa. Ensure the blend is smooth and well balanced.

2. Take a buttered waffle mold, then grate it. Apply the mound to the batter and place it in the basket of an AirFryer. Cook until all sides tan.

3. Create a cavity and sprinkle with jalapenos, olives, and salsa.

Nutrition: Calories: 12, Fat: 5g, Protein: 7g.

Mediterranean Waffles

(Ready in about 20 mins | Servings 2 | Normal)

Ingredients:

- 1 1/2 tablespoon of almond flour
- Three eggs
- 2 tsp. of dried basil
- 2 Tsp.of dried parsley

- Salt and pepper
- 3 tbsp.of butter
- 1 cup of coleslaw

Directions:

1. The AirFryer is preheated to 250 °F. Combine the ingredients in a shallow bowl, except for the coleslaw.

2. Ensure the blend is consistent and well balanced. Take a buttered waffle mold, then grate it. Apply the mold to the batter and place it in the basket of an AirFryer. Cook until all sides tan. Develop and fill a cavity with the coleslaw, and serve.

Nutrition: Calories: 3, Fat: 3g, Protein: 5g

Pudding of Cranberry

(Ready in about 26 mins | Servings 3 | Normal)

Ingredients:

1 cup of cranberry juice

2 cups of milk

Two tbsp. of cornflour

Three tbsp. of glazed sugar

Three tbsp. of butter, unsalted

Directions:

1. In a saucepan, boil the milk and the sugar and add the cranberry juice's custard powder until the paste is thick.

2. Preheat the Fryer for five minutes to 300 °F. Put the platter in the basket and cool down to 250 °F. Cook on for 10 minutes and set to cool down.

Nutrition: Calories: 5, Fat: 4g, Protein: 2g.

Butterscotch Cake

(Ready in about 20 mins | Servings 2 | Normal)

Ingredients:

- 1 tbsp. of butter, unsalted
- 2 tbsp. of freshwater
- 2 tsp. of vanilla extract
- Two tbsp. of yellow sucrose
- 1 cup of cornflour
- Half cup of condensed milk

Directions:

Put the ingredients together and stir before the mixture becomes smooth. Prepare a tin of butter, greasing it. Move the liquid into the container.

2. Preheat the Fryer for five minutes at 300 Fahrenheit. You ought to blend in the basket pan, then cover it. Check that the cake's getting upright. Serve and enjoy.

Nutrition: Calories: 9, Fat: 5g, Protein: 3g.

Kiwi Custard

(Ready in about 21 mins | Servings 2 | Normal)

Ingredients:

- 1 cup of kiwi slices
- 2 cups of milk
- 2 tbsp. of mine custard
- 3 tbsp. of glazed sugar
- 3 tbsp. of butter unsalted

Directions:

1. In a saucepan, boil the milk and the sugar and add the custard powder, the kiwi slices and whisk until the mixture is thick.

2. Preheat the Fryer for five minutes to 300 °F. Place the platter in the pan basket and cool down to 250 °F. Heat 10 minutes and ready to cool down.

Nutrition: Calories: 6, Fat: 3g, Protein: 2g.

CustardFruit

(Ready in about 21 mins | Servings 3 | Normal)

Ingredients:

- 1 cup of fruit mixed in
- 2 cups of milk
- 2 tbsp. of mine custard
- 3 tbsp. of glazed sugar
- 3 tbsp. of butter unsalted

Directions:

1. In a saucepan, boil the milk and the sugar and add the custard powder, the combined fruits and whisk until the mixture is thick.

2. Preheat the Fryer for five minutes to 300 °F. Place the platter in the pan basket and cool down to 250 °F. Heat 10 minutes and ready to cool down.

Nutrition: Calories: 12, Fat: 5g, Protein: 3g.

Deep-FriedPuff Pastry Pie

(Ready in about 14 mins | Servings 2 | Normal)

Ingredients:

- Pastry: 200 grams
- 200g of clean sink
- Sugar to try
- Vegetable oil to the taste

Directions:

1. Split the plums
2. Cut the batter
3. Print the dough out and cover it in half the oven, sprinkle with pre-sugar
4. Preheat olive oil
5. Fry the patties until golden brown
6. Place the prepared pies on a paper towel to remove the excess oil.

Nutrition: Calories: 189, Fat: 2g, Protein: 4g.

Cooked Deep-Fried Bananas

(Ready in about 14 mins | Servings 2 | Normal)

Ingredients:

- Eight bananas
- 1 lemon
- 0.5 cup of flour
- 1 tablespoon of sugar
- 0.5 teaspoon of salt

Directions:

1. Knead the flour batter with a bowl of water and salt.
2. Shave out bananas.
3. Start preparing in the batter, roll 2-3 times and fry to 180 °F, oil till brown.
4. Place bananas on napkins dry.
5. Serve hot, sprinkle with powdered sugar and arrange with circles of lemon.

Nutrition: Calories: 200, Fat: 1.0g, Protein: 2g.

Deep-frying

(Ready in about 16 mins | Servings 2 | Normal)

Ingredients:

- 200g cottage cheese
- Three eggs
- Three spoonfuls of sugar
- Five soda teaspoons
- Five salt teaspoon
- 100g of sage cream
- 1 powdered sprinkling sugar
- Five cups of vegetable oil

Directions:
1. Cottage cheese, milk, sugar, soda, salt, blend, and match.
2. Form the curd mass balls.
3. Warm the vegetable oil in a deep fryer, put the balls in it, and fry for 10-15 minutes.
4. Pretty cool.
5. Top end sprinkled with icing sugar and served at the table with sour cream. **Nutrition:** Calories: 201, Fat: 2.01g, Protein: 3g.

Cottage CheeseDonuts / The "Remember Childhood" Balls

(Ready in about 16 mins | Servings 2 | Normal)
Ingredients:
- 200 to 250g of flour
- 200 grams of soft cheese cottage
- 1 egg
- 3-4 tablespoons of sugar
- Optional vanilla
- 0.5 teaspoons of baking powder
- A splash of salt
- To dust with powdered sugar
- Vegetable oil to deep-fried

Directions:
1. Place the egg in a cup, then add a pinch of salt, sugar, and whisk well.
2. Apply the cheese to the cottage and whisk well.
3. Mix the flour gently with the baking powder, then knead the dough.
4. Tiny balls from a test roll.
5. One minute to cook the curd fried donuts.
6. End the donuts laid on a towel or paper to make something out of the outpouring of Fat: Sprinkle with diced sugar and serve.
Nutrition: Calories: 209, Fat: 2g, Protein: 2g.

Curd Donuts

(Ready in about 17 mins | Servings 3 | Normal)

Ingredients:

- 600 g of cottage cheese
- 1 cup of sugar
- 4 eggs
- 1 bag of sugar vanilla
- 2 cups of fine flour
- 1 soda teaspoon (with a slide)
- A splash of salt
- Semolina
- Vegetable oil (fry)

Directions:

1. Include salt (a drop of salt), add sugar (+ vanilla), and cottage cheese eggs, whisk well.
2. Include the soda (if the cheese in the cottage is acidic, don't have to remove soda, if not bad-extinguish with vinegar) and flour, mix the batter. (They should be soft).
3. Shape balls from the test (if necessary, moisturize the hands with the water or vegetable oil lubricates), crumble in the seedlings, and cook, in deep frying, until finished.
4. Optionally, finished donuts can be wrapped in powdered sugar.

Nutrition: Calories: 212, Fat: 1g, Protein: 2g.

Apples Donuts

(Ready in about 14 mins | Servings 2 | Normal)

Ingredients:

- 5 apples
- Batter
- 2eggs
- 250g of flour
- 100ml of milk
- Five tablespoons of sugar (can be adjusted to taste or doubled)
- Vanilla

To sprinkle:

- Powdered sugar

To deep-fry:

- About 1 liter of vegetable oil

Directions:

1. Peel apples, cut them into rings, and remove their heart.
2. Get the batter ready. Stir the eggs and the flour, vanillin, and sugar together. Milk add gradually apply, but the clay didn't get very liquid.
3. Load oil and steam onto the brazier. You'll need to limit oil consumption. Take a small brazier or a deep bottom saucepan and fry one donut.
4. Apple rings sunk into a batter and inserted in deep frying. Fry of two sides before brown gold.
5. Put the fried donuts on a tray where you put the paper on the bottom napkin because they absorb all the extra fat.
6. Spray with icing sugar and put the donuts into another dish.

Nutrition: Calories: 213, Fat: 1g, Protein: 2g.

Donuts-OnPowdered Milk Balls

(Ready in about 14 mins | Servings 2 | Normal)

Ingredients:

- Four pieces of eggs
- 1 teaspoon of baking powder
- 200 to 250g of condensed milk
- 2 cups of vegetable oil
- 650–700g of flour

Directions:

1. Knead the dough with all the ingredients.
2. Roll the balls.
3. We heat the fryer in the fry and fry it.

Nutrition: Calories: 156, Fat: 1g, Protein: 0.4g.

Onion Rings

(Ready in about 12 mins | Servings 2 | Normal)

Ingredients:

- 3 onions
- 1 spoonful of flour
- 2 eggs
- 2 tablespoons of sliced bread
- Pepper and salt
- 4 cheese slices (for sandwiches)
- Roasting oil (300-400 ml for deep frying)

Directions:
1. Peel the onion, cut it into 5-7 mm rings.
2. Remove the rings, remove the film (so it doesn't get bitter).
3. Cheese is sliced into plates of 5–7 mm.
4. We lay cheese here between two rings (in between them) and connect the rings.
5. Bake in flour, in an onion, in minced bread, in an egg, in breadcrumbs.
6. Fry them for 2-3 minutes with hot oil on both sides.
Nutrition: Calories: 233, Fat: 1g, Protein: 2g.

Chebureks on a Batter

(Ready in about 15 mins | Servings 3 | Normal)
Ingredients:
- 3-3.5 glass of flour
- 1.5 cups of boiling water
- Salt

Filling with:
- 500 gr of stuffing
- 1 large onion
- Pepper and salt
- Sunflower cooking oil

Directions:
1. Pour 1.5 cups of boiling water into a pot, spill 1 cup of flour, comb, hold, stir, for about a minute, on a small fire. Let it cool. Add 2-2.5 cups of flour, then knead the dough.
2. Chop the onion finely, blend with sliced meat and add salt and pepper. You may add a couple of spoonful of cold water for juiciness.
3. Shape the chebureks, fry over a moderate flame in a deep-fried pan.
Nutrition: Calories: 190, Fat: 1g, Protein: 2g.

Cutlets Potatoes

(Ready in about 18 mins | Servings 2 | Normal)
Ingredients:
- 2 potatoes
- 20g of hard cheese
- 5g of greening
- 3tsp of pepper
- 30g of breadcrumbs

- 2 Batter's Eggs
- 4tbsp of vegetable cooking oil

Directions:

1. Let the potatoes boil.
2. Add salt and pepper before producing mashed potatoes. Thick. Mix the puree but be sure not to be too liquid.
3. Grate the cheese on a grinder, cut the ham if you want, but we slice the greens finely.
4. Put everything in the puree and blend well.
5. Form the cutlet's hands, dip it in an egg, roll it in the breadcrumbs.
6. We dump cutlets in deep-frying oil and fry until golden brown.

Nutrition: Calories: 200, Fat: 1g, Protein: 2g.

CushionedFried Cherries

(Ready in about 19 mins | Servings 2 | Normal)

Ingredients:

- Dough
- 1 egg
- 2 cups of glass flour (took wheat and rye, 1:1)
- Salt and sugar
- Less than 1⁄2 glass of water

Filling with:

- 1 glass of frozen or fresh pit cherries
- 3-4 tbsp. of sugar
- 1.5 starch teaspoon
- Vegetable frying oil

Directions:

1. Also added some seasoning in the dough here, but it is not entirely.
2. Knead the steep bread, wrap it in a sack of cellophane and leave for 30 minutes.
3. Mix the sugar and starch with cherry thaw if necessary.
4. Shape the dough in a thin layer (approximately 3 mm), cut into squares, or another suitable type for you. We laid a few cherries on the square. Fill the second square and cover the rims.
5. In a frying pan or deep frying pan, fry them in oil. Do not track, as soon as the crust was ruddy-then ready.

Nutrition: Calories: 200, Fat: 1g, Protein: 2g.

AmericanCorn-Dog

(Ready in about 18 mins | Servings 3 | Normal)

Ingredients:

- 140g of cornflour/polenta
- 140g of wheat flour
- 240ml of milk
- 3g of baking dough powder
- 12 pieces of sausages with cheese
- Salt to the taste
- 24 pcs of bamboo spindles
- 1 pcs egg
- Vegetable oil to deep-fried

Directions:

1. Mix the egg in the milk for the dough and eventually move into the dry place materials. The dough's consistency is something of a pancake.

2. Place the dough, for proof, for fifteen min.

3. We propose splitting the regular sausages into two, for convenience parts or baby-sausage.

4. Heat the deep fryers. Take sausage equally in the dough and fry for around 3-4 minutes, until a ruddy crust.

5. Serve usually with ketchup, mustard, or mayonnaise.

Nutrition: Calories: 178, Fat: 2g, Protein: 3g.

Peanut Butter

(Ready in about 13 mins | Servings 8 | Normal)

Ingredients

- 1 cup of smooth peanut butter no-sugar-added
- 1/3 cup of erythritol granular
- 1 big egg
- 1 teaspoon of vanilla extract

Directions:

1. Combine all the ingredients in a bowl until smooth. For 2 more minutes, begin stirring, and the mixture begins to thicken.

2. Roll out the mixture into eight balls and gently press to flatten out into 2 "circular discs.

3. Cut parchment to match your air-freezer and Set it in a basket. Put the cookies on the

basket Parchment—function as required in batches.

4 Change the temperature and set the timer to 320° F for eight minutes. 5 Flip the 6-minute mark over the cookies. Serve and enjoy!

Nutrition: Calories: 222, Fat: 2g, Protein: 3g.

Puffs with Cinnamon Cream

(Ready in about 24 mins | Servings 8 | Normal)

Ingredients

- Eight puffs (1 per serving) yields
- 1/2 cup of finely blanched almond flour
- 1/2 cup of low carb Protein: vanilla powder
- 1⁄2 cup of erythritol granular
- 1/2 teaspoon powder for baking
- 1 large egg
- 5 pieces of unsalted butter, melted
- 2 ounces of full-Fat: cream cheese
- 1/4 cup erythritol powder
- 1/4 cinnamon in a teaspoon
- 2 cups of heavy cream to whip
- 1/2 cubicle of vanilla extract

Directions:

1. Blend the almond flour, Protein: powder, erythritol granular, in a big dish, baking powder, egg, and butter until there is a dish form of soft dough.

2. Place the dough for 20 minutes in the fridge. Wet The Wet Water your face, and roll the dough into eight balls.

3. Cut a piece of parchment to match your basket with an AirFryer. When required, put the dough in batches Balls on top of parchment in an AirFryer basket.

4. Set the temperature to 380° F, then set the timer for six minutes.

5. Flip puffs of cream halfway through the cooking time.

6. Remove the puffs when the timer beeps and allow them to cool.

7. Beat the cream cheese in a medium saucepan, powdered Erythritol, cream, cinnamon, and vanilla until they're soft.

8. Put the mixture in a pastry bag or bag for storage. Snipped to the top. Cut the bottom of a small whole. Fill each of the puffs and apply some of the cream mixtures.

9. Store in an airtight jar for 2 days in the freezer.

Nutrition: Calories:112, Fat: 2g, Protein: 3g.

Bread by Caramel Monkey

(Ready in about 28 mins | Servings 5 | Normal)
Ingredients

- 1/2 cup finely blanched almond flour
- 1/2 cup vanilla low-carb Protein: powder
- 3/4 cup erythritol granular, broken down
- 1/2 cubicle baking powder
- 8 tablespoons of salted, melted, and sliced butter
- full-Fat: cream cheese 1 ounce, softened
- 1 big egg
- 1/4 cup heavy cream for whipping
- extract 1/2 teaspoon of vanilla

Directions:
1. Add almond flour, and protein in a large bowl powder, erythritol with 1/2 cup, baking powder, 5 tablespoons sugar, egg, and cream cheese.It will form a sticky dough.
2. Place the dough for 20 minutes in the fridge. It's going to roll into balls, be firm enough. Wet your hands with the aid of hot water, and twelve balls roll in. Bring the balls in a round of 6"baking dish.
3. Melt in a medium saucepan over medium heat the remaining butter with erythritol remaining. Higher heat and whisk until the mixture has become golden, then apply vanilla and cream. Separate from the sun and remove from the heat. Enable it for a few minutes to thicken while you are to keep boiling.
4. When the mixture is cooling, put the baking dish in the pan freezer basket.
5. Adjust the temperature and set the timer to 320° F for six minutes.
6. Turn the monkey's bread over when the timer beeps. Slide it back onto a plate and into the baking pan. Cook an extra 4 minutes before all the tops are turned brown.
7. Spill the caramel sauce over the bread of the ape and cook for 2 more minutes. Let cool absolutely until being served.
Nutrition: Calories: 332, Fat: 2g, Protein: 3g.

Danish Cream Cheese

(Ready in about 24 mins | Servings 4 | Normal)
Ingredients

- 3/4 cup of finely ground almond flour
- 1 cup of mozzarella shredded cheese
- 5 ounces of full-Fat: cream cheese, sliced

- 2 big yolks of egg
- 3/4 cup of erythritol powder, break
- 2 teaspoons of vanilla extract

Directions:
1. Apply the almond flour in a large microwave-safe tub, mozzarella, and cream cheese of 1 ounce. Mix and then, mix and then, 1-minute microwave.
2. Stir in the cup and add the egg yolks. Continue to stir before the dough shapes elastic. To the dough, add 1/2 cup of erythritol and 1 vanilla paste.
3. To match your AirFryer basket, cut a piece of parchment. Wet your hands with warm water, and tap the dough in a rectangle 1/4"large.
4. Combine the remaining cream cheese in a medium cup, and erythritol, and vanilla. Put this cream cheese in the mixture. Mixture the dough rectangle on the right side and fold. Turn the dough to the left side and press to seal. Place it in the basket of an AirFryer.
5. Set the temperature to 330° F, then set the timer for 15 Minutes.
6. Flip over the Danish one after 7 minutes.
7. Remove the Danish from the timer when the timer beeps. Parchment and cause to cool completely before cooling.
Nutrition: Calories: 234, Fat: 2g, Protein: 3g.

Danish Raspberry Bites

(Ready in about 24 mins | Servings 4 | Normal)
Ingredients:
- 1 cup of finely blanched almond flour
- 1 teaspoon of baking powder
- Three tablespoons of swerving granular
- 2 ounces of cream cheese with full fat, softened
- 1 big egg
- 10 teaspoons of raspberry sugar-free preserves

Directions:
1. In a wide tub, add all the ingredients except preserves before developing a wet dough.
2. Position the bowl for 20 minutes in the freezer until the dough is cool and roll into a ball.
3. Roll the dough into 10 balls and push the dough softly; each ball is centered. Place the preserves of 1 teaspoon in each ball centered.
4. Cut a piece of parchment to match your basket with an AirFryer. Place every bite of Danish on the parchment, press gently down to flatten the rim.
5. Change the temperature and set the timer to 400° F for 7 minutes.
6. Allow them to cool entirely before moving. Otherwise, they will cool completely before moving.
Nutrition: Calories: 234, Fat: 2g, Protein: 3g.

Cookie Balls of almond butter

(Ready in about 15 mins | Servings 10 | Normal)

Ingredients:

- ten balls yield (1 ball per serving)
- 1 cup of butter with almonds
- 1 big egg
- 1 teaspoon of vanilla
- 1/4 cup of low-carb Protein: powder
- 1/4 cup of erythritol powder
- 1/4 cup of unsweetened crushed coconut
- 1/4 cup of chocolate chips that are low-carb, sugar-free
- One and a half teaspoons of cinnamon

Directions:

1. Mix the almond butter and the egg in a big tub. Add in vanilla, Protein: powder, and erythritol.
2. Fold in coconut, chocolate, and cinnamon flakes. Roll into 1-inch balls. Place the balls in a 6-inch circular baking pan and place them into an AirFryer basket.
3. Set the temperature to 320° F, then set the timer for ten minutes.
4. Enable to cool to the full. Store in your airtight container for up to 4 days in the fridge.

Nutrition: Calories: 190, Fat: 3g, Protein: 4g.

Cinnamon Pork Rinds

(Ready in about 15 mins | Servings 10 | Normal)

Ingredients:

- Two ounces of rind pork
- 2 tablespoons of melted, unsalted butter
- 1/2 teaspoon of cinnamon
- 1/4 cup of erythritol powder

Directions:

1. Throw the pork rinds and butter in a large tub. Sprinkle, then toss equally with cinnamon and erythritol to coat.
2. Insert pork rinds into the basket of the AirFryer.
3. Set the temperature to 400° F, then set the timer for five minutes.
4. Immediately serve.

Nutrition: Calories: 223, Fat: 3g, Protein: 4g.

Brownies Pecan

(Ready in about 30 mins | Servings 6 | Normal)
Ingredients

- 1/2 cup of finely blanched almond flour
- 1/2 cup of erythritol powder
- 2 tablespoons of unsweetened ground chocolate
- 1/2 tsp. of baking powder
- 1/4 cup of unsalted, melted butter
- 1 big egg
- 1/4 cup of pecans
- 1/4 cup of chocolate chips that are low-carb, sugar-free

Directions:

1. Combine the almond flour, erythritol, chocolate, and sugar in a large dish. Add powder to prepare. Stir in egg and butter.
2. Add in the chocolate chips and pecans. Place the pan in the Air Fryer basket in a 6" circular baking pan.
3. Change the temperature and set the timer to 300° F for twenty minutes.
4. Put a toothpick in the middle would be inserted until completely cooked. Come out clean, let it cool down for 20 minutes, and firm up.

Nutrition: Calories: 234, Fat: 5g, Protein: 6g.

Mini Cheesecake

(Ready in about 30 mins | Servings 2 | Normal)
Ingredients

- 1/2 cup of walnuts
- 2 tbsp. of salted butter
- 2 spoonful of granular erythritol
- 4 ounces of cream cheese full-Fat:, softened
- 1 big egg
- 1/2 tsp. of vanilla extract
- 1/8 cup of erythritol powder

Directions:

1. In a bowl, combine walnuts, butter, and granular erythritol. Mix until components stick together, and it forms a dough.
2. Press the dough into a 4"springform pan and insert it into the AirFryer basket.
3. Set the temperature to 400° F, then set the timer for five minutes.

4. Remove the crust when the timer beeps, and let it cool.
5. Mix cream cheese with egg in a medium saucepan, vanilla extract, and powdered up to smooth erythritol.
6. On top of the baked walnut crust, a spoonful of mixture and place it in the basket of an AirFryer.
7. Set the temperature to 300°F, then set the timer for 10 minutes.
8. Once done, refrigerate 2 hours before serving.
Nutrition: Calories: 334, Fat: 5g, Protein: 6g.

Micro Cheesecake with Chocolate Espresso

(Ready in about 30 mins | Servings 2 | Normal)
Ingredients:
- 1/2 cup of walnuts
- 2 teaspoons of butter, salted
- 2 teaspoons of erythritol, granulated
- 4 ounces of cream cheese full-Fat:, melted
- 1 big egg
- 1/2 cubicle of vanilla extract
- 2 tablespoons of erythritol powder
- 2 tablespoons of unsweetened raw cocoa
- 1 espresso of teaspoon material

Directions:
1. In a cup, mix walnuts, sugar, and granular erythritol. Mix until the elements stick together and shape the dough.
2. Into a 4-inch springform tub, press the dough and position it in the basket with the AirFryer.
3. Adjust the temperature and set the timer to 400° F for five minutes.
4. Strip crust and let it cool as timer beeps.
5. Blend cream cheese with egg in a medium dish, powdered erythritol, vanilla extract, cocoa powder, shake, and espresso until smooth.
6. On top of the baked walnut shell, a spoonful of mixture and place it in the basket of an AirFryer.
7. Set the temperature at 300° F, and set the timer for 10 minutes.
8. Once finished, before serving, chill for 2 hours.
Nutrition: Calories: 221, Fat: 5g, Protein: 6g.

Bread Mini Chocolate Chip Tray

(Ready in about 35 mins | Servings 3 | Normal)

Ingredients

- 1/2 cup of finely blanched almond flour
- 1/4 cup of erythritol powder
- 2 tbsp. of unsalted, melted butter
- 1 big egg
- 1/2 cup of unflavored gelatin
- 1/2 cubicle of baking powder
- 1/2 teaspoon of vanilla extract
- 2 teaspoons of low-carb chocolate chips free of sugar

Directions:

1. Mix erythritol and almond flour in a large tub. Stir in the butter, egg, and gelatin once fused.

2. Apply the baking powder and vanilla to the mixture and then fold in. Add the chips of cocoa, pour flour into a 6"pastry tub. Drop the pan into the basket for the AirFryer.

3. Change the temperature and set the timer to 300° F for 7 minutes.

4. The top will be golden brown when fully baked, and they will come out clean with a toothpick inserted in the middle. Let them come out clean. Cool off for at least ten minutes.

Nutrition: Calories: 343, Fat: 3g, Protein: 6g.

Crispy Blackberry

(Ready in about 15 mins | Servings 4 | Normal)

Ingredients

- 2 cups of blackberry
- 1/3 cup of erythritol powder
- 2 tbsp of lemon juice
- 1/4 teaspoon of gum xanthine
- 1 cup of crunchy granola (Find it in chapter 2)

Directions:

1. Throw blackberries, erythritol, lemon juice, and xanthan gum into a wide bowl.

2. Pour into a 6-inch circular baking dish and top with foil. Put the basket into the AirFryer.

3.Change the temperature to 350° F and timer configuration for 12 minutes.

4. Take the foil off and stir as the timer beeps.

5. Sprinkle with granola and serve.

Nutrition: Calories: 453, Fat: 3g, Protein: 6g.

Doughnut Holes Protein: Powder

(Ready in about 31 mins | Servings 12 | Normal)

Ingredients:

- Twelve holes (2 per serving) yields
- 1/2 cup of finely ground almond flour blanched
- 1/2 cup of low carb Protein: vanilla powder
- ½ cup of granulated erythritol
- 1/2 teaspoon of baking powder
- 1 big egg
- 5 spoonsful of unsalted butter, melted
- 1/2 teaspoon of vanilla extract

Directions:

1. In a large tub, combine all the ingredients. Place it for 20 minutes in the freezer.
2. Wet the water in your hands and roll the dough into it. Make a dozen balls.
3. To match your AirFryer basket, cut a piece of parchment. Running as appropriate in batches, put doughnut holes in the AirFryer basket atop the parchment.
4. Change the temperature and set the timer to 380° F for six minutes.
5. Halfway through the preparation, open doughnut holes.
6. Before serving, let it cool down. Put in the basket fryer. Change the temperature to 320° F and timer setup for 3 minutes or until it's golden on top.
7. Serve them warm and enjoy.

Nutrition: Calories: 453, Fat: 3g, Protein: 6g.

Spice Pumpkin Pecans

(Ready in about 11 mins | Servings 4 | Normal)

Ingredients:

- 1 cup full of pecans
- 1/4 cup of erythritol granular
- 1 big white egg
- 1/2 teaspoon of cinnamon field
- 1/2 tsp. of spice pumpkin pie
- 1/2 cubicle of vanilla extract

Directions:

1. Put all the ingredients into a large bowl before the pecans are ready. Place it in the basket of an AirFryer.
2. Change the temperature and set the timer to 300° F for six minutes.
3. During cooking, toss two or three times.
4. Make to cool to the max—stock in an airtight place a container for up to three days.

Nutrition: Calories: 334, Fat: 5g, Protein: 3g.

Mug Cake with Coconut Flour

(Ready in about 11 mins | Servings 4 | Normal)

Ingredients

- 1 big egg
- 2 spoonful of coconut flour
- 2 cups of heavy cream to whip
- 2 spoonsful of granular erythritol
- Vanilla extract: 1/4 teaspoon
- 1/4 tsp of baking powder

Directions:

1. Whisk egg in a 4"ramekin, then add the remaining egg Ingredients: Extract until smooth. Put the fryer in the AirFryer basket.

2. Change the temperature to 300° F and timer configuration to 25 minutes. A toothpick can appear when done. Enjoy straight out with a ramekin using a spoon. Serve hot.

Nutrition: Calories: 124, Fat: 5g, Protein: 3g.

Coconut FlakesToasted

(Ready in about 15 mins | Servings 2 | Normal) **Ingredients:**

- 1 cup of coconut flakes
- 2 lbs. of coconut oil
- 1/4 cup of granular erythritol
- 1/8 teaspoon of salt

Directions:

1. Throw the coconut flakes and oil in a large tub before tossing before re-coating. Sprinkle with erythritol and salt.

2. In an AirFryer, place the coconut flakes in the basket.

3. Set the temperature to 300° F, then set the timer for three minutes.

4. Throw the flakes while remaining 1 minute. Put one more, so just a minute if you would like a golden coconut flake

5.Storage in an airtight container for 5 or 6 days.

Nutrition: Calories: 156, Fat:4g, Protein: 2g.

Maple Bacon, coated in Chocolate

(Ready in about 15 mins | Servings 2 | Normal)

Ingredients:

- 8 slices of sugar-free bacon
- 1 tablespoon of erythritol, granulated
- 1/3 cup of low carbon chocolate chips without sugar
- 1 tablespoon of coconut oil
- 1/2 teaspoon of maple extract

Directions:

1. Apply bacon to the basket of the AirFryer and spray with erythritol.
2. Change the temperature to 350° F and timer configuration for 12 minutes.
3. Switch the bacon halfway through the duration of baking. Make the check at 9 minutes to the desired doneness. (Smaller AirFryers cook even faster.)
4. When the bacon is done, set it to cool aside.
5. Put the chocolate in a small microwave-safe bowl; addcoconut oil and chips. Microwave 30 seconds long, and shake with maple extract.
6. Put the bacon on a parchment sheet. Drizzles chocolate over bacon and put to cool in the refrigerator for 5 minutes or so.
Nutrition: Calories: 156, Fat: 4g, Protein: 2g.

Cake with Vanilla Pound

(Ready in about 35 mins | Servings 6 | Normal)
Ingredients
- 1 cup of finely ground almond flour, blanched
- 1/4 cup of melted, salted butter
- 1/2 cup of erythritol granular
- 1 teaspoon of vanilla extract
- 1 teaspoon of baking powder
- 1/2 cup of low-Fat: crème Fraiche
- 1 ounce of cream cheese with full Fat:, softened
- 2 eggs

Directions:
1. Combine the almond flour and butter in a large tub, and add erythritol.
2. Apply the vanilla, baking soda, sour cream cheese, and baking powder and blend well until well mixed. Add an egg and just spice things together.
3. In a 6"round baking tray, place the batter through AirFryers.
4. Change the temperature and set the timer to 300° F for 25 minutes.
5. When the cake is finished, put a toothpick in the middle. It'll come out clean. It shouldn't feel damp in the middle. Enable it to totally cool; otherwise, the cake will crumble.
Nutrition: Calories: 230, Fat: 3g, Protein: 1g.

Mayo Chocolate Cake

(Ready in about 35 min | Servings 6 | Normal)

Ingredients

- 1 cup of finely ground almond flour, blanched,
- 1/4 cup of melted, salted butter
- 1/2 cup of plus
- 1 spoonful of granular erythritol
- 1 vanilla teaspoon extract
- 1/4 cup of full-bodied mayonnaise
- 1/4 cup of unsweetened powdered chocolate
- 2 large eggs

Directions:

1. Mix all the ingredients in a large bowl until smooth.
2. In a 6"round baking tray, pour the batter. Put the batter in the Basket for AirFryers.
3. Adjust the temperature and set the timer to 300° F for 25 minutes.
4. A toothpick implanted in the middle will come when it's finished Cleanout. Enable the cake to cool, or it will crumble when moved.

Nutrition: Calories: 234, Fat: 2g, Protein: 2g.

Pumpkin Cookie Frosting and Cream Cheese

(Ready in about 35 mins | Servings 6 | Normal)

Ingredients:

- 1/2 cup of finely blanched almond flour
- 1/2 cup of erythritol powder, split
- 2 tablespoons of melted butter
- 1 big egg
- 1/2 cup of unflavored gelatin
- 1/2 teaspoon of baking powder
- 1/2 teaspoon of vanilla extract
- 1/2 tsp. of spice pumpkin pie
- 2 tablespoons of purified organic pumpkin
- 1/2 teaspoon of ground cinnamon, cut
- 1/4 cup of low carbon chocolate chips without sugar
- 3 ounces of cream cheese with full Fat:, softened

Directions:

1. Combine the almond flour and 1/4 cup of the milk in a wide dish, erythritol. Add butter, egg, and gelatin until readymerged.
2. Apply the baking powder, vanilla, pumpkin pie seasoning, Pumpkin purée, and cinnamon, then fold in chocolate flakes.
3. In a 6" round baking pan, put the pan in the basket of an AirFryer.
4. Set the temperature to 300° F, then set the timer for seven minutes.

5. The top will be golden brown and brown when fully baked. The inserted toothpick in the middle comes out clean. Cool for 20 minutes, at least.

6.Make the frosting: combine in a wide tub, the remaining cream cheese, cinnamon, and remaining erythritol. Use an electric mixer, beat until fluffy. Spread over cooled cookie. If needed, garnish it with extra cinnamon.

Nutrition: Calories: 117, Fat: 2, Protein: 4g.

Coconut Pineapples and Yogurt Dip

(Ready in about 25 mins | Servings 4 | Normal)

Ingredients:

- 2 ounces of dried coconut flakes
- 1 sprig of mint, finely chopped
- ½ medium size pineapple
- 8 ounces of vanilla yogurt

Directions:

1. Heat the AirFryer to 390°F.

2. Slice the pineapple into chips (sticks) and dip them into the diced coconut to allow the coconut to stick to them.

3. Place the sticks in the fryer basket and cook for about 10 minutes.

4. Stir the mint leaves into the vanilla yogurt. Serve with pineapple sticks.

Nutrition: Calories: 277 kcal.

Stuffed Apple Bake

(Ready in about 15 mins | Servings 4 | Normal)

Ingredients:

- 4 medium-sized apples, cored
- 6 teaspoons of sugar
- 4 tablespoons of breadcrumbs
- 2 tablespoons of butter
- 1 teaspoon of mixed spice
- 1½ ounce of mixed seeds
- 1 lemon zest

Directions:

1. Score the apples' skin with a knife around the circumference to prevent them from dividing during baking.

2. Mix the sugar, breadcrumbs, butter, zest, spice, and mixed seeds in a bowl and stuff the apples with the mixture.

3. Heat the AirFryer at 356°F and bake the stuffed apples for 10 minutes.
Nutrition: Calories:267 kcal.

. Sesame and Poppy Cheese Cookies

(Ready in about 30 mins | Servings 10 | Normal)
Ingredients:
- 7 tablespoons of cream
- ¾ cup of grated Gruyere cheese
- 3 teaspoons of milk
- 2 egg yolks, beaten
- 1 teaspoon of paprika powder
- 5.2 ounces of butter
- 2/3 cup of flour
- ½ teaspoon of baking powder
- ½ teaspoon of salt
- Poppy seeds and sesame seeds for garnishing

Directions:
1. Mix the cheese, butter, salt, cream, and paprika in a bowl until smooth.
2. Mix the baking powder and flour and sieve over a flat surface.Place the cheese-butter mixture on the flour and knead together to form a soft dough. Roll out the dough until thin and then cut into cookie shapes.
3. Mix the milk and eggs and use to coat the cookies using a brush. Sprinkle the poppy and sesame seed on top of the cookies.
4. Place in the AirFryer basket and bake at 340°F for 12 minutes.
Nutrition: Calories:210 kcal.

Banana and Chocolate Muffins

(Ready in about 35 mins | Servings 6-8 | Normal)
Ingredients:
- 3 medium-sized bananas, mashed
- 4 tablespoons of cocoa
- ¾ cup of wheat flour
- ¾ cup of chocolate chips
- ¾ cup of plain flour
- ½ cup of sugar
- ¼ teaspoon of baking powder

- 1 egg, whisked
- 1 teaspoon of baking soda
- 1/3 cup of vegetable oil

Directions:

1. Mix the bananas, egg, and oil in a bowl. Stir in both flours, cocoa, baking soda, baking flour, and sugar using a wooden spatula until thoroughly mixed.
2. Put in the chocolate chips and mix slightly.
3. Grease your muffin pan with oil and spoon the batter into the holes.
4. Heat the AirFryer to 347°F and bake the muffins in it for 25 minutes. Allow to cool for about 15 minutes, then place on a wire rack.

Nutrition: Calories: 225 kcal.

Sweet Cinnamon Bananas Sticks

(Ready in about 25 mins | Servings 6-8 | Normal)

Ingredients:

- 8 ounces of breadcrumbs
- 8 ripe bananas, peeled and halved
- 7 teaspoons of sugar
- 4 ounces of cornflour
- 3 tablespoons of coconut oil
- 2 large eggs, whisked
- 2 teaspoons of cinnamon

Directions:

1. Put the coconut oil in a pan over medium heat. Put in the breadcrumbs and stir for 4 minutes until slightly golden. Remove from heat and transfer to a shallow dish.
2. Roll the bananas first in the cornflour, then dip them in the eggs and lastly in the breadcrumbs to coat.
3. Place the coated bananas in the cooking basket. Mix the cinnamon and sugar in a bowl thoroughly and sprinkle the mixture on the bananas to cover them.
4. Slide the basket into the AirFryer and cook for 10 minutes at 280°F. When done, shake off excess crumbs.

Nutrition: Calories:187 kcal.

Berry and Apricot Crumble

(Ready in about 30 mins | Servings 6 | Normal)

Ingredients:

- 2½ ounces of butter

- 2¼ cups of apricot
- ½ pound of flour
- 8 tablespoons of sugar
- 6 teaspoons of lemon juice
- 5½ ounces of fresh blackberries
- Salt to the taste

Directions:

1. Cut the apricots into 2 and take out the stone, then cut into cubes.

2. Put them in a bowl and add 2 tablespoons of sugar, the blackberries, and lemon juice and stir. Pour and spread the mixture evenly in an oven dish.

3. Place the flour in a bowl and add 6 tablespoons of sugar, butter, salt, and a little water and mix thoroughly. Rub the mixture with your fingertips until crumbly.

4. Heat your AirFryer to 390°F.

5. Spread the mixture on the fruits and press down lightly.

6. Put into the AirFryer basket and bake for 20 minutes until the crumble appears golden.

Nutrition: Calories: 235 kcal.

Strawberry and Chocolate Cream Cupcake

(Ready in about 42 mins | Servings 4 | Normal)

Ingredients:

- 1 pound of refined flour
- 3 eggs
- 4 tablespoons of strawberry sauce
- 6 ounces of icing sugar
- 1 large strawberry, cut into 4
- ½ pound of cream cheese
- 6 ounces of peanut butter
- 1 teaspoon of vanilla extract
- 1 teaspoon of cocoa powder
- ½ pound of hard butter for frosting
- 2 teaspoons of beet powder
- A few crushed colorful chocolates, crushed

Directions:

1. Make a batter by mixing the flour, cocoa, peanut butter, icing sugar, beet powder, and eggs using an electric mixer. Pour the batter into cupcake molds.

2. Heat your AirFryer for 5 minutes at 360°F. Place the cupcakes in the AirFryer and reduce heat to 340°F. Bake for 12 minutes.

3. Remove the cakes from the fryer; cool for 10 minutes.

4. Combine the icing sugar, hard butter, and vanilla in an electric mixer and whisk until

smooth.

5. Add the frosting on the cupcakes and sprinkle with strawberry sauce, the crushed chocolates, and top with a piece of strawberry.

Nutrition: Calories:256 kcal.

Strawberry Ring Cake

(Ready in about 45 mins | Servings 4 | Normal)

Ingredients:
- 1 egg
- 3½ tablespoons of butter
- 3 strawberries, mashed
- ½ teaspoon of cinnamon
- 2.6 ounces of sugar
- 8 ounces of flour
- 2 tablespoons of maple syrup
- A pinch of salt

Directions:

1. Heat AirFryer to 320°F. Spray a small ring cake pan with oil spray.

2. Put the sugar and butter into a bowl and mix until creamy. Add the mashed strawberries, eggs, and maple syrup and beat the mixture until smooth.

3. Sieve in the flour, cinnamon, and salt and mix to form a batter. Pour the batter into the ring cake pan and level with a spoon. Insert the cake pan into the AirFryer basket.

4. Bake for 30 minutes until a knife inserted in the cake's core comes out clean.

Nutrition: Calories:255 kcal.

Chocolate Cake

(Ready in about 20 mins | Servings 4 | Normal)

Ingredients:
- ½ cup of chopped dark chocolate, melted
- 8 tablespoons of butter, melted
- 5 tablespoons of sugar
- ½ teaspoon of coffee
- 1 teaspoon of baking powder
- 2 eggs
- 1 small lemon, juiced
- 1/3 cup of flour

- ¼ teaspoon of salt

Directions:

1. Add the melted chocolate and the butter and lemon together and mix.

2. Put the egg, coffee, and sugar in a mixing bowl and whisk until creamy. Add the chocolate-butter mixture and mix. Add and stir the baking powder, flour, and salt. Mix the batter gently.

3. Heat your AirFryer to 356°F.

4. Put the batter into a greased baking dish and place it in the fryer basket. Air fry for 10 minutes or until firm.

Nutrition: Calories:196 kcal.

Air Fried Marble Cake

(Ready in about 27 mins | Servings 6 | Normal)

Ingredients:

- 7 tablespoons of caster sugar
- ½ cup of flour
- 4 eggs, whisked
- 1 teaspoon of baking powder
- 5 teaspoons of cocoa powder
- 2/3 cup of butter, melted
- ½ teaspoon of lime juice

Directions:

1. Heat your AirFryer to 356°F.

2. Mix 3 tablespoons of melted butter with the cocoa powder to form a paste.

3. Add the sugar to the remaining butter and mix thoroughly. Stir in the eggs, flour, and baking powder and mix thoroughly until smooth. Pour in the lime and stir.

4. Place a greased baking pan into the AirFryer and allow it to heat for a minute.

5. Pour some of the batters into the hot bake, add a layer of the chocolate mixture, then the butter, chocolate, and top with the batter. Use a skewer to create a swirl.

6. Place in the AirFryer and bake for 17 minutes. The cake should be cooled while in the pan before removing it. Enjoy!

Nutrition: Calories:235 kcal.

Why buy the Ninja Foodi

If you're looking for all-in-one kitchen equipment, the Ninja Foodi is the best option. My deep fryer, stove, and slow cooker were all turned off by the Ninja Foodi in the kit cooker.

- Let's take a look at some of the reasons why it is advisable to get a Ninja Foodi.

In addition to being a slow cooker that can sauté and sear, the Ninja Foodi can also be used as a pressure cooker and an air fryer, and it comes with two interchangeable pressure and crisping covers. The Ninja Foodi is capable of preparing a variety of dishes, including pork, chicken, asparagus, steaks, multi-grain, stews, rice, French fries, kalbi, and more.
After you discover what you can cook with the Ninja Foodi by just following the simple instructions and recipes, you will be motivated to experiment with new ingredients and dishes. In my kitchen, I am happy to have a Ninja Foodi on board.

- Why is it necessary to buy a Ninja Foodi?

The Ninja Foodi pressure cooker has completely blown my expectations away. The pressure cooker, crisper/air fryer, and cooker features are constantly in use in my kitchen.
In general, my family likes the Ninja Foodi and are looking forward to seeing what next I can come up with it.

- Here are the reasons why it is necessary to buy a Ninja Foodi

1.   **Extraordinary Time Saver**
You can prepare a whole meal for more than four people in just a pot in approximately 30 minutes, using ingredients that are taken directly from the freezer or refrigerator. This includes veggies and meat.
When pressure is applied to the food cooker, it cooks 70 percent quicker than regular stovetop cooking.

2.   **It helps you save money.**
In addition to being easy to use, a pressure cooker softens a variety of meats, as everyone is aware. By allowing you to purchase cheaper cuts of meat, the Ninja Foodi will help you save money. An additional benefit was that I became an Epicurean Chef, cooking delicious dishes with tender cuts of meat while spending less time in the kitchen and also using fewer ingredients in my recipes.

3. Multi-cooking functions combined in one device

When it comes to cooking, the Ninja Foodi provides a variety of alternatives with its slow cooking, pressure cooking, steaming, and searing/sauté modes.

When it comes to cooking, you may utilize the TenderCrisp lid. This lid can be used alone or in conjunction with any of the other Ninja Foodi cooking features. Dehydrate, Broil, and Bake/Roast are some of the options available on the TenderCrisp lid. The buttons are really easy to use. The Ninja boasts a bright, computerized touchscreen LED light with particular cooking features that may be controlled through the touchscreen. After you've selected the cooking temperature, duration, and function, you will press the Start button. When the specified cooking time has expired, your food will begin to cook. It will automatically switch to the "Keep Warm" option for up to 12 hours, or until you turn off the Ninja Foodi.

4. Healthy Cooking with Low Fat

Since it does not use any oil to fry, the Ninja Foodi Air-Frying has recently become popular over the last several years.

When compared to deep-fat frying, using the Air-Crisping lid with TenderCrisp tech may lower fat by up to 75% without affecting the flavor. Using fewer fats and oils while preparing your meals is better for your family's overall health. It also has a stronger taste.

5. It enhances the flavor and moisture of the meat.

If you cook your meals in a pressure cooker first, they will retain their natural juices, which is beneficial. As it coats your meal with a coating of crispy brown deliciousness, the Ai-Crisping lid with TenderCrisp technology traps these juices within.

6. With a large cooking capacity, this unit is built to last longer.

This Ninja Foodi is built to last for many years of severe usage in the kitchen. A massive, 6.5-qt or 8-qt variant with a nonstick, ceramic-coated pot is also included. It also has a 4-qt ceramic-coated Cook & Crisp Basket, a stainless steel reversible pressure cover, and a rack crisping lid. The Ninja Foodi comes with a one-year warranty from the production company. All the safety precautions of the Ninja Foodi have been approved by the Underwriters Laboratories.

7. Clean-up is quite straightforward.

All the Ninja Foodi's replaceable pieces may be washed in the dishwasher. However, hand washing is recommended for ceramic-coated interior pots to guarantee a longer life lifetime. To make cleaning easier, softly coat the stainless steel grid with cooking oil. It helps to clean up the pot extremely quickly and easily, particularly after broiling or baking cuts of meat.

It is one of life's greatest pleasures to master the art of cooking. In addition to keeping our tummies filled, it allows us to stay connected with family and friends. The Ninja Foodi enables you to create delicious meals that your guests will be eager to have repeatedly. Throughout history, cooking has evolved and progressed from the time that humans first learned to cook via fundamental skills such as grilling over an open fire to the time when we began to cook with pans, pots, and ovens. Cooking has steadily improved and advanced throughout history.

When you just have to work with one kind of cookware, cooking is a pleasure, rather than the headache of having to deal with a large number of cooking equipment components, according to my perspective. So why not create a single piece of equipment that has all these features? This guide will teach you how to use Ninja Foodi and all of its functions.

Ninja Foodi is a pressure cooker and also an air fryer. It enables you to produce meals that would otherwise be hard to prepare with regular cooking equipment, such as soups. So whether you are in the mood for chicken wings or a sweet treat like sea salt caramel popcorn, the Ninja Foodi can satisfy your cravings!

How to use the Ninja Foodi

The Ninja Foodi is used in the same way as other air fryers and pressure cookers, except for the fact that it is an all-in-one cooking equipment. The use of the Ninja Foodi as a pressure cooker requires the use of the pressure-cooking cover and also the understanding of the functions of the various buttons, such as Pressure and Sear/Sauté. In addition, there will be a need for you to change the parameters of the Pressure. They will be utilized with buttons like Bake/Roast, Air Crisp, and other air frying functions. The crisping lid is included with the air frying functions.

1. **Preheating:** Preheating the Ninja Foodi's inside pot before adding the food is important. Ensure the internal part of the pot has been preheated for at least 5 minutes before placing the ingredients. It is the conventional method of cooking on the stovetop or in the oven, in which preheating is required to properly prepare the oven or pot for cooking.

The use of water in pressure cooking is necessary since steam is required for the procedure to be successful, and some kind of moisture initiates the procedure. As a result, before pressure cooking foods, you need to add at least half a cup of water to the pot to ensure that your cooking is accomplished.

2. **The Lids:** The Ninja Foodi comes with two key lids: the Air Crisping Lid, which is used for air frying, and the Pressure Lid, which is used for high-pressure cooking. Make good use of each lid according to the instructions provided by the recipe you are now using.

3. **Use the inside pot every time:** The Ninja Foodi detects and overrides if the inner pot isn't placed in the pot before cooking, which is surprising. It's a smart piece of equipment! As a result, before using any of the pressure-cooking or air-frying modes, make sure you always keep the inner pot completely secured in place.

The Ninja Foodi Function Buttons are as follows:

You will discover that using the Ninja Foodi may be intimidating at first since there are so many different buttons on the device that you aren't sure of their functions.

1.   Air Crisp Button
The Air Crisp button allows you to activate the air frying function, which can be used to prepare a variety of foods by simply heating them. Cook your preferred frozen items, such as onion rings, French fries, and chicken nuggets, by using the Air Crisp function in combination with the Cook & Crisp Basket. Many foods may even be prepared without the use of oil. Make care to shake the basket at least once throughout the crisping process to get the best tasting results possible.

2.   Sear/Saute Button
The Sear / Sauté button allows you to use your Ninja Foodi as a cooktop by heating the food on it. It's great for sautéing meat, veggies, and other foods in large batches. In addition to having a large amount of surface area for searing meats and sautéing vegetables, the Ninja Foodi features five different temperature settings for the cooktop. Use the Ninja Foodi the same way as you would use your cooktop, switching between low, medium-low, medium, medium-high, and high settings as needed. You may go from a gentle simmer to an intensely hot sear in a matter of minutes.

3.   Slow Cook Button
With the Ninja Foodi, you can cook at several speeds, including low and high slow. When you use the Slow Cook option, you can prepare meals that need several hours of cooking at low temperatures. Alternatively, if you like the convenience of placing all of the ingredients into a single pot in the morning and arriving home to a well-cooked meal, the Slow Cook mode will be your most often used feature. If you like, you can even leave the Ninja Foodi overnight and come back to find everything perfect and in good condition the next day. The Steam button allows you to cook anything from fish to vegetables at an exceptionally high temperature without using any oil. Cooking with steam absorbs moisture into your food while also retaining taste and maintaining the texture of your dish. Fill the cooking pot halfway with water and place the Reversible Rack in the lowest position. Place your food on top of the rack and seal the cover in place with a lid.

4.   Bake or roast button
The Bake or Roast button is quite easy to use. If you are not in the mood to use your oven or are preparing recipes that require baking, the Ninja Foodi can be used as a micro convection oven to bake your preferred baked dishes and roast meats in a fraction of the time it would take in your regular oven. It requires just 4 to 5 minutes to warm the Ninja Foodi, which is much less time than it would take in your conventional oven.

5. **Dehydrate Button**

It is possible to dehydrate items into jerky without using the Dehydrate button, however, using the Dehydrate button will assist you in getting rid of any extra oil or when the recipe calls for it. As soon as you press the Dehydrate button, the Crisping Lid reduces the fan speed to ensure that water is removed slowly and gradually. Make your fruit and vegetable chips or flavor your jerky without the additional sugar and additives found in store-bought varieties.

Which Ninja Foodi has the dehydrator? All of the Ninja Foodi OP301 models contain a dehydrator, except the OP101 5-quart. The FD401 8-quart deluxe and Ninja OP401 dehydrator is one of the Ninja Foodi dehydrators.

6. **Broil Button**

If you're in the mood to grill anything or prepare some BBQ, the Broil button is what you're looking for. Broil is the highest temperature setting available on the Crisping Lid, and it is the quickest and most straightforward method for preparing crispier seared meats. With the Ninja Foodi's broil mode, it's like having an upside-down barbeque grill at your disposal.

7. **Keep Warm Button**

After the cooking period for slow cooking, steaming, or pressure cooking is completed, the Keep Warm mode is activated automatically. Ninja Foodi is designed to remain in this mode for a total of 12 hours. If you wish to turn it off before the 12 hours are over, you may use the warm button on the control panel.

8. **Power Button**

In this case, the Power button speaks for itself.

9. **Start / Stop Button**

To set the temperature, time, or pressure, either the Start or Stop button is pressed.

10. **Temperature button**

The Temp buttons are made up of arrows that allow you to adjust the temperature up and down.

What is Tendercrisp Technology and how does it work?

Ninja Foodi is more than simply a kitchen device that combines an air fryer and a pressure cooker into a single unit. The Tender Crispy Technology is also included in Ninja Foodi. When using this method, the meat or vegetables are given a lovely golden-brown finish, as opposed to other pressure cookers, which leave the food looking pallid.

Also made possible by Tender Crispy Technology is the Ninja Foodi's ability to have all of these capabilities functioning at the same time in a single device. Many things are possible because of technological advancements, such as cooking frozen foods, making them crispy, and inventing dishes that are otherwise impossible to achieve using conventional cooking techniques.

- **Cooking with an all-in-one pot is quite convenient.**
Use TenderCrisp Technology to transform dull soups and stews into one-pot meals that are ready in minutes. Preparing stews, casseroles, chilis, and desserts under pressure is a great way to save time. Then add biscuits, cheese, or a crust to finish it off. Use the Crisping Lid to bake the biscuits, broil the cheese, or crisp the crust by simply switching the top to the crisping position.

- **Cook from Frozen to Crispy.**
The Ninja Foodi is also capable of cooking meals straight from frozen. Pressure is used to swiftly defrost and soften frozen meat, while the Crisping Lid is used to crisp the exterior of the meat. You won't have to worry about uneven defrosting in the microwave or waiting hours for your food to defrost on the kitchen counter anymore.

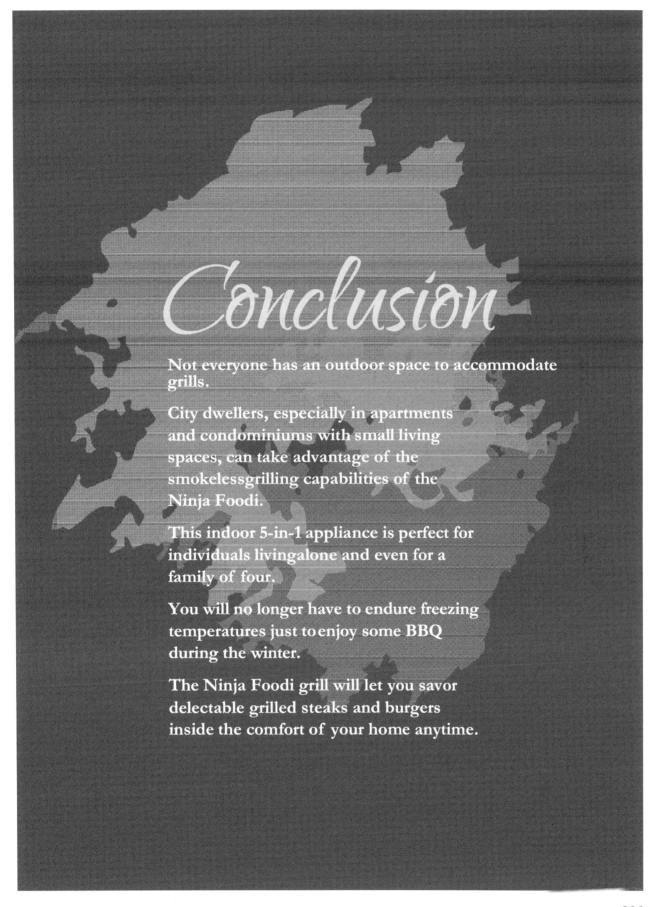

Conclusion

Not everyone has an outdoor space to accommodate grills.

City dwellers, especially in apartments and condominiums with small living spaces, can take advantage of the smokelessgrilling capabilities of the Ninja Foodi.

This indoor 5-in-1 appliance is perfect for individuals livingalone and even for a family of four.

You will no longer have to endure freezing temperatures just to enjoy some BBQ during the winter.

The Ninja Foodi grill will let you savor delectable grilled steaks and burgers inside the comfort of your home anytime.

Alphabetic Index